UNIVERSITY OF NORTH CAROLINA

STUDIES IN COMPARATIVE LITERATURE

NUMBER 57

Sales through University of North Carolina Press
Chapel Hill, N.C. 27514
Orders from countries other than U.S. and Canada:
Feffer & Simons, Inc.
31 Union Square, New York, N.Y. 10003

AMPHITRYON

Three Plays in New Verse Translations

PLAUTUS: AMPHITRUO

translated by James H. Mantinband

MOLIÈRE: AMPHITRYON

translated by Charles E. Passage

KLEIST: AMPHITRYON

translated by Charles E. Passage

TOGETHER WITH A COMPREHENSIVE ACCOUNT
OF THE EVOLUTION OF THE LEGEND
AND ITS SUBSEQUENT HISTORY ON THE STAGE.

CHAPEL HILL
THE UNIVERSITY OF NORTH CAROLINA PRESS
1974

Library of Congress Cataloging in Publication Data

Main entry under title:
Amphitryon: three plays in new verse translation.

(University of North Carolina Studies in
Comparative Literature, no. 57)

1. Amphitryon—Drama. I. Mantinband, James
H., tr. II. Passage, Charles E., tr. III. Plautus,
Titus Maccius. Amphitruo. English. 1973.
IV. Molière, Jean Baptiste Poquelin, 1622–1673.
Amphitryon. English. 1973. V. Kleist, Heinrich
von, 1777–1811. Amphitryon. English. 1973.
VI. Series: North Carolina. University. Studies
in Comparative Literature, no. 57.

PN6120.A6A43   808.82′9′351   73-14955

ISBN 0-8078-7057-9

TABLE OF CONTENTS

Table of Contents

PREFACE

Most levels of poetic worth are represented in the long history of dramas on the theme of Amphitryon. It is the primary purpose of the present volume to offer the three most significant of these plays in fresh translation into English verse: Plautus' Latin tragicomedy of *Amphitruo*, probably to be dated to the 190's B.C. and sole survivor of a dozen or more Greek and Roman tragedies and comedies on the subject; Molière's French comedy of *Amphitryon* of 1668; and Heinrich von Kleist's German *Amphitryon* of 1807, which was begun as a blank verse translation of Molière's play and subtitled "A Comedy after Molière," but which was so modified by unique poetic invention as to make it a near-tragedy and a very different work. Considerations of space forbade the inclusion of two interesting twentieth-century versions, the comic *Amphitryon 38* of Jean Giraudoux (1929) and the serious *Zweimal Amphitryon* of Georg Kaiser (1944), to say nothing of valuable older plays.

Some readers may frown upon our filling out of the lacuna in Plautus' text with the "interpolated scenes" composed by Cardinal Hermolaus Barbarus in the 1480's, some sixteen centuries later than the surrounding matter. It may be objected that for four hundred years after 1480 readers were misled into thinking they had the complete ancient *Amphitruo* before them and that we have been unwise in reintroducing what classical scholars finally succeeded in excising. We included the "interpolated scenes" mainly because Molière and Kleist read them as integral parts of the text. Judgment of the adaptation procedures of these authors requires a knowledge of these scenes. Moreover, the substituted lines are in themselves so poetically apt as to justify inclusion on their intrinsic merit. And they have a historical value of their own. The practice of recent Plautus editors has been to indicate at a certain point that pages are missing from all manuscripts and to print, in brackets, the approximately twenty lines preserved in quotation by grammarians of late antiquity from those pages. We print these lines in an appendix to the translation.

Our second objective was to give an account of the origins of the Amphitryon legend and of the astonishingly long line of its dramatic development. In dealing with the legend, we have listed and summarized the ancient sources, but we advance no new interpretation of them. Nor do we venture into the unsure field of Oriental analogues. Homer and Hesiod allude to the story, which they supposed to have occurred prior to the Trojan War and long before their own times. Long after their times the ancient dramas spanned four centuries. The mythographic authors wrote later than that. Our Plautus fragments come chiefly from Roman Numidia and Mauretania, now Algeria, in the fourth century of the Christian era, and corroborative details about the myth come from Byzantium-Constantinople of the times of the Crusaders. Thus a survey of the Amphitryon matter constitutes a demonstration in miniature of the unity of classical civilization through more than two millennia.

In dealing with the dramatic history of Amphitryon from the late Middle Ages to the present, we intend a succinct review of the literary continuum amid which the masterpieces of Molière and Kleist materialized. Our guidelines were Örjan Lindberger's book, *The Transformations of Amphitryon* (1956) and Professor L. R. Shero's article, *Alcmena and Amphitryon in Ancient and Modern Drama* in *Transactions and Proceedings of the American Philological Association*, LXXXVII (1956), pp. 192–238. Some checks were made in these two writers' sources, Friedrich Leo's *Plautinische Forschungen* (1912) and K. von Reinhardstoettner's *Plautus: Spätere Bearbeitungen Plautinischer Lustspiele* (1886), but we have not searched for new items to add to the Amphitryon list.

For the shadings of the historical perspectives, for the comments and opinions expressed, the present writers assume responsibility. Our hope is that students and general readers of drama and of comparative literature will find this book both enjoyable and helpful.

C. E. P.

J. H. M.

I. AMPHITRYON IN CLASSICAL ANTIQUITY

1. THE LEGEND OF AMPHITRYON

In the fourteenth Book of the *Iliad* Hera, with a guileful purpose, comes to Zeus on Mount Ida to say that she is about to set off on a journey. The king of the gods genially replies that she may journey some other time because at this moment he is aflame with conjugal desire for her. Neither goddess nor mortal woman, he says, has ever so incited his passion as Hera does right now, and he cites a series of instances to illustrate his point. Fifth of the mortal women whom he enumerates is Alkmene, who in Thebes bore him a son, Herakles (lines 323–4).

In the eleventh Book of the *Odyssey*, when the far-wandering hero has crossed the river of Ocean and arrived at Persephone's shore, he follows each detail of Circe's bidding in order to call up the ghosts of the dead. With his sword he digs a trench, pours into it first honey mixed with milk, then wine, then water, then glistening barley, and lastly he beheads two sheep whose blood drains into the pit. Thirstily the dead come swarming toward him, his recently lost comrade Elpenor first, then the seer Teiresias who has words for homeward guidance, then Odysseus' own mother, who is followed in turn by an extended series of ladies once the wives and daughters of great men. Most of these ladies endured sad or tragic fates—the wife-mother of Oedipus, Phaedra, Ariadne, Procris, and the like. One of them is "Alkmene, Amphitryon's wife, who lay in the arms of mighty Zeus and bore a hero, Herakles" (lines 266–8).

Both poems mention Alkmene in a list of famous women. The context of the *Iliad* list is quite literally jovial in tone; the context of the *Odyssey* list is somber, verging on the tragic. So far as the brief allusions show, the focus of attention is on Alkmene as mortal mother of Herakles by the seed of Zeus. The first quotation names Thebes as the place of the portentous birth and the second quotation gives the name of Alkmene's husband—pre-

1

sumably a mortal—as Amphitryon. But in an earlier passage of the *Iliad* (Book V, line 392) there is an unmistakable allusion to Herakles as "the strong son of Amphitryon." All subsequent evidence concurs to resolve the apparent contradiction: divine Zeus was the father of Herakles, mortal Amphitryon was Herakles' foster-father. Centuries later, in Euripides' drama of *The Raging Herakles,* composed between 424 and 416 B.C., the hero will not only refer to Amphitryon as his father but, in lines 1258–65, will say that, though Zeus was his actual begetter, he nevertheless regards Amphitryon as his true father.

The few details gleaned from the *Iliad* and the *Odyssey* thus accord perfectly with the later versions of the story known to us, but it would be rash to assume that all the attendant circumstances from those later versions were necessarily known at the time of the epic poems. The story may have been complete and only partially revealed in allusion, or it may have been an embryonic story whose details had yet to grow. We cannot even discern whether the story was basically tragic or comic.

At any rate, some story about Alkmene, Amphitryon's wife, as mother of Herakles was alluded to in the *Iliad,* or at least in the form of the *Iliad* which has been preserved. If we suggest a round date for the *Iliad* between 850 and 800 B.C. we shall be in agreement with Herodotus (II, 53) and with many, though not all, modern scholars. Homer, as author of the *Iliad,* was recalling bygone days of the Trojan War, which seems to have had a historical counterpart around 1200 B.C., if not in the specific decade of 1194–1184 proposed by Eratosthenes, and Zeus's love for Alkmene is cited as predating that war. Scholars who suspect the preserved text of the *Iliad* of containing more than one post-Homeric interpolation will need to adjust these claims to later dates, but none will deny that Greeks of the classical fifth century B.C. assigned Alkmene and Herakles to a heroic age prior to the Trojan War. Unquestionably the story, in some form, was in existence by 500 B.C. and the present writers incline to the belief that it was in existence more than three centuries before that.

Great uncertainty attends upon the dates for the writer Hesiod and upon the attribution of his works. The poem of the *Works and Days* is generally accepted as his; the poem of the *Theogony* may well be his, but with later modifications. In a recent edition of the latter, with commentary, (1966), M. L. West accepts its essential authenticity, dates it between 730 and 700 B.C., and takes as genuine certain passages doubted by other specialists. Line 526 of the *Theogony* mentions "Alkmene's heroic son Herakles" as slayer of the eagle that tormented Prometheus. West believes that Hesiod wrote this line, whereas Norman O. Brown, a recent (1953) American translator of the poem, feels that the line is part of a set of lines added by an unknown later poet. Lines 943–4, as part of a catalogue of Zeus's terrestrial amours, speak of Alkmene who lay with Zeus and gave birth to Herakles. Norman O. Brown finds the passage authentic; M. L. West believes all lines after line 900 are by a later writer.

In the form transmitted to us, the *Theogony* ends with lines which permit a transition into a different poem, which is thought to be "Hesiodic" without being by Hesiod and which is known by alternate titles as *The Catalogue of Women* or the *Ehoiai*— the "Or-Like's." It enumerates famous women, introducing each case with the words "Or like (her who . . .)" and the last of the series speaks of Alkmene, who alone was left to her parents when the Taphians, famous shipmen, slew all her brothers.

Appended to the *Ehoiai* is still another poem—originally an independent work, West believes—with the separate title of *The Shield of Herakles* (Aspis Herakleous). Its 480 hexameters are intact, whereas the text of the *Ehoiai* is fragmentary, and it begins: "Or like her who . . ." Ostensibly its subject is the slaying of the robber Kyknos (Cycnus) by Herakles, though a disproportionate space is allotted to a description of the hero's shield, whence the title of the work. The first fifty-six lines deal with Alkmene. She is the beautiful daughter of Elektryon; she married Amphitryon, came to Thebes with him, but denied herself as wife until he should have destroyed the Taphians and the Teleboeans (or Teleboans) who had slain her brothers. As for Amphitryon himself, his story is complex and the poem leaves it obscure, presumably because readers of the poem could supply it of themselves. He came to Thebes, though that was not his city, and he had slain Alkmene's father Elektryon "in anger about the oxen." His allies in war are the Boeotians, the Phocians, and the Locrians, i.e. the three adjacent peoples along the northern shore of the Gulf of Corinth. Westward beyond the narrow neck of the Gulf of Corinth and thence northward past Ithaca lie islands called the Taphian Islands. ("Taphos" means "tomb.")

Thus far to line 27, where the text abruptly shifts to Zeus, who is meditating the begetting of a hero who will defend both gods and men against destruction. In a single night Alkmene is possessed, first by Zeus, then by Amphitryon, who has just returned from his war. The poem does not specify that Zeus assumed Amphitryon's shape, but we are all but compelled to supply that detail for so virtuous a wife as Alkmene. Twin sons are subsequently born, heroic Herakles by the divine sire, the somewhat less heroic Iphikles by the mortal one. At line 57 the text hurries on to the feats of the grown Herakles, who is clearly Zeus's defender of gods and men.

Lest we dismiss all this as idle storifying by firelight of long ago, it is well to cite a passage from the soberly reliable Herodotus who wrote after 450 B.C. in an era about which there is no mystery or uncertainty. Amid a discussion of old forms of the Greek alphabet, which he attributes to the remote time of Cadmus, Herodotus says (V, 59):

> "I myself saw Cadmean characters engraved upon some tripods in the temple of Apollo Ismenias in Boeotian Thebes, ... One of the tripods has the following inscription:
>
> Me did Amphitryon place, from the far Teleboans coming.
>
> This would be about the age of Laius, the son of Labdacus, the son of Polydorus, the son of Cadmus."

Scholars concerned with dating the introduction of the alphabet into Greece may puzzle over what these "Cadmean characters" may have been, but we, who are here concerned only with the beginnings of the Amphitryon story, note simply that Herodotus, at some time after 450 B.C., viewed an inscription which he considered to be of remote antiquity and that this inscription consisted of a line of verse which alluded to Amphitryon's return to Thebes after a war with the Teleboans.

A book that might have clarified Alkmene's story for us was the prose handbook of mythology composed at Athens by Pherecydes of Leros in the first half of the fifth century B.C., but only tantalizing fragments of it remain to us. That contemporary of

Aeschylus and of the young Sophocles is likely to have given the tale in a form not yet modified, or only little modified, by the sophistication of the classical era or by the dramatic poets.

What we do have, however, is a much later work based partly on it and likewise in Greek prose, entitled *The Library* (Bibliothēkē). This dry but straightforward book seems to have passed all but unnoticed until the ninth century A.D., when Byzantine scholars made liberal use of it. They styled its author Apollodorus, perhaps in the mistaken notion that it was written by the famous Athenian grammarian of that name—whose partially known works contradict this one outright. Possibly the compiler of *The Library* was also named Apollodorus. His very century is unknown. The first two hundred years of the Christian era are thought to be the most likely period for him. The Byzantines termed him "the Athenian"—as Apollodorus the grammarian was—and an editor of 1873 felt he could detect a few Athenian local allusions in the text. "Apollodorus" must, then, have been a Roman subject in the heyday of Roman might, yet never once does he mention Rome or the power of Rome, not even when his narration of a myth involves Italian geography. Such studied avoidance of the masters of the civilized world may betoken a Greek sorehead who would not be reconciled to the provincial status of his native land. A man of that sort might well choose to write about the old Greek myths, ignoring Roman intrusions into them and Roman modifications of them. Happily this deliberate antiquarianism best serves our purpose in the present case. We are, moreover, reassured by his indifference to literary ornament, and we note that when he works from sources accessible to us—Homer, Sophocles, Euripides, Apollonius of Rhodes—he is remarkably accurate. Thus when, in *The Library*, II, iv, he outlines the Amphitryon-Alkmene story and cites Pherecydes in the process, we feel we have an account as close as possible to what had been written in Athens between 500 and 450 B.C.

In the tangled skein of genealogy presented we learn that Amphitryon and Alkmene were first cousins to each other and grandchildren of Perseus and Andromeda, who in former days had ruled Tiryns and Mycenae. The ruler at Mycenae is now Elektryon, the father of Alkmene and of nine sons. His right to the throne is challenged by six great-great-great-nephews—the text is highly implausible here—who are the sons of Pterelaus and the grandsons of Taphius. This latter had colonized the island of Taphos and called his people Teleboans—the text explains: from *tēlou ebē*—"he went far." When Elektryon paid no heed to the demands of these six great-great-great-nephews they drove away his cattle. All nine of Elektryon's sons and five of the six great-great-great-nephews perished in the ensuing struggle. The attackers left the raided cattle with the king of Elis before sailing off to Taphos. Outraged Elektryon pursued these Taphians/Teleboans, leaving his daughter Alkmene with her cousin Amphitryon, who swore an oath to respect her virginity. But Amphitryon, to his uncle's annoyance, ransomed the cattle from the king of Elis, and, as uncle and nephew were rounding up the reclaimed herd, Amphitryon hurled a club at an unruly cow, the club glanced off the cow's head, struck Elektryon, and killed him outright. As a result, the dead man's brother Sthenelus, who now seized power, banished Amphitryon as a murderer until, as law required, a foreigner should perform the ceremony of purification over him. Amphitryon went accordingly to Creon, King of Thebes, taking Alkmene with him, but she refused to marry him until he had avenged her nine brothers slain. With Creon's aid he sailed on that punitive expedition to Taphos, where he prevailed only after a daughter of King Pterelaus pulled out a golden and magically life-preserving hair from her father's head.

But ("Apollodorus" continues) before Amphitryon got home, Zeus assumed the shape of Amphitryon, announced to Alkmene that her nine brothers had been avenged, and through a night thrice the normal length of nights enjoyed her love. When on the following night Amphitryon arrived, he was bewildered by Alkmene's report, but the seer Teiresias explained to him what had happened. Subsequently Alkmene bore twin sons, Herakles by Zeus and Iphikles by Amphitryon.

Then follows the tale of how Hera, out of jealousy, sent two serpents to kill the infant boys and how infant Herakles strangled the monsters with his tiny hands. But, "Apollodorus" adds, Pherecydes had it that Amphitryon himself put the two serpents with the children in order to determine which of the twins was his own child. The terror of infant Iphikles revealed that *he* was the mortal offspring.

By coincidence we have a bit of this narrative preserved in Pherecydes' own words in a fragment numbered 13 b which is contained in an Alexandrian scholar's marginal commentary on the allusion to Alkmene in the eleventh Book of the *Odyssey*. The fragment speaks of Alkmene's refusal of herself to Amphitryon until her brothers are avenged, of Zeus's assumption of Amhpitryon's shape, and of Amphitryon's presentation of a drinking cup as a marriage gift. The cup was originally a gift from the god Poseidon to King Pterelaus' grandfather, so that it serves both as marriage gift and as vengeance-token. Scholars have guessed that it was originally a vengeance-token only and that the early fifth century Pherecydes was "civilizing" a story from the cruder past by making it also a marriage gift. Scholars have further guessed that Pherecydes injected the motif of Zeus's shape-shifting in order to possess the chaste bride, again by way of "civilizing" a harsher, older version of the story. If these guesses are correct, the story did not acquire the indispensable ingredient of all our subsequent Amphitryon dramas until after 500 B.C.

Next, *The Library* proceeds to a full-scale account of the Twelve Labors of Herakles, for, as in the "Hesiodic" *Shield of Herakles,* the succinct account of the hero's earthly mother and divine father serves as a mere prelude to the principal narrative about the hero himself. Amphitryon, meanwhile, remains an incidental figure. In fact, we are surprised at the amount of attention given him by "Apollodorus." The era is the heroic age of Greece prior to the Trojan War and some of the involved genealogies must reflect historical dynastic struggles at the once great capital of Mycenae. The House of Perseus is clearly in decline and the House of Atreus is about to come to power, for three of Amphitryon's uncles married daughters of Pelops, and Sthenelus, the uncle who banished him as a murderer and seized power for himself, appoints his wife's brothers, Atreus and Thyestes, to the thrones of lesser cities in his domain. With the mention of these names we sense a transition to a wholly different story cycle. Amphitryon and Alkmene, therefore, were cousins of Agamemnon and Menelaus.

Only small details from this complex background matter found their way into the dramatic tradition, which focused attention

on events in Thebes after the Taphians/Teleboans had been
overcome. Into this phase of the tale Pherecydes and "Apollodorus," between them, bring the motifs of the triple night, Zeus's
impersonation of Amphitryon, and the god's anticipation of
Amphitryon's victory narrative, as well as King Pterelaus' drinking cup as recognition-token and the bewilderment of the homecoming hero. Still, certain motifs vital to the dramas are not yet
mentioned. There is no hint of the roles of Mercury and Sosia,
no confrontation of husband with impersonating god, no recourse to witnesses of the husband's whereabouts. The story as
a whole shows no flicker of comedy, yet, since the heroine survives
to bear her twins and since no one else dies, it does not seem to
be a tragedy either. Only hindsight on our part can identify the
dramatic nucleus in the Theban episode at all. The interpretive
role of the seer Teiresias, we observe, has dramatic potential, yet
this motif is only faintly echoed by Plautus and will otherwise—
except perhaps for Sophocles—be wholly absent from the known
plays about Amphitryon. So far, the story remains a mere for-
word to the life of Herakles.

The same eagerness to get on with the feats of the adult
Herakles characterizes the Theban birth-story as reported by
Diodorus Siculus. This Sicilian Greek, contemporary of Julius
Caesar and of the early reign of Augustus, composed a markedly
Rome-oriented history-and-geography of the world in forty
Books, entitled *The Library of History* (Bibliothēkē Historikē),
fifteen of which survive. Myth, understood as "ancient history,"
occupies the long Book IV, in which Herakles plays an important
part. The triple night at Thebes is mentioned as being required
for the procreation of so great a hero, and such was Alkmene's
chastity, we are told, that the god was obliged to impersonate
her husband. Then Diodorus makes the curious statement that
Zeus felt no love whatsoever for Alkmene, his sole purpose being
to beget the heroic child. So odd a statement, without clarification, suggests that the writer became entangled in the thread of
that motif which somehow made the procreation of Herakles
necessary for the defense of both gods and men from destruction.
Nothing at all is said about Amphitryon, or about Teiresias'
interpretation of events, or even about the war with the Taph-
ians/Teleboans. Trouble in heaven is reported, however, with

Hera's jealousy, which is not, as we would expect, so much wifely as it is directed against Zeus's candidate (Herakles) for dynastic succession in the House of Perseus. With the help of her daughter, the goddess of childbirth, Hera delayed Alkmene's delivery while hastening the birth of the throne-candidate of her choice. The matter of the strangled serpents is reported in a single sentence, but only infant Herakles is involved; there is no mention of twins.

Nor does Ovid cast any light upon the dramatic tradition. The fifteen Books of his famous Latin poem of the *Metamorphoses*, which was completed in the year 7 A.D., devotes only a couple of pages of its Book IX (lines 275–323) to Alcmena. There the heroine is presented in a kind of genre portrait, as an aged woman relating to her recently widowed daughter-in-law the anguish she endured long ago in giving birth to Hercules. Seven days and seven nights her excruciating labor pangs continued, because Juno (Hera) willed it so—we are not told why. And when the goddess of childbirth came at Alcmena's prayer, the goddess maliciously sat with knees crossed and fingers interlocked to prevent the child's delivery. Then a red-haired servant named Galanthis went out and told the goddess that Alcmena's child had been born. For sheer dismay the goddess leaped to her feet and flung her hands aloft—whereupon Hercules promptly came into the world. Out of spite, the goddess metamorphosed the maid Galanthis into a red-furred weasel.

Besides the foregoing sources of information about the Amphitryon legend there are at least a dozen others, incidental ones, scattered down the length and breadth of classical antiquity: two or three lines of Pindar's seventh Isthmian Ode of the early fifth century B.C.; allusions in Theocritus's twenty-fourth Idyll of the third century B.C.; allusions in Fables 28 and 29 of Gaius Julius Hyginus, who died in 17 A.D.; remarks by scholiasts of unknown dates in the manuscript margins of authors from Homer forwards; passing comments by the Byzantine scholar John Tzetzes, who died around 1180 A.D.; and so on. They are all listed by Robert Graves in Section 118 of *The Greek Myths* (Volume II, pp. 87–88) and collated by him into the synthetic account of Amphitryon and Alkmene that he gives there. They add little to what has been reviewed here.

2. THE CLASSICAL AMPHITRYON DRAMAS:
TRAGEDY

Meanwhile a dramatic tradition of the Amphitryon theme had developed, which must have differed somewhat from the mythological tradition just outlined.

Aeschylus, who died in 456 B.C., wrote a tragedy of *Alkmene*, which is lost. The evidence for its existence consists of a single word quoted from it by the lexicographer Hesychius in late antiquity and it has been suspected that Hesychius may have made an error of identification. Sophocles composed a tragic *Amphitryon*, of which we possess one obscure sentence and two isolated words quoted out of context. The suggestion that this was not a tragedy but a satyr play has long since been rejected, but there is slight evidence to support the suggestion that its tragic conflict was resolved by the intervention of Teiresias. At some time between ca. 451 and 422 B.C. the tragedian Ion of Chios is known to have written an *Alkmene*. From it three fragments remain, of about two words each.

From the lost tragedy of *Alkmene* by Euripides we have seventeen definite fragments and three or four dubious ones, but something of its nature may be inferred from the opening of Plautus' comedy *The Rope* (Rudens), where the slave Sceparnio comes out of his house on the North African coast and exclaims:

> "Immortal gods, what a storm Neptune sent down on us last night! The wind took the roof off the house. What am I saying? That wasn't a wind, but Euripides' *Alkmene!*"

In 1872 the German scholar Engelmann first pointed out that two painted vases (of the third century B.C.), now in the British Museum, may well depict the final scene from Euripides' lost play. The painter of the first of these not only signed his name, Python, in the upper border, but labeled each of the figures, so there is no doubt as to their identities. Two men, superscribed Antenor and Amphitryon, are setting torches to the left and right sides respectively of a pyre on which is seated Alkmene. She looks neither at them nor at the flames but rather toward the figure marked Zeus in the upper left, whose torso projects above a wavy line suggestive of a cloud. Lightning-bolts are

The vase painted by Python.

F 193

Another Amphitryon vase

striking near the feet of the two men, oversetting a libation container at Antenor's feet, while from the sky two "rainy Hyades" are emptying jars of water to extinguish the fire. Over Alkmene is spanned a rainbow, beneath which a multitude of dots must signify rain. Eos, goddess of the dawn, occupies the upper right-hand corner of the picture.—The second vase painting resembles the first but the figures are not labeled, Zeus is absent, and there is only one man setting a torch to the pyre. The painting is unsigned.

Python's painting must not be taken as representing a scene from a stage performance actually viewed by fifth century audiences, but rather as an assemblage, in pictorial terms, of the elements that composed such a stage performance. Significantly, the painting reports matters not mentioned by the mythographers and these matters accord well with the spirit of Euripides. With fair confidence we may then assume that in Euripides' play Amphitryon set about burning Alkmene alive as an adulteress and that Zeus, as *deus ex machina,* intervened with thunder, lightning, and rain to avert the innocent lady's death, presumably at the hour of dawn. Quite possibly Alkmene had denied herself to Amphitryon until he avenged her brothers and he returned from the Taphian war to find her pregnant. If, as Engelmann believed, she took refuge at an altar and her husband left her there and built the funeral pyre around her and the altar together, we have an arresting example of Euripidean tragic invention. The implication of the jest in Plautus' *Rudens* is that there must have been melodramatic sound effects in imitation of violent tempest to accompany this scene.

The focus of the Euripidean drama must, then, have been upon a husband's jealousy and a wife falsely accused of adultery; almost inevitably the god's impersonation of the husband must have been the chief factor of complication. Given Zeus's immortality and the fact that both husband and wife survived, it is hard to see how any of the fifth century Amphitryon tragedies can have been other than near-calamities averted at the last minute, in Sophocles' drama by the intervention of Teiresias the seer and in Euripides' drama by Zeus as *deus ex machina.* With Sophocles, whose play bore the hero's name, we might expect action to center upon the husband whose harsh *hybris* is subdued to awe; with Euripides, we fancy, the blamelessly suffering wife might have been the center of attention in the play that bore her name. But with Aeschylus, whose work was also entitled for the heroine, and who was often preoccupied with the accomodation of conflicting religious values, we are left hopelessly guessing. About the focus of attention in the tragic *Alkmene* of Ion of Chios we know nothing at all.

3. THE CLASSICAL AMPHITRYON DRAMAS: COMEDY

To the same fifth century B.C. as these tragedies belonged the genre of the brilliant, witty, ribald "Old Comedy," which was usually political and civic in content and which addressed itself to personalities and issues of the moment. Beginning small with Epicharmus just before and just after 500 B.C., and broadening through successive decades, it attained its highest development with Aristophanes, whose extant plays are the only representatives preserved to us of this extraordinary art form. Papyrus finds in Egypt since the 1890's, however, have revealed a significant sub-genre of "Old Comedy" which spoofed both gods and heroes and applied lofty diction to absurd situations, yet still managed to deal in political satire. Fragments of such a work of 430 B.C. by the poet Cratinus, entitled *Dionysalexandros,* and the same poet's *Nemesis* of 429 B.C., both burlesqued Homer's Helen, a character normally treated in tragedy. In the latter of these, the goddess Nemesis is represented as having laid the egg from which Helen was born, and one of the rediscovered papyri contains the hilarious words of Zeus as he brings the egg to Leda and in exalted diction bids her sit on it till it hatches. This zany story of the heroine with two mothers was somehow set parallel—we do not know exactly how—to Pericles, his mistress, his wife, and his illegitimate child, thus combining merry spoof with serious political criticism. Within this sub-genre of "Old Comedy" are probably to be listed the *Amphitryon* of Archippus, represented by seven insignificant fragments, and *The Long Night* (Nyx makra) by a writer named Plato, surnamed "Comicus" to distinguish him from the famous philosopher. The five fragments from this play are quite as unhelpful as those from Archippus.

When catastrophic defeat befell Athens at the end of the Peloponnesian War in 404 B.C., the political-social "Old Comedy" came to a sudden end. The last plays of Aristophanes himself betoken the change, particularly *Wealth* (Plutus), his final work, which was produced in 388 B.C. The "Middle Comedy" of the fourth century jested at foibles of the human race rather than at living politicians and public figures, but was none the less popular for it. The scholar Athenaeus, around 200 A.D., mentions a reading repertory of eight hundred Middle Comedies, every last one of which is lost. Our knowledge of these works is derived from fragments and indirect report, but they were apparently rather harsh in their portrayal of human vices and foibles. Aristotle in the *Poetics* describes the characters as "worse than ourselves." What is certain, however, is that "Middle Comedy" widely exploited that sub-genre of "Old Comedy" represented by Cratinus and took up with zest the travesty of myth and legend that were normally tragic material—minus all political satire.

Parenthetically it should be mentioned that tragedies continued to be composed in the fourth century, especially in the manner of Euripides, though our knowledge of them is slight. A tragic *Alkmene* was written by Dionysus the Elder, the famous tyrant of Syracuse in Sicily, before 367 B.C.; a later author has preserved for us three quoted lines from it. A fourth century tragedy of *Alkmene* by Astydamas the Younger is known only from its title in a list of that author's works. We also have two lines from an *Amphitryon* by a poet named Aeschylus of Alexandria, of uncertain date but probably from the third century B.C.

In the latter 300's "New Comedy" emerged with such poets as Diphilus, Philemon, Demophilus, and above all Menander (342–291 B.C.). These plays constituted a genteel verse comedy of manners and dealt in love stories, in stories of kidnapped children restored, of families separated and reunited, and in stories of intrigues by clever slaves. Again a very extensive repertory has been completely lost, although lucky finds in Egypt since 1897 have recovered substantial portions of four comedies

by Menander and in 1959 there was published the complete
text of Menander's *Dyskolos* (The Curmudgeon). Of the "New
Comedy" poets, Philemon is known to have written a *Long
Night* on the Amphitryon theme. Two tiny fragments from it
do not permit us to ascertain either its general nature or its
relation to the work of the same title by Plato "Comicus" a
hundred years earlier.

In the Greek colonies of southern Italy there was developed a
specialized form of comedy later called "Rhinthonic" for its
most famous practitioner, Rhinthon, who flourished between
304 and 285 B.C. In this sub-genre, barefooted actors with gro-
tesquely padded bellies and posteriors and wearing out-sized, pro-
truding phalli, turned the myths of the gods topsy-turvy. One
of the thirty-eight tragicomedies of Rhinthon—all lost—is known
to have been an *Amphitryon*. A south-Italian vase painting in
the Vatican Museum was identified by Winckelmann in the
eighteenth century as relating to the Amphitryon story and very
possibly to Rhinthon's version of that story. It portrays Mercury
holding a lamp to guide a grizzled and lecherous Jupiter as the
latter is about to set up a ladder to reach a lady in an upper
window. If the lady is Alcmena—and this is only a guess—*this*
Jupiter came to his desire by means rather more prosaic than
shape-shifting.

It was, however, not Rhinthonic burlesque from southern Italy
but rather Greek "New Comedy" from Greece that was introduced in Rome in 240 B.C., in Latin language adaptation for
the Roman audience, by Livius Andronicus. The innovation was
a success and more adaptations of "New Comedies" followed,
as well as of Greek tragedies. Within five years (235 B.C.) Livius
Andronicus had a significant competitor in Gnaeus Naevius.
Haphazard fragments in quotation by later writers are all that
remain from the considerable production of both these authors,
but their younger contemporary, Plautus, fared better, with
twenty comedies preserved more or less intact, the earliest works
of Latin literature to be so preserved. All twenty are presumed
to be adaptations from Greek originals. In some cases their
prologues cite title and author of the source work, in other cases
scholars are able to establish provenience with fair certainty, and

Zeus with ladder, Mecury with a light, below Alcmena in the window.

in still other cases the source work is wholly unascertainable. One of them, for instance, is known to be from Demophilus, two from Diphilus, two from Philemon, and two from Menander. For *Amphitruo*, which is probably to be dated to the 190's B.C., the source is unknown, though at one time or another Archippus, Plato "Comicus," and Rhinthon have all been proposed.

Chronological order makes us close this survey of classical Amphitryon dramas with tragedies in the Latin language. Roman tragedy flourished primarily in the names of Quintus Ennius, a contemporary of Plautus; in Marcus Pacuvius, who was a young man in Plautus' advanced years; and in Lucius Accius, who was born after Plautus' death and who lived until approximately 86 B.C. The production of all three is now represented by bare titles and miscellaneous quotations, but among the forty-five titles attributed to Accius there is an *Amphitruo*. Further, a tragedy entitled *Alcumena* is mentioned, unaccompanied by any author's name, in a grammarian's list of titles that showed the intrusive vowel u in Greek names. Although this grammarian, Marius Victorinus by name, wrote in the fourth century A.D., there is no reason to doubt that his five-hundred-year-old information was correct on this point as in the citing of a lost Latin *Alcumeo* and a lost Latin *Tecumesa* which Greeks would have termed "Alkmeon" and "Tekmessa" respectively. Since it is known that Gaius Julius Caesar Strabo, who was killed in 87 B.C., was the first Roman to omit these intrusive u's, the unidentified author of *Alcumena* was probably a contemporary of Accius.

There is a span of four hundred years from the lost *Alkmene* of Aeschylus to the lost *Amphitruo* of Accius, and in that span are comprised fourteen plays. In Greek: seven tragedies, three of them by the supreme tragic poets, two "Old Comedies," one "New Comedy," and one mythological travesty; in Latin: one adaptation of a Greek "New Comedy" by Plautus, one tragedy by an unknown author, and one tragedy by a poet highly esteemed in literary Rome (who may have worked on the basis of Sophocles' text). Of these fourteen works, only Plautus' adaptation survives. Clearly it is impossible to assess accurately the dramatic tradition constituted by these lost works, and just as clearly it is impossible to deduce from Plautus' *Amphitruo* the essential qualities and procedures of his predecessors, especially of the tragedians.

Certain observations can, however, be made about the dramas in contrast to the legend. Neither the complex genealogies nor the remote dynastic struggles within the House of Perseus, as reported by "Apollodorus," can have furnished more than incidental details for the plays, whether tragic or comic. Family trees grow in the study, not on the stage, and throne disputes of long ago may well delimit a dramatic situation but they cannot constitute a dramatic essence. Similarly, the birth of Herakles may well be the goal toward which a drama moves, but an infant cannot be an acting personage. The stageworthy matter in the legend has to involve primarily the Theban triangle of Zeus, Alkmene, and Amphitryon, in other words precisely that portion of the story that is hurried over by the legend reporters. This fact is all the more mystifying in that all the sources reviewed, save for Homer and Hesiod, were composed *after* the four-hundred-year dramatic tradition had ended. "Apollodorus," Diodorus, and Ovid cannot have been ignorant of the plays, yet they wrote as if the plays had never existed. We suspect that an independent book-tradition of mythography must account for their omissions. We are left with the ironic result that these authors, while telling us much, withheld precisely the things which we most want to learn.

4. ROMAN DRAMA AND PLAUTUS

From very early Roman times dramatic potential lay, undeveloped, in the "Fescennine verses," which took their name either from an Etrurian town called Fescennia or from the word *fascinum*—"black magic," and, by extension, a diverting charm against black magic. These short pieces of bawdy verse-repartee coupled with bawdy songs continued in use for centuries at harvest and vintage festivals, at weddings and military triumphs, but they involved no impersonation and underwent no direct literary development. The verse form used was the "Saturnian," a two-part line which some think had three *accents* in each half, in accordance with a native Italian accentual prosody, though this notion is much disputed. At any rate, the form was so old as to be ascribed to the earthly reign of the god Saturn.

In the fourth and third centuries B.C. the *satura* held dramatic promise. We may imagine it to have been a plotless skit using Saturnians in its dialogue sections and interspersed with songs and dances, thus justifying the likeliest etymology of the word as "a medley." Livy reports that it was first known in Rome in 364 B.C., when Etruscan performers were invited to give such "medleys" as part of a religious exercise against plague. Events conspired, however, to divert the *satura* from the direction of drama, so that by complex evolution it turned ultimately into verse satire.

A tributary stream feeding directly into Roman comedy, and doubtless a more important one than we are able to assess from meager reports, was the *fabula Atellana,* an early third century B.C. import, originally in Oscan dialect, from (it is said) the town of Atella, just north of Naples. What we know of it so resembles the Italian *commedia dell'arte* of hundreds of years later that some people have claimed it was the ancestor of the latter, but the claim is beyond proof or disproof. It used stock clowns with names like *Maccus* the fool, *Pappus* the slow-witted oldster, *Manducus* the glutton, *Dossenus* the hunchback, *Bucco* the fat man, and put them through successive adventures of rustic farce. After 150 B.C. two authors, Pomponius and Novius, made written verse plays about these characters, somewhat perhaps as the eighteenth century writers Goldoni and Gozzi did with the old *commedia dell'arte* figures, but we possess no more than the titles of these literary *Atellanae,* e.g. *Maccus as a Soldier, Maccus as a Girl, Maccus as a Tavernkeeper.* This, however, was two generations after Plautus.

Roman drama proper, and indeed Roman literature, began with Livius Andronicus, a Greek imported as a slave from Tarentum in the heel of Italy after the conquest of the southern extremities of the peninsula. By a translation of the *Odyssey* into Latin Saturnians he brought Greek epic to the Romans, and in 240 B.C. he produced the first of a series of tragedies and comedies on Greek subjects translated and adapted by him. The new genre, which could draw on the wealth of Greek classicism, was directly exploited by a competitior, Gnaeus Naevius, who

was probably a native of Rome itself and whose first plays were
given in 235 B.C. The foreign subject matter must have left
some elements of his audiences unsatisfied, because Naevius
composed a number of plays on themes taken from Roman history, thus creating a new genre called the *fabula praetextata.*
As for his comedies, they apparently had about them some of
that old political salt of the Aristophanic variety, because around
205 he was in jail for offense to certain prominent families—the
Metelli, perhaps, whose high office in the state, one of his preserved lines says, was achieved "by Fate." Ultimately he died in
exile in North Africa, around 200 B.C.

From Livius Andronicus less than a hundred lines remain,
from Naevius about twice that number. The earliest plays—in
fact, the earliest works of Latin literature—to be preserved in
their entirety are those by Plautus. We have twenty of them,
with here and there a page missing, and shattered fragments of
one more. Presumabily these are the twenty-one edited around
50 B.C. by the scholar Marcus Terentius Varro and sifted by
him from a hundred and thirty comedies that had been indis-
criminately called Plautine.

Scholars deduce that our comic poet was born about 254 B.C.,
in the Umbrian town of Sarsina, it is said, over the Apennine
watershed from the source of the Tiber and facing toward the
Adriatic. It lay close to the border of the north Italian Gauls,
whom conquest had not yet brought under Roman dominion.
He may have been a slave, or perhaps a freedman (ex-slave), and
of course he was not a Roman citizen. As a young man he came
to The City and was there associated in some capacity or other
with plays. There was a tradition that he accumulated some
capital by so doing, went on a trading journey in which he lost
everything, and was obliged to turn a baker's grindstones upon
his penniless return; from that situation he extricated himself
by composing three comedies. These biographical details are
known only from a single sentence of the little article about true
and spurious Plautine plays which Aulus Gellius inserted, three
hundred and fifty years later, into that huge scrapbook of his
which he entitled *Attic Nights.* When he was granted Roman
citizenship he took the name of Titus Maccius Plautus—the
given name (*praenomen*), some think, from his father; the *nomen*

of Maccius, which corresponds to our family names, in allusion to Maccus the fool of the Atellan farces, which suggests he may have been a performer in that character; and the *cognomen* of Plautus (or Plotus)—"Flatfoot"—the *cognomen* being often a nickname. Public success seems to have come to him around age forty, which would be around 214 B.C.

An allusion to the imprisonment of Naevius in the comedy of *The Braggart Soldier* (Miles gloriosus) dates that work around 205. It is known that his comedy *Stichus* was produced in 200 and his *Pseudolus* in 191. Cicero mentions that he died in 184. Now it happens that *The Braggart Soldier* is metrically conservative and contains only one lyric passage, whereas *Stichus* has decidedly more lyric matter, and *Pseudolus* abounds in lyric passages and shows considerable metrical variety. Scholars therefore infer that *The Braggart Soldier* is probably the earliest of the twenty-one canonical plays and that a rough chronology can be established for the others on the basis of metrics and style. *Amphitruo* would then appear to be late among the twenty-one extant works. Lost early works before 205 are doubtless to be assumed. Other criteria for dating seem unreliable. Length of text, for instance, varies widely and apparently at random, from 1,437 lines in *The Braggart Soldier* to 729 lines in *Curculio*. Quality varies just as widely, from splendid to perfunctory.

The circumstances of production of these plays differed somewhat from those of Greek drama and, needless to say, were unlike anything familiar to our own experience. Both *saturae* and the new plays on Greek themes had long been given annually in September as part of the four-day Roman Games (*ludi Romani*) and in November at the Plebeian Games (*ludi plebeii*). Late in Plautus' life, in 194, plays were first added to the *ludi Megalenses* of the April festival in honor of the goddess Cybele and somewhat earlier to the *ludi Apollinares* held in July in honor of Apollo. Further, there might be plays as part of the celebration of a military triumph and, strange as it may seem, at the funerals of distinguished persons. It is hard to see how our author could have accumulated money for a trading venture by working at drama in any capacity for a total of perhaps ten days a year.

A generation after his death, in 154, construction was begun on a stone theater, but by senatorial order it was demolished and no permanent structure was created until Pompey's theater of 55 B.C. Two more such, the theaters of Cornelius Balbus and of Marcellus, graced the capital by 13 A.D., while succeeding decades saw elaborate stone theaters built in every large and medium-sized city in the Empire. Two of the best preserved of these are to be found now in the southern French city of Orange (Arausio) and at the abandoned site of Timgad (Thaumagadi) in Algeria. But for the time of Plautus we are obliged to imagine open air performances, probably in the vicinity of the temple of the deity being honored, with wooden stages built for the occasion and removed after the festival was over. Audiences faced a long, narrow stage from which four or five steps led down to the flat space of the "orchestra," where senators were seated, no doubt in light, portable chairs. The "orchestra" was no longer a dancing circle for the Greek chorus and, to judge by those later permanent Roman theatres, it was a half-circle rather than the full circle customary with the Greeks.

In order to say more, we are at this point compelled to specify what authority we are following. J. Wight Duff's standard and traditional *Literary History of Rome,* thrice reprinted from its original edition of 1909, states that audiences, except for senators, stood; that the stage, which might be as much as sixty yards in length, contained rudimentary painted scenery, and that no masks were worn by actors until fifty years after Plautus' time. For Duff, the reference to seats in the prologue to *Amphitruo* (line 65) indicates that either part or the whole of that prologue was written by someone else than Plautus, perhaps for a revival of the play in some later generation. These contentions, and others, are contradicted outright by W. Beare's *The Roman Stage* (third edition, 1963), and, all things considered, we have found ourselves persuaded by Professor Beare's arguments. Not only does he cite cases in the texts of the plays—and not merely in prologues and closings where textual modification could be most readily introduced for a revival production—where there is unmistakable reference to seated spectators, but he points out that the public officials who staged the plays as a means of winning favor at the next elections would not have been likely to oblige the voters to stand through a two-to-three-hour performance, especially when those people knew of Greek theaters with seating facilities no further away than Pompeii. Clearly these are controversial matters, but Beare works primarily from the closest kind of reading of Plautus' texts, whereas, he says, previous scholars have gathered statements and inferences from imperial times about those elaborate structures which we have mentioned and uncritically applied them to the period around 200 B.C.

With Beare, then, we envisage an audience seated and not standing; a slope of wooden benches built, like the stage, especially for the occasion and removed when the festival was over; actors who did wear masks—as all Greek drama hitherto had done; no stage scenery, but rather the plain front wall of the actors' dressing room and storage building, penetrated by the usual three sets of inward-opening double doors, which led to whatever places the dramatic poet indicated in his text. In tragedy, that plain wall was, by virtue of the poet's statement and the audience's imagination, a temple or palace façade; in comedy it was, by virtue of the same factors, the façade of two or three houses whose doors opened onto the public street. The much debated *angiportus* was not a narrow passageway between the houses and at right angles to the stage, but the entrance to houses on the next street over; the audiences supplied from everyday reality the back-yard interconnections that the *angiportus* made possible. No object was permanently on stage except for an altar at center-front. Plautus, like Shakespeare, began with an empty stage platform, indicated in the text anything that had to be brought on stage, arranged for its removal as part of the play's action, and cleared the stage of all actors at the end. No indoors action was ever represented, and such indoors action as occurs in the plays is verbally reported by on-stage actors who may, perhaps, gesture toward one of the open doors through which they claim to see what they are describing. There was no stage curtain (as there was in later times). The comedies were designed for continuous performance, the division into Acts being the superimposed work of editors of Rome's Classical age.

It is possible that Plautus was poet, producer, and actor, and that he was a member or master of a regular troupe, in which case he would stand as an ancient parallel to Molière, but none

of these points is certain except that he was a dramatic poet.
Later practice knew a troupe master (*dominus gregis*) with
actors who were slaves owned outright by him and whom he could
reward or physically punish according to the merits of their
performances. This troupe master usually bought a script, con-
tracted with the annually elected magistrates called *aediles* for
the furnishing of costumes and other necessaries, and himself, as
actor primarum, took the leading role. Commonly a freedman
and with slaves for troupe members, neither he nor they enjoyed
any social prestige. In Rome the acting profession was never
looked upon with favor, though in Cicero's day the famous actor
Roscius might associate with persons of rank. By imperial times
even this slight advance was lost, and when actresses were finally
allowed to perform, the profession became synonymous with
harlotry.

In the matter of costume our two authorities are again at odds.
Beare rules out as anachronistic the fairly detailed accounts of
it given by Julius Pollux, who was a professor of rhetoric at
Athens around 180 A.D., and by Aelius Donatus, who some time
in the fourth century A.D. wrote a commentary on Terence. It
may be mentioned that these two accounts are not in full agreement with each other. We have preferred to accept Beare's strict
—perhaps over-strict—deductions from the text and from known
habits of Plautus' era.

The comedy initiated by Livius Andronicus in 240 B.C. was,
by definition, Greek New Comedy in adaptation. Thus all comedies of Plautus and Terence are nominally set in Greece, most
commonly in Athens but occasionally in other Greek towns.
Plautus' *The Rope* (Rudens), as we have mentioned, is set on
the North African coast near the *Greek* colony of Cyrene. All
characters are therefore nominally Greeks and wear Greek dress.
The basic item of this costume was a linen or woolen *chiton*
(Latin *tunica*), normally sleeveless, which was pulled on over
the head and girded at the waist by a belt, over which it could
be bloused to different lengths. Over this might be worn a
woolen wrap called *himation,* which was draped about the
shoulders and attached with a brooch. In Latin this wrap was
called a *pallium* for men, a *palla* for women. Hence the technical
term for this genre of comedy: *fabula palliata.* The toga-clad

audience, therefore, always viewed stage characters who were foreigners wearing foreign costume.

Colors must have varied, but Beare rejects Pollux' color-rules —red or purple mantle over white linen for young men, "flowery" mantle over "dyed" tunics for pimps, yellow or sky-blue for old women, etc., as well as Donatus' color-rules—purple for the rich, red for the poor, yellow for harlots, etc. There was sufficient difference between male and female costume to make it possible for a man to disguise himself as a woman in Plautus' *Casina.* Slaves dressed pretty much like their masters. Rustics might be clad in goatskins. In comedy all characters wore either fastened sandals or unfastened slippers. The Latin word for the latter was *soccus,* a term which came to stand for comedy itself, as in Milton's *L'Allegro,* line 132: "If Jonsons learned Sock be on," whereas the footgear for tragic actors was the *cothurnus* (English: buskin), a thick sole cross-laced over the foot and half way up the lower leg. In *Amphitruo,* Sosia, Mercury, Amphitryon, and Jupiter all wear hats, like the travelers they are or claim to be, presumably the broad-brimmed Greek *petasos,* which was provided with a chin-strap that might hold the hat in position on the head or allow it to dangle at the nape of the neck. Soldiers might also wear these, as well as a bright-colored cape called a *chlamys.*

Costume in Plautus' time, Beare feels, was more likely simple than elaborate, with the simplicity compensated for by elaborately styled masks. These fitted not only over the face but over the entire head and included hair—white hair for old men, black hair for young men, and frequently, but not invariably, red hair for slaves. Both costume and mask had to be quickly changed backstage—in one case within a space of six lines of text—by actors doubling in the different roles.

Tragedy, on the other hand, may well have employed gorgeous, non-realistic costume and must have been altogether a more expensive sort of drama to mount. Its splendor was its ultimate downfall, for by the imperial age those gorgeous costumes smothered both poetic and human content. Likewise the exalted diction of tragedy had no very long distance to go before it arrived at mannered bombast. In the opening scene of *Amphitruo* Plautus makes Mercury and Sosia exchange a few lines in

the tragic manner for comic effect, for example Mercury's inquiry
(line 341):

> Whither walkest thou, O stranger,
>   with Vulcan enclosèd in yon horn?
> (Quo ambulas tu, qui Volcanum in cornu conclusum geris?)

—meaning, of course, "Where are you going with that lighted
lantern?"

Most vexed of all Plautine questions is that of how the lines
of the text were delivered in performance. On a few points there
is agreement: the prologues were spoken; there were no choral
interludes; passages in iambic senarii (hexameter) were spoken.
It is also certain that portions of the text were musical, that the
music was composed by someone other than the author—usually
a slave, and that the music was subordinated to the words. Further, we know that a boy with a clarinet-like instrument called
tibiae—"pipes"—was on stage through most of the performance
and that he moved from actor to actor, supporting the delivery
of lines with musical accompaniment. We have no idea what he
played, other than that he marked the complex and frequently
changing rhythms. We do know that he blew different notes, else
a drummer would have done just as well, but it is easier to
imagine that he repeated a rhythmic phrase over and over, perhaps in alternating registers or with slight variations, so long
as a given meter was in use by the actor, than it is to imagine
that he played a melody, in our sense of the term, through to its
close. We may further imagine that he cued the actor to the
next rhythmic change—and we cannot overstress the point that
Plautus' meters vary amazingly and rapidly, in some cases from
line to line. More mysterious is: what did the actor do against
this accompaniment? It is all but certain that he did *not* sing.
There is nothing in Plautus that corresponded to an operatic
aria or a musical comedy "number" that spectators could whistle
or sing on the way home. On the other hand, the actor did not
speak to the piper's music. Intermediate between speech and
song are: chanted declamation, which is closer to speech, and
recitative, which is closer to song. Beyond this point of deduc-
tion only subjective fancy can go, especially since we know next

Five figures, the one in the middle being "the flute-lad" playing a double flute.

to nothing about Roman music and not very much about Greek music.

The fourth century A.D. writer Donatus states that the sign "DV"—for *diverbium* (dialogue)—was indicated in manuscripts over spoken sections. Some preserved manuscripts contain a few such "DV's," but also certain "C's," which must stand for *canticum,* a word more cautiously translated as "musical" than as "song." Of the 20,000 lines of Plautine comedy only 8,200 are iambic senarii, which scholars agree were spoken. Anyone can pick out more exciting passages which he would readily mark with a "C," in meters bearing such discouraging names as: bacchiacs, choriambics, cretics, glyconics, sotadeans, anapestic dimeter catalectic and anapestic dimeter acatalectic, and so on. But (as Beare asks) what about some 1,300 seven-foot iambics, some 400 eight-foot iambics, and whole scenes in trochaic lines of seven and a half feet? Would these be "DV's" or "C's?" If this question could be answered we could decide whether a comedy of Plautus was primarily musical or primarily dramatic. In any event, we may be sure that the over-all effect was like neither *The School for Scandal* nor *The Merry Widow,* and we feel that the often suggested parallel with Gilbert and Sullivan operetta, while containing some truth, is really more misleading than helpful.

Moreover, the actors sometimes danced and it was their regular practice to accompany their lines with elaborate miming gestures. Livy may have been thinking of his own Classical era when he professed to relate an ancedote about Livius Andronicus of two hundred years before, but the anecdote is still enlightening. In a certain performance Livius Andronicus went hoarse from repeated encores of a musical passage. When the crowd demanded more, he called over a boy to do the vocal part while he himself stood aside from the boy and the piper and silently mimed the *canticum.*

Pausing for a moment to allow fancy to assimilate all these details, we imagine people gathering in bright September weather near a temple of Jupiter, in whose honor the Roman Games are being held. Those who prefer the acrobatic show have stayed behind. It is midday, for, contrary to Greek usage,

noon to mid-afternoon, not the morning, was play time, and
probably only one play is to be given, not the Greek sequence
of three or four. The occasion is both a religious and, as we
would say, a national holiday, and the crowd is motley. There
are ladies present, both respectable and not-so-respectable, and
both may (or may not) be prepared for quips that the actors
may aim at them in asides to the audience. The presence of
senators is the chief guarantee of audience decorum. Possibly the
senators signal for the performance to begin. The Greek or semi-
Greek subject matter of the play being by no means familiar to
everyone, the author has sent out a Prologue to identify the
scene of action, to sketch in the story situation, and to cajole the
spectators into settling down. The Prologue retires. Masked characters whom he has named come onto the long, narrow stage,
either from one of the three sets of double doors, which the
Prologue said was the entrance to the house of so-and-so, or from
the far end of the stage platform at the actors' left, which by
convention was understood to be "from the forum" or "from
the center of town," or from the opposite end of the stage platform which by convention was understood to be "from the
harbor" or "from the country." Full sunlight pours down unin-
terruptedly, even if the action is alleged to take place in darkness. Much like a Shakespearean actor, Sosia, in the opening
scene of *Amphitruo,* will signify pitch-black nighttime by carrying a lantern. A conversational passage in recited iambic senarii
gets the story going, but it is not long before the piper-lad comes
and a musical section carries the story forward, for there are
no time-suspended solos in this drama. The acoustics are such
that all the actors must use full lung-power. The trainer has
urged them to make the case endings of nouns and the personal
endings of verbs audible to the back rows. Bits of stage business
are broadly played. A good joke may have to be followed by a
pause so audience laughter will not cover up the better come-
back joke. The long stage makes it possible for an actor to stand
plausibly apart and make third-party asides to the audience
about the center-stage dialogue. New arrivals on stage, however,
may fail to see other actors by simply taking care not to look
their way until the moment when their lines come to the surprised exclamation at their presence. A dance or a musical sec-

tion may take the audience's fancy so much that it has to be repeated to satisfy them. Among the spectators there are individuals who especially appreciate good vocal display or effective miming gestures, and there are some who may even have received a little token of money in advance to be especially appreciative of either the author's work or some actor's performance. At last the comedy is brought to its conclusion and one of the actors steps forward to invite applause. If that applause is enthusiastic, the candidates for election, who have paid for all this, hope that audience memories will not fail to be enthusiastic when the next voting comes around.

5. PLAUTUS' *Amphitruo*

As the reader opens the book of Plautus' *Amphitruo* he encounters two separate plot-summaries in verse, "Argument I" and "Argument II" respectively, of which the first is an acrostic that spells out the title of the play. The other comedies are likewise prefaced with verses of the one sort or of both. None are by Plautus. They are more likely the by-products of bibliophile pastime than playbills for revival performances.

The prologue spoken by Mercury is the longest in Plautus' works, consisting of 152 iambic senarii. With Beare we regard it as genuine, rejecting the traditional disqualification on account of the reference in line 65 to seats for the audience. These 152 lines are reckoned as part of the total play-text of 1,146 lines, though the passage missing after line 1,034 may have added as much as another 300 lines to the total. Compare Molière's 1,943 lines and Kleist's 2,362. Mercury begins with the cajoling of spectators' interest and attention—the *captatio benevolentiae*—but he undercuts his flattery with rather sharp quips and he has much to say before he gets down to the practical business of introducing the play proper in the last third of his speech. In between, he wittily tantalizes the audience by talk about the god Jupiter and the human actor playing the role of Jupiter, creates dismay by announcing a tragedy and then whets curiosity by declaring for a tragicomedy, and also alludes to hired applauders and hired hecklers of actors and to the political equivalents of each at election time. Ultimately this all comes down to subtle flattery of the spectators as voting citizens and as proper judges of dramatic performance.

As opposed to seven Plautine prologues where the Greek source work is named, sometimes both by title and by author, this one passes over that point in silence and scholars have been unable to identify any of the known—but lost—Greek Amphitryon comedies as the source. As a tragicomedy and as a burlesque of a divine myth, this play stands somewhat apart from Plautus' other nineteen preserved plays and may well reflect an origin in "Middle Comedy" rather than in "New Comedy."

A question much more vexed and much more vexing asks whether there were *two* Greek sources. It seems absurd to ask about two when we cannot identify even one, but there is a notion long held and much debated as to whether Roman prac-tice regularly telescoped two Greek plays into one by a process termed *contaminatio*. The question becomes even more vexing when we note that it arises out of a few lines in the prologue to Terence's play *The Woman of Andros* (Andria), dated 166 B.C., eighteen years after Plautus' death.

Reading between the lines of the *Andria* prologue, we discern that the Roman audiences craved dramas as good as the cele-brated Greek ones but in their own language, that Terence was a conscientious translator-adapter, and that there were jealous literary cliques in Rome. Such a clique is known to have centered on one Luscius Lanuvinus, a disappointed poet, and though Terence mentions no names, it is likely that this man and his supporters were the "enemies" alluded to in the prologue. The "enemies" have accused the youthful dramatist of spoiling good Greek plays by combining elements of two of them to make one Latin work. The word for "spoil" is *contaminare*. Terence pro-ceeds to state that in composing his *Andria* he had indeed used both Menander's *Andria* and Menander's *Perinthia,* since those two works were similar anyway. With neither Menander play available to us, we do not know exactly what the combination involved. The fourth century A.D. scholar Donatus, who did have all three works at hand, reports that the two Greek plays had a similar passage, one in monologue and one in dialogue, and that Terence has a dialogue at that point. Otherwise Do-natus found the *Perinthia* completely different from the Greek

Andria, but he did find a three-line passage near the end of the Roman *Andria* that seemed to be borrowed from still another play of Menander's. This is all quite bewildering and we have a feeling that it was a matter of a tempest in a teapot. At any rate, Terence admits the basic truth of his "enemies' " rumors, claims to have achieved better results that way, and assuages audience fears of being cheated. Then he goes on to say that the "enemies" are automatically attacking Naevius, Plautus, and Ennius by their remarks, and that *he* prefers the "carelessness"—*negligentia* —of these older authors to the "carefulness" of his opponents. On this basis arose a scholarly tradition that all Roman playwrights dovetailed two Greek sources to make one Latin work.

In the twentieth century the doctrine of *contaminatio* has become ever more suspect among scholars. For one thing, the word *contaminare* in all known contexts means "to spoil" and no clear-cut case has yet been found where it means "to combine." But the quarrel is abstruse and we may best avoid difficulties by saying that Plautus, who in seven prologues mentioned one and only one source work, is likely to have regularly used one and only one source work at a time, but that he treated that one very freely—"carelessly"—adding and subtracting elements with a shrewd eye to the needs and tastes of his clientele.

Yet a nagging doubt persists. The distinguished Plautine scholar Friedrich Leo, writing two generations ago, felt it likely that *Amphitruo* did depend on two Greek sources, not one, and he pointed to the confused biology of the work. In the prologue Mercury explains that Alcmena is simultaneously pregnant by Amphitryon and by Jupiter and in lines 481–2 he adds: ten months by the former, seven months by the latter. It matters not at all that this is fanciful gynecology, but it does matter esthetically that Jupiter has ordained a night of triple length in order to enjoy the passionate embraces of a woman destined to give birth to twins a few hours hence. Leo felt that this odd circumstance was most plausibly accounted for by the author's use of two quite different Greek sources, one in which Jupiter appeared at the hour of Herakles' birth after having begotten him upon Alcmena seven months previously and one in which Jupiter spent the triple night with Alcmena and at its close announced the hero's birth at a future date. The French scholar G. Michaut reproved Leo for taking a comic work with excessive literal-mindedness. To which we retort that even comic fantasy has limits. By all poetic rights the triple night of passion should be Jupiter's first encounter with Alcmena and there is plausibility in Leo's suggestion that two disparate Greek sources have been combined here, perhaps "carelessly." On the other hand, it is possible that Plautus' single Greek source had already "carelessly" joined two mythological versions. Of all the Plautus-inspired *Amphitryons* of later ages, only Jean Rotrou's *Les Sosies* of 1638 ventured to clarify this point; there the triple night *is* Jupiter's first encounter with Alcmena, but the god abrogates the laws of Nature by divine fiat in order to make birth ensue within hours after the act of procreation.

At line 19 of the prologue Mercury formally announced his name to the audience: ". . . my name is MERCURY" (nomen Mercuriost mihi); at line 141 he speaks of Amphitryon's slave "of whom I bear this shape" (quoius ego fero hanc imaginem). We infer that the Mercury-actor wore a slave's costume and that he was not recognizable as the god Mercury until he introduced himself. Perhaps the actor delivered the prologue while holding his mask in his hand; then, at the point where he explains that he *will have* these little winglets on his hat (Ego has habebo . . . in petaso pinulas) to distinguish himself from the real Sosia, he perhaps put the mask on. The mask fitted over the entire head and included both hair and hat. It would be theatrically effective if he did. Then as Mercury-Sosia he would gesture toward the real Sosia whose approach he heralds. Thus the transition from prologue to dramatic action would be smoothed and the audience would enjoy inspecting the two identical personages.

Sosia comes up carrying a lantern, sole indication of the story's pitch darkness in the scene enacted under the noonday Roman sun. Otherwise the spoken word must conjure the illusion of night. He approaches from actors' right (or audience left), the direction regularly understood to be "from the harbor." Mercury waits for him in front of the middle pair of inward-opening double doors which now, by his own statement, are the main entrance into Amphitryon's house. The other two pairs of double doors, to right and left of the central one, will be ignored in this play, because no other house is involved in the story.

It is odd that Sosia should walk up from the harbor and odder
still that he should retraverse that road no less than five times
in the course of the play, which is to say in a single day, for
Thebes is a landlocked city fifteen miles from both its ancient
"out-ports," Anthedon to the north and Creusis to the south.
Of the two, Anthedon, on the Gulf of Corinth, faces out toward
the islands of the Taphians/Teleboans whence Amphitryon has
just returned by ship. To say that Plautus here indulged in
fantasy geography similar to Shakespeare's "seacoast of Bo-
hemia" is to deny the all-but-total certainty that he was trans-
lating a Greek text. But what Greek was capable of such a
blunder? It is perhaps best to assume that either Plautus or the
Greek, or both, used a stage convention which gave any Greek
city an "out-port" some distance off, as the Piraeus was four and
a half miles from Athens. (See also our note to line 404 on the
"harbor of Persicus.")

Sosia's monologue is highly amusing as he describes in detail
the battle in which he did *not* take part. It must have been even
more amusing to the recent veterans of the Second Punic War,
which ended in 201 B.C. A soldier's cowardice, comically portrayed, is always fun for the survivors of a recent war. We note
that it was a land battle, where we might have expected a naval
engagement against islanders, and that it was won by Amphitryon's *legions*. Plautus regularly Romanized details in his adaptations from the Greek and seems to have relished the resulting
anomalies. It has been suggested that Sosia's battle-narrative may
be a parody of some tragedy of Ennius, but it could quite as
easily be another application of the unfailing humor of "the
braggart soldier," which Plautus had exploited before.

As for all that beating and violent talk of beating that goes
on in this very long scene between Mercury and Sosia, we may
take it as harmless Punch and Judy violence, for Sosia is basically
a clown character and clowns are those who get slapped. The
actors must, of course, go through the motions of violence and
Sosia must talk of having "a meal of fists," but he cannot really
be struck resoundingly and repeatedly on the jaw if his perish-
able linen mask is to identify him as Sosia through the rest of
the play.

At the end of this longest single scene in Plautus' works—

310 lines—Sosia beats an ignominious retreat, whereupon Mercury delivers a kind of second prologue, consisting of thirty-six lines in the "speaking" meter, iambic senarii, outlining for the audience what is to come. *He* will mix everything up, Jupiter will sort everything out again, and all will eventually turn out well. The need for mixing everything up is left unexplained. The play requires it, Mercury was the traditional rogue among the gods, and motivation is the wrong thing to ask for at this point.

Mercury, as pseudo-Sosia attendant upon the orders of the pseudo-Amphitryon, remains on stage as Jupiter takes his pre-dawn farewell of Alcmena, presenting her with King Pterelas' golden goblet just before he leaves. It is an odd moment for such a presentation; more logically it would have been made upon arrival. We detect that in the source work—or in the source work of the source work—the goblet must have been what old German practice termed a *Morgengabe,* a gift from husband to wife on the morning after consummation of the marriage. This dorus," but it squares ill with the fact that Jupiter begot Herakles ancient datum of the myth is clear from Pherecydes and "Apollo-upon Alcmena seven months before.

At line 543 Jupiter-Amphitryon bids Mercury-Sosia go on ahead, himself tarries for one more parting line to Alcmena, and, when she has retired within the house, delivers five lines to dismiss Night at last and to allow Day to begin its course. At this point the Classical editor inserted the direction: "Act II." As in Shakespeare's practice, however, there was no break here; Jupiter retired and the stage was immediately taken over by Amphitryon and Sosia. These two are coming up from the harbor, hence they approach from the far end of the stage at audience-left; Jupiter must therefore make his exit toward the far end of the stage to audience-right, since he must neither encounter them nor go back into the house. The newcomers must stop more than once for conversation in their walk up the long stage so as not to arrive too close to the house entrance before Alcmena has had time to come out and deliver her *canticum* on courage. She has twenty-one lines and they have six before she exclaims, "Why, look, it's my husband!" Follows then the excellent 200-line scene of the husband-wife confrontation and quarrel, with Sosia making clown comments throughout. At the end of it, Amphitryon stalks off to find in Naucrates a witness for his night's whereabouts, Sosia trails after him, and Alcmena speaks a 3-line soliloquy that confirms the sincerity of all that she has said heretofore. At this point the editor inserted "Act III."

Jupiter opens this third Act in quiet iambic senarii of confidences to the audience. The altogether serious subject of adultery on the part of a nobleman's wife has been broached, divorce has been threatened, and a Roman audience needed reassurance as to Jupiter's intentions relative both to the innocent lady and to their promised comedy. Alcmena is mollified by the pseudo-husband, and Jupiter sends Sosia—the real Sosia —to invite ship-captain Blepharo to a little dinner of rejoicing. When all three have left the stage, Mercury enters in breathless haste, not because there is any dramatic need of breathless haste but because, in his slave costume, he is giving a hilarious imitation of the "running slave" (servus currens). Such were to be seen any day in the streets of Rome, haughty messengers jostling crowds and ordering everyone out of their way in order to speed some errand for an impatient master. Seeing a messenger-*god* behaving this way would surely create mirth in the audience. Actually, Mercury's only errand is a further confidence to the audience about how he means to do some more mixing up: he will go up on the roof, pretend to be drunk, and goad master-of-the-house Amphitryon into fury beyond anything yet seen.

Along comes Amphitryon in foul mood. Naucrates was nowhere to be found. He has hunted for him all over the city without success. He tries the door of his house; it is locked. He calls, only to be answered from the roof (of the building where stage properties were stored and actors changed costume) by, his own slave Sosia. Mercury-Sosia affects drunken insolence to the furthest limits, Amphitryon is wild with rage, and . . . suddenly the ancient manuscript fails us for several pages. It is not certain where the editor drew the line between Act III and Act IV, and modern editors make that division at different points. All, however, are agreed that the text resumes late in Act IV.

At the resuming place, ship-captain Blepharo is on stage between the two Amphitryons and on the point of renouncing all effort at distinguishing the real one. The real one is ready to explode with baffled fury, and when Blepharo walks away and Jupiter-Amphitryon retires within the house, he rushes to batter down his own door. At that instant a bolt of lightning strikes him down and as he falls to the ground the peals of thunder roll over him.

He lies there unconscious while the editor, as it were, inserts the caption: "Act V" and as the maid servant Bromia comes stumbling in terror out of the house. The real reason for her presence is, of course, to inform the spectators of the events and marvels that have occurred in the last few minutes. Her Messenger's Speech is strongly reminiscent of such speeches just before the final scenes in various tragedies of Euripides, and given the fact that Plautus, as we know from the line in *Rudens,* was familiar with Euripides' tragedy of *Alkmene,* we can only wonder whether any element of parody was intended here. We would also like to know in what play of the preceding year it was that Jupiter appeared right on stage as a *deus ex machina.* Mercury speaks of it in the prologue, lines 91–92, as if it had been a new experience for the audience. Perhaps we have a kind of parody of *that* play. More likely, however, is that the thunder-machine (bronteîon) was a sure attention-getter, along with the "high-periactus" or "flash." The latter was a three-sided revolving stand, probably with lightning-flashes painted against dark background on each side, which was mounted on the roof and set whirling on a spindle. Bromia's narrative is serious enough, but the recital of such portentous happenings by a slave woman would, for a Roman audience, hold the serious words within the limits of comedy.

Most of Act V is given over to Amphitryon's dazed reviving and his piecemeal learning from his maid about all that has happened. The absurdity of the great warrior's plight in this scene is evident to readers of any century. Again the roll of thunder, and then the strikingly Euripidean-type epiphany of Jupiter in full majesty (on the roof of the scene building). Dutifully, Amphitryon accedes to the divine pronouncements and the play closes as the Amphitryon actor steps forward and solicits applause from the spectators.

The characterizations in this play are theatrically vivid. To

inquire more deeply into them than that would defeat the purposes of comedy and the author's intentions, but we may remark
that Amphitryon is humanly plausible throughout. If he speaks
roughly to his slave Sosia, that was expected of him, and if he
speaks roughly to Alcmena, that was understandable in the circumstances; but he is nowhere ignoble. Thoroughly human and
convincingly realistic is Sosia, who stars in hard luck all the way
but who will emerge safe after all. Alcmena is admirably portrayed as a plucky young wife, loyal and devoted to her husband,
but without a trace of sentimental vapors, humanly dignified,
and totally sincere. She is even thoughtful enough to beg Jupiter-
Amphitryon to refrain from unkind words to Mercury-Sosia (line
540). If we say that Jupiter acts within the limits of his divine
prerogatives and that Mercury abets him while enjoying his own
mischievous devices on the side, we have said about all that
should be said. There is no cosmic meaning behind all this. In
the matter of religious values, we would do best to meditate—
at some other time—how the Romans, like the Greeks, could
alternately laugh at and revere their gods, and how the gods, on
their side, found both laughter and reverence acceptable.

It was not impiety that made *Amphitruo* a daring play, but
the fact that the story carried the author into two areas where
Roman social taboo was most sensitive: in the portrayal of
adultery and in the portrayal of a (Roman) nobleman flouted
by his own slave. The adultery proved, of course to be no
adultery at all and the slave that flouted his master was really a
god flouting a mortal. The distinction may seem tenuous to us,
but it was for Plautus a hard-and-fast line between success and
personal disaster. Alcmena's unimpeachable goodness was necessary if the poet was to get away with his adultery theme, and
even her list of truisms in her opening *canticum* about courage
may be seen as an extra effort on Plautus' part to guarantee to
the audience that she has every right attitude for a young
(Roman) matron.

In *Amphitruo* there are five principal roles: Mercury, Sosia,
Jupiter, Alcmena, and Amphitryon, and two small roles for ship-
captain Blepharo and maid servant Bromia. There is also a
mute role for the maid servant Thessala, who appears only once
(in Act II), her functions being, first, to provide female com-

panionship for propriety's sake when the lady of the house sets
foot out of doors without her husband to escort her, and second,
to fetch the golden goblet at her mistress' bidding. Seven speaking parts in all. We do not know how many actors were used to
perform these seven parts. Greek practice was to distribute all
roles among three actors, each of whom, by virtue of quickly
changed masks and very simple costumes, shared in playing any
given character, and among the three of them they accounted
for every spoken word. From very late Roman writers, Donatus
of the fourth century A.D. being one, there are confusing statements about more on-stage characters in Roman practice than in
Greek practice. Almost certainly these remarks refer to extras,
primarily to attendants upon a nobleman. Amphitryon, in his
last speech in Act II (lines 853–4), abruptly says, "Here, Sosia,
take these men inside." (tu, Sosia, duc hos intro.) No men had
been mentioned, and the impersonality of *hos* ("these," mascu-
line plural) indicates that the men were of no dramatic importance. Amphitryon must, then, have appeared, for dignity's
sake, with two or more attendant noblemen whose only function was to stand and wait. Professor Beare, however, cautiously
limits himself to saying that a troupe of four or five actors could
play any scene in Plautus. As a matter of fact, three actors, following the usual Greek practice, could enact *Amphitruo* quite
as well as four or five. The diagram on the facing page shows one
possible distribution of lines to Actors 1, 2, and 3. The reader
may work out other possible arrangements at will.

Plautus' adaptations of Greek originals are lusty and ex-
uberant, quite in contrast to his successor Terence, who more
studiedly conformed to what we know of the "New Comedy"
sources used by both authors. Plautus is colloquial (as Cicero
remarked), given to puns, *double-entendres,* and comical lists,
to direct jibes at the audience, to moderate indecencies, and to
farcical improprieties like stage vomiting, stage belching, and
stage dousing of characters with accidentally emptied slopjars
or deliberately emptied pails of water. Political issues he discreetly avoided.

Many of these characteristics hold true for *Amphitruo,* yet
there is a unique quality in this work which the prologue defines
as a tragicomedy. It has its share of slapstick farce, yet it is also

Line	Actor No. 1	Actor No. 2	Actor No. 3
Prologue 1 152	1 ↓ Mercury		
Act I 153 550	Mercury ↓ 543	153 ↓ Sosia 462 499 ↓ Jupiter 550	499 ↓ Alcmena 545
Act II 551 860	551 ↓ Amphitryon 854	633 ↓ Alcmena 860	551 ↓ Sosia 857
Act III 861 1008	956 ↓ Sosia 969 984 ↓ Mercury 1008	882 ↓ Alcmena 973	861 ↓ Jupiter 983
Act IV 1009 1034 . . . . . 1035 1052	1021 ↓ Mercury 1034 . . . . . 1035 ↓ Jupiter 1039	1009 ↓ Amphitryon 1034 . . . . . 1035 ↓ Amphitryon	. . . . . 1035 ↓ Blepharo 1038
Act V 1053 1146	1131 ↓ Jupiter 1143	↓ Amphitryon 1146	1053 ↓ Bromia 1127

Note—We follow the Oxford edition of Plautus in beginning Act IV at line 1009; other editors are not all in agreement on that point.

peppered with more cerebral wit. The baffled Sosia of Act I exclaims: "But I swear by Jupiter that *I* am Sosia . . . ," and Mercury replies:

> And I swear by Mercury
> that Jupiter does not believe you.

It shares with the *Menaechmi* the situational humor afforded by doubles, but the dignified figure of Alcmena, faintly tinged as she is with a tragic hue, restrains the farce. The whole last Act plays on the level of high comedy, so that the drama ends on an uncharacteristically sober, but not somber, note.

The musical component, which must have been extremely important for the work, is lost beyond recall. As for the metrical pyrotechnics, only advanced students of Latin have access to them. About a dozen different meters are used and there are some forty points of change from one to another of these. Even in a Classical poet like Vergil scansion can be made difficult by vowel elisions or hiatus, but Vergil has nothing like the complexities of Plautus, with his arbitrary shortenings of long vowels and his unexpected resolutions of long syllables into two short ones. Even Cicero complained that the meters seemed sometimes to be non-meters. To reproduce this sort of thing in English, or in any modern language, is impossible. In general, the present translation renders iambics and trochaics by roughly equivalent English iambics and trochaics, whereas in the sections of greater diversity a rhymed doggerel has been used, which we hope is Plautine in spirit even if rhyme was unknown in ancient Latin.

English puns have been introduced where there were Latin puns; the sense may differ but the effect is similar. The primary objective was to recapture the coarse, rapid, zany *vis comica*— the comic vigor—that was Plautus' trademark.

AMPHITRUO

A
Tragicomedy

by

Titus Maccius Plautus

translated by

James H. Mantinband

AMPHITRUO

ARGUMENT I (Acrostic)

Alcmena's charms inspired Jupiter with love,
Making him assume the shape of her own husband,
Paragon of virtue, battling for his country.
His servant Mercury, in the guise of Sosia,
Inveigles both that servant and the returning master.
Then Amphitryon charges his wife with adultery,
Remembering the things she said. And Blepharo
Umpires, but cannot tell which is Amphitryon.
Out comes the truth at last: Alcmena gives birth to twins.

ARGUMENT II

Whilst Amphitryon fought with his enemies
The Teleboeans, Jupiter assumed his shape,
And took the loan of his wife Alcmena for a night,
While Mercury took on the form of Sosia,
An absent slave. The two of them deceived Alcmena.
After the real Amphitryon and Sosia
Returned, they were deluded both in wondrous wise
Husband and wife began to quarrel bitterly,
Until a peal of thunder told them both
That Jupiter himself was the adulterer.

PROLOGUE

[spoken by the god MERCURY]

Whereas all you good folks want me to make you prosper,
and bring you fortune in your buyings and your sellings,
and handsome profits in your business arrangements;
and whereas you would wish, at home and overseas,
to find prosperity in all your speculations,
to consummate your present and your future deals
with ample, fat returns, both now and evermore;
and whereas you would have me bearer of good tidings
for you and yours—reporting and announcing things
which most redound to what is for your common good—   10
(for you must know that all the gods have made Yours Truly
responsible for messages and business deals)—
whereas you want my blessings in these varied matters,
and profits, everlasting and perennial—
then kindly keep your mouths shut during the performance
and all be fair, unbiased judges of our play!
    Now let me tell you why I'm here and at whose command,
and at the same time let me tell you who I am.
JUPITER sent me and my name is MERCURY.
My father sent me here to ask you for a favor,   20
although he knows quite well that anything he tells you
you'll take as a command, because he understands
you fear the name of Jove—as all men better had!
But anyway, he ordered me to be polite
and ask you nicely, as befits a suppliant—
for really, the same Jupiter who sent me here
is just as scared of trouble as any one of you:
his mother was a woman, his father was a man—
no wonder, then, that he looks out for Number One.
The same thing goes for me, the son of Jupiter: 30
if he gets into trouble, I'm sure to catch some too.

41

And this is why I come in peace and bring you peace.
Now what I ask is right and proper, and easy too,
and I am right and you are right—so *that*'s all right.
For it's unjust to ask just men for unjust things,
and downright stupid to ask just things from unjust men—
they just don't know what's just—if they did they wouldn't do it!
So now please all give heed to what I'm going to say:
our wishes should be your wishes too. My father and I
deserve no less than this from you and from your city.   40
For why should I, like other gods in tragedies,
like Neptune, Virtue, Victory, Mars and Bellona,
whom we've seen all rehashing their benefits to you—
why should I tell you of all the splendid things
my father, Ruler of the Gods, has done for you?
My father never had that most obnoxious habit
of throwing all his benefits in people's faces,
because he knows quite well how grateful you must be,
and anyway, he realizes that you deserve them.

    Now for the favor that I've come to ask you for,   50
and then I'll tell you all about our tragedy.
—What's wrong? Why do you frown? Because I said the play
would be a tragedy? But I'm a god—I'll change it:
I'll change the play from tragedy to comedy,
if that's what you want, without a single change of lines!
Well, yes or no? would you like that? What a dunce I am!
As if I didn't know what you want—and me a god!
I understand exactly what you have in mind:
I'll scramble them and make a tragi-comedy.
It wouldn't do to make it only comedy,   60
not with gods and kings parading on the stage.
What do you think? But wait—it has a slave part too.
I'll make it what I said, a tragi-comedy.

    Now for the favor Jupiter told me to ask.
He wants the officers to search the theater
from row to row and seat to seat and front to back,
and if they find claqueurs for any party at all,
they'll confiscate their togas and hold them all as bail.
Yes, and if any parties have been lobbying
and trying to secure the prize, either in person   70

or by letter or by intermediate agent,
or if the Aediles should be guilty of corruption,
Jupiter says the penalty should be the same
as that which deals with Unfair Campaign Practices.
You win your wars by qualities of worth and merit
and not by bribery and underhanded tactics.
Why shouldn't this apply to actors as well as others?
The prizes should be won for merit, not by claques.
Actors who act well get all the applause they need,
providing that the judges know their business.   80
And here's another order from my father Jove:
officials will be watching all the actors too.
If any one of them has hired claques for himself,
or hecklers either, or if anyone steals scenes,
his costume will be ripped to shreds—with him inside it!
No need to wonder why great Jupiter himself
is so concerned for actors—no need to be surprised—
for Jove himself is an actor in this comedy.
What? You're surprised? As if this were a new departure,
that Jupiter himself has turned to histrionics?   80
Why, only last year, when the actors prayed to Jove,
right on the stage he appeared—a *Deus ex Machina*!
Of course, he's always taking part in tragedies.
So Jupiter will have a part in our play today,
and so will I. Now please pay very close attention
while I explain the story of our comedy.
     This city here is Thebes. In that house over there
Amphitryon lives, an Argive citizen by birth.
He's married to Alcmena, who is Electrus' daughter.
Right now Amphitryon is off with the Theban army,   100
and the Thebans are at war with the Teleboeans.
Before Amphitryon himself left for the war,
he got his wife Alcmena pregnant. Now I don't need
to tell you folks what kind of god my father is:
you all know about his roving eye for the fairer sex,
and what a lover he can be when the fancy takes him.
Well, it seems he's fallen in love with this Alcmena,
and he has borrowed her—without her husband's knowledge.
The long and short of it is—he's got her pregnant too!

Now do you get the lay of the land? Thus poor Alcmena   110
is pregnant both by her husband *and* by Jupiter.
In fact, my father's with her now, this very minute,
and that's why he has made the night last so much longer,
while he's enjoying his beloved, but, you see,
he's taken the appearance of Amphitryon.
Now, don't be too surprised at this costume of mine,
for I'm supposed to represent a slave, you see.
I'm playing a brand-new version of an ancient tale,
and that is why I'm all dressed up in this new costume.
Now, as I've already told you, my father is inside,   120
and he's the spit-and-image of Amphitryon,
so all the slaves who see him think that's who he is,
for he can change his appearance any time he pleases.
And I have taken the form of Sosia, his slave,
who went off to the war with Amphitryon his master—
so I can play the servant to my amorous father,
and still not have the house-slaves ask me who I am
when they see me doing chores around the house.
So when they think that I'm a slave and one of them,
no one will ask me who I am and what I'm doing.   130
    Did I tell you Jupiter's inside with her,
lying in the arms of his newest heart's delight?
And he's telling Alcmena all about the battle
and everything that's happened. She thinks he's her husband
when all the while he's really Jupiter. Well then,
he's telling her how he put the enemy to flight
and all the medals and awards that he received.
We actually stole all of Amphitryon's medals—
you really have it made when you're an immortal god!
Today Amphitryon is coming home from the war   140
with Sosia his slave, the one whose part I'm playing.
Now, just so you'll recognize which one is which,
I'll always wear these little winglets on my hat.
My father will have a golden tassel on his hat.
Amphitryon will not have any distinguishing marks.
But no one on the stage will see these magic signs:
only you in the audience will be able to see them.

Aha! Here comes Amphitryon's servant Sosia,
he's coming from the harbor with a lantern now.
I'll chase him from the house as soon as he arrives.   150
Attention now: you'll find it worth your while to see
a cast including Jupiter and Mercury!

Act I

SOSIA: Who ever heard of a braver, bolder,
            more courageous man than me?
    I know how these young blades cut up,
            but still I walk alone at night.
    But say, what in the world would I do
            if the cops should lock me up in jail?
    Tomorrow I'd be taken out
            of stir, and get a beating, too—
    never even have a chance
            to say a word in self-defense—
    no help from my master—everyone
            would say I had it coming, too.
    Those eight big brutes would play an anvil
            chorus on my wretched body!
            That's the only kind of welcome   160
            I would get on my return.
            And it's all my master's fault,
            with such impatience does he burn.
    The very idea of sending me
            out from the harbor this time of night!
    Why the devil couldn't he wait
            at least until the sky gets light?
    It's a hard life being a rich man's slave:
    It shouldn't happen to a knave.
    Night and day, they never end it;
    No rest for the weary; I can't recommend it.
    The rich man, not a thing does he do,   170
    But whatever he says, that goes for you.

All's fair in love and domestic service;
    But that rich man—how great his nerve is!
Always thinking up extra work,
    that's their very favorite quirk.
Well, grin and bear it, that's the ticket;
    otherwise you'd never stick it.
MERCURY: I'm the one that ought to be griping
    as my sweaty brow I'm wiping!
Yesterday I was free and genial;
    today, alas! I am a menial;
while this fellow, born to be a slave,
    he's the one to rant and rave.
SOSIA: It's a beating for me. Damn, if
    I haven't gone and completely forgot   180
to thank the gods for my safe arrival.
    Now I'm really in the soup.
If the immortal gods decide
    to give to me my just desserts,
then I'm really done for,
    my face would be pounded to a pudding,
seeing how ungrateful I've been
    and after all they've done for me.
MERCURY (aside): It's a wise slave that knows his own fodder.
SOSIA: Something that I never thought
    would happen (nor did anyone else!)
has happened, namely and to wit,
    we're all returning safe and sound.
All our troops have come back safely,
    mission accomplished, enemy slain.
The mighty battle is all finished,
    and our foes are finished too.
The city that has caused the death
    of many Thebans good and true,   190
by our strength and military
    prowess it has been laid low—
and mostly by the skill and luck
    of my own master Amphitryon.
For he has given loot and land
    and glory to his countrymen,

and established Creon firmly
   on the throne of the Theban state.
He's sent me on ahead from the harbor
   to tell his wife the happy news:
how the land was saved, and all
   because of his brilliant leadership.
Now, let me see: how shall I tell her
   the story when I get to the house?
If I embroider the truth a little,
   that'll be nothing new for me.
For when they were in the thick of the fight,
   I was in the thick of flight!
But I'll pretend that I was there
   and tell it just the way I heard.   200
I'd better get in practice first
   and rehearse the way I'm going to tell—
exactly what words I'm going to use;
   let's see: here's how I will begin:
No sooner had we arrived, that is,
   no sooner had we touched the land,
when first of all Amphitryon
   calls his most reliable officers
and tells them to deliver an ultimatum to the Teleboeans:
if they wished to avoid a war
   and give up everything they stole,
and return what they had plundered,
   he would call the whole thing off;
the Argives all would leave the land
   and its inhabitants in peace;
but if they were of another mind
   and would not give him what he asked,
then he with all his might and main
   would lay a siege around the town.   210
Now, when Amphitryon's men had given
   this ultimatum to the foe,
they, relying on their strength,
   confiding in their courage too,

made a haughty, arrogant
  reply to our ambassadors;
they said they could defend themselves
  and all their families by force,
and that we should leave the country,
  taking all our troops along.
When Amphitryon heard this answer
  from the returning delegates,
at once he led his army out
  of the camp. The Teleboeans too
led out their troops in battle formation,
  shining in their splendid armor.
Both sides took their places that day,
soldiers in all their paraphernalia;   220
our legions formed in the usual way,
the enemy in all their regalia.
The leaders marched out as the troops retreated,
and held a pow-pow behind the lines.
They agreed that whoever was defeated
would give up lands and homes and shrines.
On this agreement the trumpets blared,
the earth rang out with the battlecry. Then
the leaders asked Jove to help those who dared,
and cheered the officers and men.   230
Every man for himself, death despising,
sword and spears were shivered and shattered,
the sky resounded, a cloud arising
from all the panting. Men fell, blood spattered.
Finally we begin to win;
enemy corpses in heaps are lying,
while we press on mid victorious din.
But still the enemy are not flying.
They all stand firm and never give way,
they'd rather die than retreat that day.   240
So there they lie, in ranks still tight.
But when Amphitryon catches sight.
he bids the cavalry charge on the right.
They attack the foe: quick as a flash
with wild war-whoops they charge, every one,

trampling the enemy in their mad dash—
     Thus justice is done!
MERCURY: He hasn't said a single word
     so far that's not the whole plain truth,
     for I myself was there the whole time
     and my father Jupiter too.
SOSIA: The enemy all turn in flight,
     and our men get their second wind.   250
     And as the Teleboeans flee,
     we hurl our missiles at their backs.
     Amphitryon himself killed their king
     Pterelas with his own hands.
     All day long the battle lasted,
     from early dawn till evening time.
     The reason I remember is—
     I went without my lunch that day.
     And not until it grew quite dark
     was there at last an end to the fight.
     Next morning all the enemy leaders
     came in tears from town to the camp:
     their hands were covered like suppliants;
     they begged our pardon for their sins,
     gave up themselves and all their possessions—
     everything, sacred and profane,
     their town and their children, to the Thebans
     to dispose of as they wished.
     Amphitryon was presented with
     a golden goblet for his bravery,   260
     which King Pterelas used to drink from. . . .
     That's how I'll tell Alcmena now.
     I'll do as my master said,
     and then I'll take myself on home.
MERCURY: Hey, he's coming this way now—
     I'll step up and meet him face to face.
     One thing sure, this fellow will never
     be allowed to reach the house.
     Seeing that I'm his spit-and-image,
     I'll have a little fun with him.

I look exactly like him, both
    in clothes and in appearance too,
so it's only fair that my
    behavior should be just like his—
sly and tricky, a scurvy knave,
    full of dodges, wiles and tricks.
Using his own weapon, trickery,
    that's how I'll drive him from the door.
What's that—he's looking at the sky.
    I'd better keep an eye on him.   270
SOSIA: Good heavens, one thing I know for sure,
    and that without any mistake:
Nocturnus, the God of Night, is drunk,
    stoned, stupefied, and sleeping it off.
The Big Dipper hasn't moved at all,
    the least little bit there in the sky,
yes, and the moon's in exactly the same
    position as when she arose.
Orion too, the Pleiades,
    and Evening Star, none of them's set.
The constellations are standing still
    and night will not give way to day.
MERCURY: Keep up the good work, Night! keep right
    on doing what my father says.
You're doing great! A great job for
    a great god—and you'll get your reward.
SOSIA: I really don't think I've ever seen
    a night as long as this one's been,
excepting maybe the time I was whipped
    and strung up by the heels all night,   280
and bless my soul if this one isn't
    even longer than that one was.
Damned if I don't think the Sun
    passed out and still is sleeping it off.
I wouldn't be surprised if he
    had one too many at dinner last night.
MERCURY: Is that what you think, you rascal, that
    the gods behave the way *you* do?
By all the gods, I'll treat you as you
    and your rotten ways and manners deserve.

Come over here, you wretch, and you'll
   meet with a slight case of calamity!
SOSIA: Where are all the lustful lechers
   who can't go to bed alone?
What a night this one would be
   to spend with one of those high-class callgirls.
MERCURY: According to this fellow, my father
   certainly has the right idea—
lying in there with Alcmena right now
   and following his heart's desire.   290
SOSIA: I'd better go in and give Alcmena
   the message my master told me to.
Who's standing outside the house this time
   of night? I don't like the looks of this.
MERCURY: What a pusillanimous coward
   this fellow is!
SOSIA: I wonder if
  maybe he's a hoodlum and
   he wants to steal the cloak off my back?
MERCURY: Scared out of his wits! Now for some fun.
SOSIA: Ye gods! My teeth are chattering.
What a welcome he will give me—
   a cordial fist right in the mouth!
He's taking pity on me, I really
   believe he is, seeing that master
kept me up all night, his fists
   will see I get a good long rest.
Oh, ye gods, I'm dead and done for!
   Look, just look at the size of him!
MERCURY: Well, I'll speak out loud to him,
   and when he hears what I have to say   300
he'll be even more afraid—
   his teeth will chatter like castanets.
Let's go now, Fists! It's a long, long time
   since you've had a good square meal.
When was it, yesterday? when you
   laid out and stripped *four* big strong men
and sent them to the land of Nod?
SOSIA: Oh, oh, I'm really done for now.

He's going to change my name from So-
    sia to Quintus—woe is me!
Already he's laid out four strong men
    and sent them to a well-earned rest.
Oh lord, I don't want to be in that number!
MERCURY: Ready, get set—here we go!
SOSIA: He's getting ready—I'm a dead duck!
MERCURY: He can't escape a beating now.
SOSIA: Who can't?
MERCURY: Anyone that comes
    this way will have a meal of fists.
SOSIA: Please, Sir, not me. It's too late for my supper,
    and I just had something to eat.   310
    So why don't you save that dinner
        until you meet a hungry man?
MERCURY: Feel the weight of this fist?
SOSIA: Oh, no!
    He's weighing his fists—I've had it now.
MERCURY: How about if I just gently
    jar him to sleep?
SOSIA: You'd save my life—
    I haven't had a good night's sleep
        for three days.
MERCURY: Well isn't that too bad?
    Why can't you learn, you silly fist,
        how to hit a man properly?
    One little touch should be enough
        to change his appearance once and for all.
SOSIA: Seems as if he's going to do
    a retouch job on my poor face.
MERCURY: Any face you hit for real
    should have the bones knocked out of it.
SOSIA: I'll be damned if he isn't going
    to fillet me like some poor fish.
    Enough of men who fillet people!
        If he sees me, I'm a goner.   320
MERCURY: I smell a man—Bad luck for him!
SOSIA: Ye gods, he's gotten wind of me.
MERCURY: He was far away before
    but now he seems right near at hand.

SOSIA: The man's a magician!
MERCURY: Oh, my fists
    are itching for a face to punch!
SOSIA: If you're about to use them on me,
    please try them out first on the wall
  to sort of break them in.
MERCURY: A voice
    has flown into my ears. . . .
SOSIA: Oh, damn!
  Poor me—I ought to have clipped its wings,
    seeing I have such a birdlike voice.
MERCURY: This fellow seems to be begging for
    a good swift kick right in the ass.
SOSIA: I have no ass, or other beasts.
MERCURY: He's asking for a load of trouble.
  Lay on!
SOSIA: I'm all tired out from that
    damned trip. I'm still seasick, in fact.
  I can't even walk emptyhanded,
    let alone with a load laid on.   330
MERCURY: Methought I heard Somebody's voice.
SOSIA: I'm saved! He doesn't know I'm here.
  He says he heard Somebody—not me,
    since my name's surely Sosia.
MERCURY: Methought I heard a voice upon
    the right, that struck me on the ear.
SOSIA: Methinks he's going to wallop *me*
    instead of my voice—to make things even.
MERCURY: Good. Here he comes this way.
SOSIA: Ye gods, I'm simply numb with fear.
  If anyone asked me where I am
    right now, I couldn't even answer.
  My legs are glued to the ground and I'm
    so scared I can't even take a step.
  Well, that's the end of my master's orders;
    that's the end of Sosia too.
  Anyway, I'm going to speak
    to him boldly and with confidence.
  Then he'll think I have some nerve
    and maybe he'll even let me alone.   340

MERCURY: Whither walkest thou, O stranger,
    with Vulcan enclosèd in yon horn?
SOSIA: What business is it of thine,
    O thou who filletest people's faces?
MERCURY: Are you a slave or are you a free man?
SOSIA: I'm whichever one I choose to be.
MERCURY: Really, no fooling?
SOSIA: Really, no fooling.
MERCURY: You're in for a beating.
SOSIA: You're a liar.
MERCURY: But now I'll make you say it was
    the truth.
SOSIA: Now, what's the point of that?
MERCURY: I want to know where you are going,
    whom you belong to, and what you want.
SOSIA: I'm coming here, and I'm my master's
    slave. Now are you satisfied?
MERCURY: Now you're really in for it.
    I'll *belay* that mouth of yours.
SOSIA: It can't be laid, it's too well chaperoned.
MERCURY: Still at it with your silly talk?
MERCURY: What are you doing near this house?
SOSIA: For that matter, what are you doing here?   350
MERCURY: Creon the king has posted sentries
    here to watch the place at night.
SOSIA: Very decent of him: we're
    away at war, so he guards the house.
  Well, off with you now. You can tell him
    the family servants have arrived.
MERCURY: What kind of family servants . . . If
    you don't buzz off, and quickly too,
  you'll soon see the kind of contempt
    that such familiarity breeds.
SOSIA: But this is where I live, I tell you.
    I'm the slave of the master here.
MERCURY: If you don't disappear you'll be treated
    like an aristocrat.
SOSIA: How come?
MERCURY: You won't walk, you'll be carried away
    once I've taken a stick to you.

SOSIA: But I keep telling you I'm one
    of the family. I'm a family slave.
MERCURY: Just see how soon you want a beating
    unless you vanish instantly.   360
SOSIA: What, you want to keep me out
    of my house, and me just back from abroad?
MERCURY: This, your house?
SOSIA: Of course it is.
MERCURY: Then who's your master, tell me that.
SOSIA: My master is Amphitryon,
    commander of the Theban troops.
  Alcmena's his wife.
MERCURY: What's that you say?
    What is your name, you gallows bird?
SOSIA: Sosia is what they call me
    here in Thebes. I'm Davus' son.
MERCURY: Then all the worse for you, coming here,
    you pillar of audacity.
  You with all your patched-up schemes
    and all your patched-up stories too.
SOSIA: I came with clothes patched up, if you like,
    but not my stories and my schemes.
MERCURY: You're telling lies again. You haven't
    come with clothes but with your feet.
SOSIA: Certainly true.
MERCURY: And you're certainly going
    to get a beating for telling lies.   370
SOSIA: I certainly don't want one . . .
MERCURY: Well,
    you're certainly getting one anyway.
  When I say certainly, it's certain,
    there's no room for any argument.
                      (Beats him.)
SOSIA: Hey, take it easy, please!
MERCURY: Do you
    still say that *you* are Sosia?
  when *I* am Sosia?
SOSIA: He's killed me!
MERCURY: That's nothing compared with what you'll get.
  Now: who's your master?

SOSIA: You are. Your fists
  have claimed me for your very own.
  Help me, Thebans, help me!
MERCURY: What!
  shouting still, you gallows bird?
  Tell me why you're here.
SOSIA: Just to
  supply you with a punching bag.
MERCURY: Whom do you belong to?
SOSIA: Amphitryon.
  I'm his servant Sosia.
MERCURY: You'll be beaten all the more
  for lying. You're not Sosia. *I* am.
SOSIA: I wish to heaven you were and that
  I was the one that was beating you. 380
MERCURY: What's that you're muttering?
SOSIA: Nothing.
MERCURY: Who's
  your master?
SOSIA: Anyone you say.
MERCURY: Yes? And what's your name now?
SOSIA: Any-
  thing you want to be my name.
MERCURY: You said you were Amphitryon's Sosia.
SOSIA: That was a mistake. I meant
  to say I was Amphitryon's as*soc-*
  *ia*te. That's what I really meant.
MERCURY: Because there's only one Sosia
  in this family. That I know quite well.
  You've made a mistake.
SOSIA: I only wish
  your fists had been mistaken too.
MERCURY: I am in fact the Sosia
  that you said that you were just now.
SOSIA: Could we have a truce so I
  could speak and not get hit again?
MERCURY: No truce, but armistice for a while,
  if you've got anything to say.
SOSIA: No, Sir, only peace will do.
  Your fists are just too much for me. 390

MERCURY: Speak, I won't hurt you.

SOSIA: Do I have
    your word for that?

MERCURY: You have my word.

SOSIA: What if you deceive me?

MERCURY: Then
    may Sosia feel Mercury's wrath!

SOSIA: Well, then, since I'm free to speak,
    and say whatever I want to say,
  I am Amphitryon's Sosia, you know.

MERCURY: What, are you starting with that again?

SOSIA: Wait, please, we made a treaty! It's
    the truth, you know.

MERCURY: Take that, you wretch!

SOSIA: Do whatever you like with me—
    you will anyway, with those fists of yours.
  But all the same, no matter what
    you do, I will not hold my tongue.

MERCURY: You'll never get away with pretending
    I'm anyone but Sosia.

SOSIA: And *you* will never get away
    with making me out to be someone else.
  We only have one Sosia in
    our family, and that one is me,
  the very same me that went away
    to the army with Amphitryon.

MERCURY: The man's completely mad!

SOSIA: You're talking
    about yourself, not about me.   400
  Am I not Sosia, Amphitryon's
    servant, you big bully, you?
  Didn't our ship arrive this very
    night from the harbor of Persicus?*
  With me aboard it? Didn't my master
    just now send me to the house?

---

* "The harbor of Persicus" renders *portus Persicus,* literally "the Persian port." The translator speculates that the phrase may represent Plautus' own misunderstanding of "the harbor of Perseus" in the unidentified Greek original text. See our note on p. 105–6.

Am I not standing in front of the house
　right now with a lantern in my hand?
Am I not awake and talking?
　Didn't this fellow just beat me up?
Didn't he, though! My aching jaws
　are telling me he certainly did.
Then what am I waiting for?
　Why don't I go right into my house?
MERCURY: *Your* house?
SOSIA:　　　　　　　　Yes, my house.
MERCURY:　　　　　　　　　　　　You're crazy,
　and an outright liar too.   410
You haven't spoken a word of truth.
　I am Amphitryon's Sosia.
Why, just tonight our ship set sail
　from the harbor of Persicus.
We besieged and captured the city
　where King Pterelas had reigned,
and we beat the Teleboean
　legions with our army too.
Amphitryon himself killed Ptere-
　las, their king, on the battlefield.
SOSIA *(aside):* I can't believe myself when I hear
　the fellow talking in this way.
He certainly knows exactly what happened
　and he's got it all down pat.
　　　　　　　(to Mercury)
What was Amphitryon presented with
　from the Teleboean spoils?
MERCURY: A golden goblet from which King Ptere-
　las was wont to drink his wine.
SOSIA *(aside):* He's got it!
　　(to Mercury)　And where is that goblet now?
MERCURY:　　It's locked up in a little chest,   420
　sealed with Amphitryon's signet ring.
SOSIA:　　What's on the seal, can you tell me that?
MERCURY: A rising sun and a four-horse chariot.
　Trying to trick me, you gallows-bird?
SOSIA *(aside):* Well, he's beaten me. I've got
　to find myself another name.

How did he ever see all that?
   Now I'll get him once and for all . . .
Something that I did by myself
   when I was all alone in the tent,
something he'll never know or be able
   to tell me, not to save his life.
                  (to Mercury)
All right, if you are Sosia,
   what were you doing in the tent
while the fighting was the thickest?
   Tell me that and I'll call it quits.
MERCURY: There was a cask of wine, and I
   poured myself a jugful of it.
SOSIA *(aside):* He's getting warm.
MERCURY: Then I drank it pure
   as it came from its mother on the vine.   430
SOSIA *(aside):* Exactly how it happened. I did
   drink a whole jugful of wine.
 This fellow must have been hiding right
   there inside of the very same jug.
MERCURY: Well, then, have I convinced you that
   you are not Sosia, as you claim?
SOSIA: You say I'm not?
MERCURY: Of course I do,
   seeing that I myself am he.
SOSIA: But I swear by Jupiter
   that *I* am Sosia—that's no lie!
MERCURY: And I swear by Mercury
   that Jupiter does not believe you.
 He'll believe my unsupported
   word against your solemn oath.
SOSIA: Then who am I, if I'm not Sosia,
   will you kindly tell me that?
MERCURY: Well, when *I* don't want to be
   Sosia, *you* can be Sosia yourself.
 Now, when I am he, clear off,
   or be whipped again, you nameless man!   440
SOSIA: Certainly when I consider
   this guy's looks, and my own as well—

for many's the time I've looked at myself
   in the mirror—we're exactly alike.
He is wearing a cap and cloak
   exactly like the ones I wear;
legs and feet and height and haircut,
   eyes, nose, lips—they're all alike;
cheeks and chin and beard and neck—
   remarkable similarity!
Now, if only his back is scarred
   like mine, then really he's my twin.
But now that I consider, I'm sure
   that I'm the same man I've always been;
I know my master and our house;
   I've got my wits; I'm in my right mind . . .
Well, then, I will just ignore
   this fellow's nonsense and knock at the door.
MERCURY: Where are you going?
SOSIA: Home.
MERCURY: If you
   should climb right into Jupiter's chariot   450
and fly away in it, even so
   you would not escape calamity.
SOSIA: Can't I even tell my own mistress
   what my master told me to?
MERCURY: Tell *your own* mistress whatever you like—
   just stay away from ours in here.
 Keep on bothering me, and you'll
   wind up a walking piece of driftwood.
SOSIA: All right, all right, I'll go! Immortal
   gods, I beg you, tell me this:
 How did I get mislaid? What happened?
   How did I lose my former shape?
 Did I forget myself and leave
   myself down by the harbor there?
 This fellow certainly has my shape—
   or at least the shape I used to have.
 I'm alive and yet they carry my image
   (more than they'll do for me when I'm dead).
 Well, I'd better go to the harbor
   and tell my master about all this.   460

Unless he doesn't recognize
    me either—I hope to God he won't!
Then I can shave my head today
    and then put on a free man's hat.
(Exit.)

MERCURY: Well, everything has gone exactly as I planned:
I've kept that confounded nuisance far away from the house
so that my father can make love to Alcmena inside.
Now when this fellow finds Amphitryon, his master,
he'll say his servant Sosia drove him away
from the house; the master will think the slave is telling lies
and never went at all to carry out his commands.
Well, then I will bamboozle them and mix things up,   470
and all the household of Amphitryon as well,
and keep it up till my father's had his fill of love
with the lady in there. Then and only then will they know
exactly what took place. Then Jupiter will restore
love and peace and harmony between the two.
Amphitryon will be simply furious with her
and he'll accuse her of infidelity. Then my father
will take a hand and read them both the riot act.
Oh yes, one thing I forgot to tell you about Alcmena:
today she'll give birth to twins, two bouncing baby boys,   480
and one of them, you see, will be a ten-month baby,
the other will be a premature child of seven months.
Amphitryon's the former's father, Jove's the latter's.
So that the younger baby has the greater father,
and vice versa. You see how matters lie . . . er, stand?
But just to make things easier for Alcmena here,
my father's seen to it that only one confinement—
a single parturition will do the job for two.
So no one will suspect her of adultery,
and their clandestine love affair will remain a secret.   490
Amphitryon, as I have said, will be informed
and he'll know the whole story. Well then? No one, surely,
will think Alcmena guilty—that would be unfair,
for gods to let mere mortals take the blame for them
and all their follies and misdeeds and peccadillos.
Well, that's enough of that. There's someone at the door.
Here comes the fake Amphitryon out of the house

along with the lady Alcmena, his wife on short-term loan.
JUPITER: Goodbye, Alcmena dear, take care
   of yourself, and keep an eye on things.
  Please don't try to do too much.
   Remember, your time is nearly due.   500
  I must go and leave you now,
   For Jove's sake, don't disown the child.
ALCMENA: Why, my dear husband, do you have
   to go away so suddenly?
JUPITER: Well, you know how much I'd prefer
   to remain with you, my dearest wife,
  but that's the army for you: when
   the general is not with his troops
  all sorts of things go wrong, you know,
   much more often than they go right.
MERCURY: Now he's taking after me:
   I'm the god of liars and rogues.
  Watch him now: how cleverly
   the old boy soothes her ruffled temper.
ALCMENA: Now at least I know how much
   you think of your poor little wife, you brute!
JUPITER: Isn't it enough to know
   I love no other woman but you?
MERCURY: Good heavens, if *she* gets wind of all
         (points up)
   your terrestrial shenanigans,   510
  I bet you'd a darn sight rather be
   Amphitryon than Jupiter.
ALCMENA: It's all very well for you to talk,
   but look at what you go and do—
  you leave me alone before
   your half of the bed is even warm.
  It was midnight when you came,
   and now you're going. Is that fair?
MERCURY: I'd better step in and play the stooge;
   a word from me would help things out.
         (to Alcmena)
  By Jove, Madam, I don't think
   there's a single mortal anywhere

who loves his wife as much as he
   loves you. He's simply crazy about you.
JUPITER: Don't I recognize you, you scoundrel?
   Away, beat it, out of my sight!
What does all this have to do
   with you, that you should come butting in
with your two obols' worth? I'll take
   my stick . . .
ALCMENA: Oh no!
JUPITER: Not another word!   520
MERCURY: Well, so much for my debut as
   a stooge. I won't try that again!
JUPITER *(to Alcmena):*
   But, my dear, as to what you said,
      you musn't be angry with me now.
I left my troops and went over the hill
   and sneaked away just to see you,
so you could hear from my own lips
   how I fought for my country's sake.
Now you know it all. I wouldn't
   have done it if I didn't love you.
MERCURY: What did I tell you? Look how he
   is buttering that poor woman up!
JUPITER: Now I must sneak back to camp
   before the others hear of this
and say that I thought more of my wife
   than the welfare of my native land.
ALCMENA: *You* don't care that you're making me cry
   by leaving me . . .
JUPITER: Hush, hush, my dear.
Don't cry, you'll make your eyes all red.
   I'll be back soon . . .
ALCMENA: You and your "soon!"   530
JUPITER: Really, it's not as if I *liked*
   to go away and leave you alone.
ALCMENA: That's awfully easy to say when you go
   away the very same night you came.
JUPITER: Please, dear, let me go. I must
   get back to camp before the dawn.

Look, here is the goblet I
  was awarded for my bravery,
the one King Pterelas used to drink from—
  whom I killed with my own hands.
Here, I want you to have it.
ALCMENA: Oh,
  my dear, if that isn't just like you!
A worthy gift, by Jupiter,
  one that does credit to the giver.
MERCURY *(aside):* No, a worthy gift *from* Jupiter,
  one that does credit to the receiver!
JUPITER *(to Mercury):*
  Will you shut up, you jailbird, or
    will I have to get rough with you?
ALCMENA: Please, Amphitryon, don't be angry
  with Sosia on my account.   540
JUPITER: Whatever you say, my love.
MERCURY: Why,
  love's made him a regular barbarian!
JUPITER: Anything else you wish, my dear?
ALCMENA: Let absence make your heart grow fonder.
MERCURY: Let's go, Amphitryon, it's getting
  light.
JUPITER: You start out, Sosia.
  I'll join you in a minute.
        (to Alcmena)   Any-
  thing else, my love?
ALCMENA: Yes, come back soon!
JUPITER: I certainly will. Before you know it,
  I'll be back, so please cheer up!
              (Exit Alcmena)
Now, Night, you've held back long enough;
  retire, and make room for Day.
Let him shine for mortals with
  his usual radiance and light,
and since last night was so much longer
  than an ordinary night,
I'll make the day be shorter, so
  things will even up, you see.

Now let Day follow Night's footsteps;
I shall follow Mercury.   550
(Exit.)

Act II

AMPHITRYON: Let's go, Sosia, follow me.
SOSIA: Coming, Sir, immediately.
AMPHITRYON: I think you are an utter rat.
SOSIA: What makes you say a thing like that?
AMPHITRYON: You say things that aren't and never were
   and never will be true.
SOSIA: Oh, Sir!
   Why can't you have some faith in me?
AMPHITRYON: Faith? You don't know how lucky you'll be
   if I don't tear your tongue out by the roots.
SOSIA: I'm your slave; you can do what suits
   your convenience. I'll tell you what took place
   and you'll never dissuade me with threats or disgrace.   560
AMPHITRYON: You scoundrel, to say you're in the house
   when you're right here with me, you louse!
SOSIA: But it's true, it's true, every word is true!
AMPHITRYON: Keep that up and I pity you.
SOSIA: That's up to you, since I'm your slave.
AMPHITRYON: What, making fun of your master, you knave?
   You're talking rubbish, no reason or rhyme.
   One man in two places at the same time!
SOSIA: But I tell you, master, it's just as I say!
AMPHITRYON: Jupiter curse you for talking this way.   570
SOSIA: What have I done?
AMPHITRYON: You're still making fun—?
SOSIA: You'd be right to scold me if it was true,
   but it's not, so give the devil his due.
AMPHITRYON: You must be drunk.
SOSIA: I wish I were.
AMPHITRYON: You've got your wish.
SOSIA: How is that, Sir?
AMPHITRYON: Just tell me, where did you get that drink?

SOSIA: I didn't.

AMPHITRYON: I don't know what to think.

SOSIA: I've told you ten times if I've told you once
    I'm at home, but another me
  is here with you. Now do you see?
    That should be clear even to a dunce.

AMPHITRYON: Get out of my sight!

SOSIA: Now what's the trouble?   580

AMPHITRYON: You're drunk or sick, or seeing things double.

SOSIA: Oh no, Sir, I really feel all right.

AMPHITRYON: You must be higher than a kite.
  But I'll soon see that you get yours,
    just wait till I get you home and indoors.
  Now follow your master, if you please,
    you and your galloping D.T.'s!
  You didn't carry my orders out,
    and now you have the colossal gall
  to make me a laughing stock by saying
    things that never happened at all
  and never could happen, you combination
    gallows bird and vampire bat!
  By Jupiter, I'll make you suffer,
    you can take my word for that.

SOSIA: Really, it isn't fair. I'm only
    trying to do what's right, you know.   590
  But all I get for my pains is more
    pains—to refute what I know is so.

AMPHITRYON: Just tell me this one thing:
    how can it possibly be true
  that you're home and here at the same time?
    Tell me that, you villain, you.

SOSIA: But I *am* right here, and I *am* at home—
    you can call me crazy if you will.
  It's just as strange to me as it is
    to you. I don't understand it still.

AMPHITRYON: How can that be?

SOSIA: I repeat, it's no
    stranger to you than it is to me.
  So help me, I didn't really believe
    that it was my own self there,

not until the other me,
    that other Sosia convinced me.
Why, he knew everything that happened
    to me on the battlefield.
Besides, he not only had my name,
    he had my whole appearance as well.
That other me is as much like this me
    as two drops of milk are alike.   600
Remember, you sent me back from the harbor
    before daybreak, a while ago?
AMPHITRYON: Yes, and what happened?
SOSIA: There I was
    at the house before I even arrived.
AMPHITRYON: Now you're talking nonsense again.
    Have you gone stark raving mad?
SOSIA: Do I look as if I had?
AMPHITRYON: Someone
    must have bewitched or enchanted you.
SOSIA: I don't know about bewitched,
    but someone's sure been be-switching me.
AMPHITRYON: Who beat you up?
SOSIA: Me. That is,
  the other me, who's back there at home.
AMPHITRYON: Wait a minute. Just give answers
    to the questions I put to you.
First, I'd like to know who in
    the world that other Sosia is.
SOSIA: Your own servant.
AMPHITRYON: I think I have
    one too many when I have you,   610
And I certainly never had any
    other Sosias but yourself.
SOSIA: Well, I'm telling you, Amphitryon,
    you will see another me
—a second Sosia, my alter ego,
    just as soon as you get home.
Looks just like me, same age, and his
    father's name is Davus too.
That's the long and short of it—
    I've become a set of twins.

AMPHITRYON: This is strange and doubly strange.
　　But tell me, did you see Alcmena?
SOSIA: Certainly not. They didn't even
　　let me set foot in the house.
AMPHITRYON: Who didn't let you?
SOSIA: 　　　　　　　　I told you,
　　the other Sosia, who beat me up.
AMPHITRYON: But who *is* that other Sosia?
SOSIA: 　Me! How many times must I tell you?
AMPHITRYON: Maybe you've been asleep and dreaming.
SOSIA: 　I've been nothing of the kind! 　　　　620
AMPHITRYON: Maybe you only thought you saw
　　another Sosia in your dreams.
SOSIA: I'm not one to fall asleep
　　when I have errands to perform.
　I was wide awake, with open
　　eyes, just as I am right now,
　talking with you—just as I was
　　when he beat me up. And so was he!
AMPHITRYON: Who's that?
SOSIA: 　　　　　　　Sosia, the other
　　me. You still don't understand?
AMPHITRYON: How can anyone understand
　　such nonsense? You're talking absolute rot.
SOSIA: You'll see what I'm talking about
　　when you see that other Sosia.
AMPHITRYON: Then come and follow me. This whole
　　affair bears looking into, for sure.
　Now will you kindly see that they
　　bring all the stuff from off the ship.
SOSIA: Don't you worry, Amphitryon,
　　I'll take care of everything. 　　　　　　630
　I'm not one to drink up orders
　　as if I were drinking a glass of wine.
AMPHITRYON: I only hope to heaven this all
　　turns out to be an awful dream.
　　　　　　(Enter Alcmena from the house.)
ALCMENA: How little pleasure life contains
　　when we compare it with the pains!

This is the common lot for all,
   into each life some rain must fall.
Sorrows follow each delight
   as surely as the day the night,
and the more our joy and laughter
   the more the tears that follow after.
I'm learning now, from my own sorrow,
   that we can never count on tomorrow.
I saw Amphitryon for just one night
   and off he went before it was light.
Now I feel alone and bereft
   since the man I love has left;
I feel more sad when we say goodbye
   than glad when we meet. And that is why   640
I am so lonely and forlorn.
   I almost wish I'd never been born.
At least there is one thing to praise:
   he'll be a hero all his days.
Yes, it's entirely another story
   if he returns with fame and glory.
I can bear these sad goodbyes
with smiling face and tearless eyes
if I then have the reward
of hearing him called a conquering lord.
For courage is the noblest prize;
   it stands before all else in our eyes,   650
preserving our safety, freedom, lives,
homes, parents, children, husbands, wives.
All other things to courage yield:
   the brave man needs no other shield.
AMPHITRYON: Goodness, how my wife will rejoice
   to see me home both safe and sound,
seeing that we love each other
   the way we do. And especially
since we've conquered the enemy—
   a thing no one thought possible—
at the very first encounter—
   all because of my leadership.

Yes, indeed, she certainly will
    be glad to see her lord and master.
SOSIA: I suppose you think my girl won't be
    every bit as glad to see me.
ALCMENA: Why look, it's my husband!
AMPHITRYON: Follow me.
ALCMENA: What's he doing back so soon?   660
  After saying he had to hurry
    away. Is this a test for me?
  Can he be trying to find out how much
    I miss him when he goes away?
  Well, by all the gods, I don't
    mind a bit if he comes back!
SOSIA: Look, Amphitryon, we'd better head
    for the ship.
AMPHITRYON: What are you talking about?
SOSIA: No one's going to give us breakfast
    on our arrival, that's for sure.
AMPHITRYON: Whatever gives you that idea?
SOSIA: We've come too late to get a meal.
AMPHITRYON: How come?
SOSIA: Because Alcmena's standing
    in front of the door and she looks full.
AMPHITRYON: Don't be silly! She was pregnant
    before we left.
SOSIA: I've had it, then!
AMPHITRYON: What do you mean?
SOSIA: I've just come home
    in time to be a waterboy.
  If your reckoning is right,
    she must be nine months gone by now.   670
AMPHITRYON: Cheer up, it's not as bad as that.
SOSIA: Cheer up, he says! I'll show him cheer!
  Just let me get my hands on a pail,
    and I'll swear by all the gods
  never to let up till I've drained
    that damned well to the last drop.
AMPHITRYON: Just come along. I'll get someone else
    to haul the water, never fear.

ALCMENA *(aside):* Maybe it would look better if
  I came to greet my "long lost" man.
AMPHITRYON: Greetings and salutations from
    Amphitryon to his loving wife,
the finest little woman in
  the whole of Thebes, if you ask me.
And every other husband in town
  will go along with me on that.
How are you, dear? Are you glad
  to see me back?
SOSIA *(aside):*   Glad isn't the word.
  A stray dog off the street would get
  a warmer welcome than he's getting.   680
AMPHITRYON: Glad to see you're coming along
  so well with your pregnancy, my love.
ALCMENA: Oh, for heaven's sake, why do you
  have to make such fun of me?
All these "greetings and salutations"
  as if you hadn't just been here
barely half an hour ago
  and as if you were just coming home.
Why must you play games and make
  believe you haven't seen me for months?
AMPHITRYON: Why, I haven't so much as laid
  eyes on you until this minute!
ALCMENA: What do you mean?
AMPHITRYON: Just what I say.
  I have learned to tell the truth.
ALCMENA: All this learning and unlearning—
  I don't like this whole business.
Trying to test me? By the way,
  why *have* you returned so soon?
Omens unfavorable? Or
  is it the weather keeping you back   690
from the war, where you were going
  only a little while ago?
AMPHITRYON: What's that? A little while ago?
ALCMENA: Stop teasing! A little while, just now.

AMPHITRYON: How can that be? "A little while"
   is not the same thing as "just now."
ALCMENA: Just some of your own medicine.
   You teased me, I'm teasing you.
  That's what you get for saying you've just
   arrived, when really you just left.
AMPHITRYON: The woman's delirious.
SOSIA: Leave her alone,
   Amphitryon, till she sleeps it off.
  Clearly she's having nightmares.
AMPHITRYON: What do
   you mean, awake and yet asleep?
ALCMENA: Certainly I'm awake, and everything
   happened just as I said it did.
  Just before dawn I saw you here,
   and this fellow was with you too.
AMPHITRYON: Where was that?
ALCMENA: Right here in the house.
AMPHITRYON: Nonsense!
SOSIA: Take it easy, Sir.   700
  Maybe the ship brought us here
   from the harbor when we all were fast asleep.
AMPHITRYON: What, are you taking her side too?
SOSIA: Well, whatever did you expect?
  When you're dealing with a lunatic
   the best thing is to humor her;
  contradicting her will only
   make her even more violent.
  If you agree she'll let you off easy . . .
AMPHITRYON: I'll show her how I'll humor her!
  What kind of a welcome is this, anyway,
   on my return from overseas?
  I don't even get a greeting.
SOSIA: You're stirring up a hornet's nest.
AMPHITRYON: Oh, shut up!
                (to Alcmena) Just one more question.
ALCMENA: Ask me anything you wish.
AMPHITRYON: Tell me, are you being stupid,
   or has the honor gone to your head?

ALCMENA: How dare you speak to me like that?
    What's the matter, Amphitryon?
AMPHITRYON: Well, up to now you always gave me
    a hearty greeting when I arrived,
  you know what I mean, the way
    a decent wife is supposed to do.
  But this time I come home to find
    that you've completely changed your tune.
ALCMENA: Goodness me, when you came yesterday
    you know how I greeted you.
  The minute you arrived I asked you
    how you were and how you had been,
  I took your hand and hugged and kissed you.
    If that's not a greeting, then what is?
SOSIA: Yesterday you greeted him?
ALCMENA: Yes, and you too, Sosia.
SOSIA: Well, Amphitryon, I hoped
    your wife would give birth to a child,
  But, alas . . .
AMPHITRYON: What is it?
SOSIA: She's
    not gaining a child, but losing her wits.
ALCMENA: Nonsense! I'm perfectly sane, and pray
    to Jove I have a normal child.
  But if you get what you deserve,
    you'll come in for a beating now
  because you put a hoodoo on me,
    you, you hoodoo-artists, you!
SOSIA: Hoodoo? Who do? You're the one
    to get beat—a beet to eat, I mean.
  You know, something you can munch on
    when you get that morning sickness.
AMPHITRYON: You saw me yesterday?
ALCMENA: Yes, how many
    times do I have to tell you that?
AMPHITRYON: In a dream?
ALCMENA: No, wide awake,
    and so were you.
AMPHITRYON: Oh, woe is me!

SOSIA: What's the matter?
AMPHITRYON: The woman's mad.
SOSIA: A sudden attack of colic, perhaps.
   Nothing like a touch of colic
      to make a person delirious.
AMPHITRYON: Tell me, please, Alcmena, when
      did you begin to feel this attack?
ALCMENA: I keep telling you that there is
      nothing at all the matter with me.   730
AMPHITRYON: Then why do you say you saw me
      yesterday, when I arrived last night?
   Had my dinner in the harbor,
      and spent the whole night on the ship?
   What is more, I haven't set foot
      in this house since we went away
   to fight the Teleboeans—and
      by the way, we conquered them, too.
ALCMENA: Really! You had dinner with me
      and slept with me too.
AMPHITRYON: What's that you say?
ALCMENA: I speak the truth.
AMPHITRYON: Not about this.
   I can't vouch for anything else.
ALCMENA: Then, at daybreak, you went back
      to the troops.
AMPHITRYON: How can that possibly be?
SOSIA: She's telling you her dream, to the best
      of her memory. Listen here, Alcmena,
   after you woke up you should have
      sacrificed to Jupiter—
   salted cakes and incense—after all,
      he's the god in charge of dreams.   740
ALCMENA: Oh, go to blazes!
SOSIA: Why don't you go—
   and see to the sacrifice as I said?
ALCMENA: There! Again he's insulting me,
      and you don't even take my side!
AMPHITRYON: Sosia, shut up!
               (to Alcmena) You say
   that I left you at dawn today?

ALCMENA: Certainly. Who else could have
    told me all about the battle?
AMPHITRYON: You know about the battle?
ALCMENA: Of course,
    since you told me about it yourself.
  How you stormed the town and killed
    King Pterelas with your own hands.
AMPHITRYON: I told you that?
ALCMENA: Of course you did,
    and Sosia was right here too.
AMPHITRYON: Sosia, did you hear any of this?
SOSIA: Where would I hear it? Certainly not.
AMPHITRYON: Ask the lady.
SOSIA: You never did,
    not in my presence anyway.
ALCMENA: Isn't it strange how he won't contradict you!
AMPHITRYON: Sosia, please look at me.   750
SOSIA: Well, I'm looking.
AMPHITRYON: I want you
    to tell me the whole truth, not to humor me.
  Did or did you not hear me
    say all the things she said I said?
SOSIA: Now I'm beginning to wonder if *you're*
    in your right mind, to ask me this.
  This is the first time that I've seen
    Alcmena, just like you yourself.
AMPHITRYON: Hear what he says?
ALCMENA: I certainly did.
  He's just as big a liar as you.
AMPHITRYON: You won't believe him or your own
  husband?
ALCMENA: Of course I won't believe.
  That's because I believe myself.
  I know it happened just as I said.
AMPHITRYON: You say I arrived yesterday?
ALCMENA: Do you deny that you left today?
AMPHITRYON: Naturally I deny it. This is
  the first time that I'm in your presence.
ALCMENA: Speaking of "presence," what about
    the goblet they "presented" you with?   760

The golden one . . . Will you deny
  you gave it to me this very day?
AMPHITRYON: I never gave you the cup, or mentioned
  it, though I was going to.
  Matter of fact, I'm still going to—
  Hey, who told you about that cup?
ALCMENA: You told me yourself, when you
  gave it to me with your own hands.
AMPHITRYON: Just a minute, please. You know,
  Sosia, something's fishy here.
  How the devil would she have known
  about the goblet I received?
  Sure you didn't see her before
  and tell her all about it, eh?
SOSIA: I didn't say a word to her—
  I didn't *see* her before you did.
AMPHITRYON: What kind of a woman did I marry?
ALCMENA: Would you like to see the cup?
AMPHITRYON: Yes, I would.
ALCMENA: Good. Thessala,
  please get the goblet my husband brought.   770
AMPHITRYON: Sosia, come here. I'd like
  to have a word in private with you.
  If she has that goblet, it
  will certainly be the strangest thing!
SOSIA: How can you believe she has it
  when you know I have it here
  locked up in this little box,
  sealed with your own signet ring?
AMPHITRYON: Seal intact?
SOSIA: Look and see.
AMPHITRYON: Just as I left it.
SOSIA: What I'd like to know,
  Why don't you have her put away
  in the bughouse?
AMPHITRYON: Yes, you're probably right.
  She's crazier than a bedbug.
                (Enter the maid with a golden goblet.)
ALCMENA: Well, Sir,
  do you see this goblet here?

What's the use of talking?

AMPHITRYON: Give me that cup!

ALCMENA: Yes, and take a good long look.
Now try to deny what stares you
in the face. Go right ahead.
Is this or is it not the bowl
they gave you on the battlefield? 780

AMPHITRYON: By Jupiter! I can't believe it!
This is it! Oh, Sosia!

SOSIA: Either that woman is the world's
champion sorceress, by God,
or else the cup is in the box.

AMPHITRYON: Well, open it, hurry up, man!

SOSIA: What would be the point? The seal's
quite intact, it hasn't been touched.
You've given birth to another Amphitryon,
I to another Sosia.
Now if the cup's had a baby too,
why, we've all become sets of twins.

AMPHITRYON: I still want to open that box!

SOSIA: All right, but first please check the seal,
Just so you won't blame me later.

AMPHITRYON: Come, get it over with, open it up
before this woman drives us out
of our minds with all her silly talk!

ALCMENA: Where do you suppose I got this
if I didn't get it from you? 790

AMPHITRYON: This bears looking into, that's certain.

SOSIA: Oh no! Oh no! By almighty Jove!

AMPHITRYON: What's the matter?

SOSIA: There's no goblet
in the box.

AMPHITRYON: What did you say?

SOSIA: I told you the truth.

AMPHITRYON: That cup had better
appear, or your own days are numbered!

ALCMENA: *This* one's appeared.

AMPHITRYON: Who gave it to you?

ALCMENA: The same person who's asking me now.

SOSIA: Oh, I get it, you're pulling my leg.
    You went and ran ahead from the ship
    secretly, and took another
        road, and took the goblet out,
    then you gave it to your wife
        and sealed the box up tight again.
AMPHITRYON: Good heavens! This delirium
    is becoming contagious now.
                    (to Alcmena)
    We arrived here yesterday,
        did you say?
ALCMENA: Yes, and when you arrived
    each of us greeted the other one
        with a great big hug and kiss.   800
SOSIA: I'm not so sure I like that last part—
    all that hugging and the kissing.
AMPHITRYON: Then?
ALCMENA: You took a bath.
AMPHITRYON: And then?
ALCMENA: You dined.
SOSIA: Ah, now we're getting somewhere!
    Keep up the good work!
AMPHITRYON: Stop interrupting!
    Go on. What happened after that?
ALCMENA: Dinner was served. You dined with me,
    and I was on the couch with you.
AMPHITRYON: On the same couch?
ALCMENA: Of course.
SOSIA: I don't
    like the looks of this dinner party.
AMPHITRYON: That's enough now, Sosia!—
    Well, what happened after dinner?
ALCMENA: You said you were tired; dinner
    was removed; we went to bed.
AMPHITRYON: Where did you sleep?
ALCMENA: With you, of course,
    as usual, in our bed. Where else?
AMPHITRYON: Ye gods, I'm ruined!
SOSIA: What's the matter?
AMPHITRYON: She has killed me, that is all!

ALCMENA: What do you mean?
AMPHITRYON: Don't speak to me!
SOSIA: What's the matter?
AMPHITRYON: All is lost!   810
   She has committed adultery—
      been seduced while I was away.
ALCMENA: Goodness, dear, what kind of a way
      is that for my own husband to talk?
AMPHITRYON: Am I your husband? Don't call me
      by pretended names, you pretender, you!
SOSIA: What a mixup if he has changed
      his sex and isn't her husband now!
ALCMENA: What have I ever done to you
      that you should speak to me like that?
AMPHITRYON: You ask me that, when you yourself
      just told me what you've done to me?
ALCMENA: What do you mean? What have I done
      wrong by spending the night with you?
AMPHITRYON: You with me? I've never heard such
      shameless, brazen insolence!
   If you have no sense of shame
      at least you could try to borrow some!
ALCMENA: Such behavior is not fitting
      for a woman in my position.   820
   Try as you may, you can never prove me
      guilty of such shamelessness.
AMPHITRYON: By all the gods, at least, you know
      who I am, don't you, Sosia?
SOSIA: Of course I do.
AMPHITRYON: Did I have dinner
      yesterday on board the ship?
ALCMENA: I have witnesses as well
      to bear me out in what I say.
SOSIA: I just don't get it at all,
      unless there is another you—
   another Amphitryon who takes your place
      and takes care of all your affairs,
   you know, does everything for you
      whenever you are out of town.

I was quite surprised, as I said,
    when I saw another Sosia,
but another Amphitryon is
    even more surprising still!
AMPHITRYON: Some wizard or magician has cast
    a spell on my poor wife, Alcmena.   830
ALCMENA: I swear by heaven, Jupiter, and
    Juno, goddess of the home
(whom I reverence and worship,
    as is fitting, above all gods),
no man excepting only you
    has ever touched my body with his.
I am completely innocent.
AMPHITRYON: I wish to heaven it were true.
ALCMENA: It is the truth, but what does it matter,
    since you don't believe in me?
AMPHITRYON: You swear confidently for
    a woman.
ALCMENA: One who is innocent
    and free from sin has a right to speak
    up boldly in her own defense.
AMPHITRYON: Yes, very bold.
ALCMENA: As befits the innocent.
AMPHITRYON: Innocent in word, not deed.
ALCMENA: The only dowry that I have—
    I do not speak in the usual sense—
is my modesty and purity,
    my honor and my decency,   840
fear of the gods, love of my parents,
    and harmonious family life—
that, and being a loyal wife
    kind and decent to her man.
SOSIA: Goodness, she's the pinnacle of
    perfection, if she's telling the truth.
AMPHITRYON: I'm so confused right now that I
    don't even know who I am any more!
SOSIA: You're Amphitryon. Just watch out
    that somebody doesn't jump your claim,
seeing the way that people are changing
    about since we got back from the war.

AMPHITRYON: Woman, I tell you that this matter
   must be looked into carefully.
ALCMENA: By all means, investigate all
   you like.
AMPHITRYON: Look here, how would it be
  If I bring your relative
   Naucrates with me from the ship?
  He was with me on the voyage.
   How about if he denies   850
  everything you say I did:
   then what should be done with you?
  Can you think of any reason
   why I should not divorce you then?
ALCMENA: None.at all, if I am guilty.
AMPHITRYON: Then it's agreed. Here, Sosia,
  take these men inside. I'll go
   find Naucrates down on the ship.
              (Exit.)
SOSIA: Now there's just the two of us,
  seriously, tell me the truth:
  Is there another Sosia
   inside, one who looks just like me?
ALCMENA: Oh, go away! The slave is worthy
  of the master.
SOSIA: All right, I'm going.
              (Exit.)
ALCMENA: Heavens! How can my husband think
  such things of me? I don't understand.
  To accuse me of such things
   without a bit of evidence!
  Oh well, my kinsman Naucrates
   will put things right—he's got some sense.   860
            (Exit.)

Act III

JUPITER: I'm that Amphitryon with the servant Sosia
  who turns into Mercury when the occasion demands.
  I'm the one who lives up there in the upper story,

and I turn into Jupiter whenever I feel like it.
But when I descend to earth and come into these parts,
then I become Amphitryon and change my costume.
The reason I'm here today is on account of you,
so as not to leave this comedy unfinished.
Also to help Alcmena in her innocence
—she's been accused by her husband of adultery.   870
It really wouldn't be right if I got her into trouble
all because of something I alone had done.
So now I'll pretend to be Amphitryon again
just as I did before, and take a hand in things,
to see if I can make them even more confused.
But later on. I'll straighten everything out again.
I'll even play the midwife for Alcmena here,
so that she gives birth, at one and the same time,
to both the children, his and mine, without any trouble.
Yes, and I've ordered Mercury to keep standing by   880
in case I need him. Now I'll have a word with Alcmena.
ALCMENA: I can't stay in this house any longer. The very idea—
accused of such disgraceful things by my own husband!
The way he tries to make undone what he has done,
and then accuses me of things I've never done!
He needn't think I'm going to take it lying down.
No, by Heaven, I won't, I simply will not stand it!
Such awful untrue accusations! No, I'll leave him
unless he apologizes and swears that he is sorry
for treating innocent people in such a disgraceful way!   890
JUPITER *(aside):* I guess it's up to me to do what she demands
if I expect to get anywhere with her again.
Since what I have done offended Amphitryon
and my affair has got him undeserving trouble,
turn-about's fair play—I have to suffer now
for everything *he* said, although I'm innocent.
ALCMENA: Well, here's the man who charges his unhappy wife
with shame and adultery!
JUPITER: A word with you, my dear.
Why, where are you going?
ALCMENA: I don't want to look at you.
How can I after all the hateful things you said?   900

JUPITER: Are we enemies now?

ALCMENA: We certainly are, unless
  you're going to tell me that this too was all a lie.

JUPITER: Don't be so annoyed!

ALCMENA·   Just keep your hands off me!
  I'll tell you this, if you had any sense at all,
  when you think your wife's done such disgraceful things
  you wouldn't want to hold any conversations with her,
  serious or not, unless you were an utter fool.

JUPITER: My saying you were bad will never make you so.
  Besides, I don't think you are. That's why I've come back:
  to put things right. I really felt quite miserable   910
  to hear that you were just a bit annoyed with me.
  Why did I do it? you will ask. Well, let me explain.
  Heavens! I didn't really think you were immoral!
  It was just a sort of test to see what would happen,
  and what you'd do, and how you'd take such a suggestion.
  That's all it was—a joke—the things I said before;
  a jovial jest, that's all. Ask Sosia, if you like.

ALCMENA: Why don't you bring my relative Naucrates here
  the way you said you would, to back up your account
  that you weren't here?

JUPITER: Now look, when something's said in jest
  it really isn't nice to take it seriously.   [920

ALCMENA: All I can say is: your "joke" has cut me to the heart.

JUPITER: Please, Alcmena dear, give me your hand, I beg you.
  Forgive me, please, and don't be angry any more.

ALCMENA: I am living refutation of your charges,
  and since my own behavior has no taint of shame,
  I won't stand for shameful language from anyone.
  Goodbye. You keep what's yours, and give me what is mine.
  Send me my servants.

JUPITER: Are you crazy?

ALCMENA: If you won't,
  I'll go alone—with Honor as my retinue.   930

JUPITER: Please, wait a minute, I'll swear to anything you like
  and say that I believe my wife is virtuous,
  and if I am deceiving you, I'll call Jove's curse
  upon Amphitryon both now and evermore!

Alcmena: Oh no! Don't say that! His blessing rather!

Jupiter: Be it so.
  For that's a powerful, trustworthy oath I gave you.
  Now are you angry with me?

Alcmena: . . . No.

Jupiter: There's my good girl!
  Life is full of little ups and downs like this,
  and every cloud, you know, must have a silver lining.
  People quarrel, then they are reconciled again.
  And you know the nicest thing about these quarrels?
  Afterwards, when they make up and are friends again   940
  they love each other twice as much as they did before.

Alcmena: You never should have said a thing like that to me,
  but since you apologize so nicely, I'll forgive you.

Jupiter: Well, ask them to prepare the sacrificial vessels
  so I can fulfill the vows I made for my safe return—
  the vows I made when I was on the battlefield.

Alcmena: I'll do as you ask.

Jupiter: And please tell Sosia to come out.
  I want him to invite the pilot Blepharo   950
  who is aboard my ship to come and lunch with us.
                    (aside)
  Now, Blepharo will get no lunch but a big surprise
  when I drag Amphitryon out by the scruff of the neck.

Alcmena *(aside):* What in the world is he talking to himself about?
  Someone's coming out the door. It's Sosia.

Sosia: Here I am, Amphitryon.
  Anything you need, just tell me.

Jupiter: Just the man I want.

Sosia: Everything
    all right now between you, Sir?
  Believe me, I'm so happy to see
    that you two have made up again.
  That's the way a slave should be—
    this is the rule that he should follow:
  always be just like the master,
    taking his cue from the master's mood.   960
  He should be sad when they are sad,
    rejoice when they are in happy mind.

Tell me, is it really true
    that you two have made up again?
JUPITER: What's the matter? Don't you know
    when a person's having a little joke?
SOSIA: Joke, did you say? I could have sworn
    you were in earnest a while ago.
JUPITER: Everything's cleared up and peace
    has been declared.
SOSIA: I'm glad of that!
JUPITER: Now I'll take care of these votive offerings
    inside.
SOSIA: That's a good idea.
JUPITER: You go down to the ship and give
    my invitation to the pilot
    Blepharo. Tell him to come
    to lunch after the sacrifice.
SOSIA: I'll be back before you think I'm there!
    (Exit.)
JUPITER: Yes, make it as fast as you can.
ALCMENA: Anything else you need, or shall I
    go inside and see to things?   970
JUPITER: Yes, you do that, please. Have every-
    thing prepared as soon as you can.
ALCMENA: You may come in whenever you like;
    I'll see that there is no delay.
                        (Exit.)
JUPITER: That's the way a conscientious,
    attentive wife should always speak.
    Now I've got them both bamboozled, mistress and slave.
    They both think I'm Amphitryon—too bad for them.
    Appear at once, divine Sosia! You hear
    what I am saying even though you are not present.
    You must keep Amphitryon away from the house
    when he returns. You may use any tricks you please.
    I want him to be deceived until I've had my fill   980
    of pleasure with my borrowed wife. So see to it
    that everything is taken care of as I wish,
    and stand by while I'm sacrificing to myself!
                        (Exit.)

MERCURY: Out of the way, clear the road,
    gangway, gangway, everyone!
Let no man be audacious enough
    to stand in the road and block my path.
Why shouldn't gods have just as much right
    to chivvy folks around this way
as any petty slave you see
    strutting about the comic stage?
They rush on, saying: "Here's the ship!"
    or: "The old man's home and good and mad!"
But I obey the Old Man Up There—
    on orders from almighty Jove.
So when I yell: "Gangway!" people
    just better gangway good and quick.   990
My father calls and I obey
    just as soon as I hear his commands.
What a dutiful son I am,
    just as a son should always be.
I play the stooge when he's in love,
    I help, advise, rejoice with him.
For when he's happy, that makes me
    the happiest person you've ever seen.
Now he's in love. Well, good for him!
    He's right to indulge himself like that.
Just what everyone ought to do . . .
    well, within limits, that is to say.
Now he wants Amphitryon fooled,
    and you have not seen anything yet!
Just wait, Spectators, I'll put on
    a superspectacle of fooling.
I'll put a wreath on my head and go
    into my drunken specialty act.
Then I'll climb upon the roof
    and from that vantage point up there   1000
I'll take care of him. He won't
    be soused, but he will sure be doused.
Then poor Sosia the slave
    will have to pay for what I've done.
Amphitryon will think that he's
    responsible—and I couldn't care less.

My job is to see to the interests
  of Jupiter and do what he says.
Watch out now, here comes Amphitryon!
  Pay attention, everyone,
you are going to see some fancy
  bamboozling, so lend me your ears!
Now I go into my drunken act.
I'll drive him crazy, and that's a fact.

Act IV

AMPHITRYON: Naucrates, the man I wanted,
  wasn't even on the ship.
Nobody seems to know what's happened
  to him. He is not at home.   1010
I've tramped around through all the streets,
  gymnasia, and pharmacies,
the market place, athletic fields,
  the Forum—in and out of stores,
the doctor and the barber, yes,
  and all the holy temples too,
and I'm all tired out with searching,
  but not a trace of Naucrates.
Well, I'd better get on home
  and ask my wife some questions, too.
See if I can find out who's
  dishonored both my spouse and house.
I would rather die than fail
  to settle this affair today.
Well, isn't that something! I can't even get
  into the house. The door is locked.
Just in keeping with everything else
  that's going on around this place.
I'll knock.—Hey there, open the door!
  —Anyone home?—Let me in!   1020
          (Mercury appears on the roof.)
MERCURY: Who'sh there at the door?
AMPHITRYON: Me.
MERCURY: Who'sh Me?

AMPHITRYON: Me that's speaking.

MERCURY: Well, Jupiter
   and all the other gods'll be mad
    at you for breaking down the door.

AMPHITRYON: What in hell are you talking about?

MERCURY: You, my friend, are in for trouble.

AMPHITRYON: Sosia!

MERCURY: That'sh me. Think I forgot
   my own name? Well, whaddya want?

AMPHITRON: What do I want? You miserable wretch,
   you, you ask me what I want?

MERCURY: Shert'n'ly I ask you. You damfool,
   you're breakin' down the door, thash all.
  Whaddya think, we get free doors
   on a government expensh account?
  All right, what are you looking at, stupid?
  Who are you and whaddya want?

AMPHITRYON: You'll be the ruination of all
   my hickory switches, you baboon!
  How dare you ask me who I am?
   Just wait till I get my hands on you!   1030

MERCURY: You musht have been a Prodigal Shon
   when you were a little boy.

AMPHITRYON: How's that?

MERCURY: Becaush—you are not asking for
   a Fatted Calf but a Broken Leg.

AMPHITRYON: Why, I'll break every bone in your body,
   you rascal, for talking to me like that!

MERCURY: I'm sacrificing to you. *(He balances a jug of water.)*

AMPHITRYON: What's that?

MERCURY: I'm gonna pour you such a libation!   1034

(Here, after line 1,034, pages containing an estimated three hundred lines
are lost from the manuscript.
   From these lost pages we have nineteen lines or parts of lines quoted by
late Roman grammarians in illustration of points of grammar or of obsolete
word usage. The nineteen fragments appear in an appendix at the end of
this translation.
   What appears here in italics is the "interpolated scenes" composed by
Cardinal Hermolaus Barbarus in the 1480's A.D., in imitation of Plautus
but wholly from his own imagination, in order to furnish a complete text.)

Amphitryon: You'll make me a libation, gallows-bird?
   If the gods haven't taken away my shape
I'll load you down with bull-whips today,
   You Saturn-type-sacrifice, you!
That's how sure you'll be of torture
   and crucifixion. Come on out,
you whipping-post!
Mercury: *What's that, you ghost?*
   Think you can scare me with your threats?
If you don't take off this very instant,
   if you knock on that door again,
if you so much as touch a finger
   to that door, I'll bash your skull in
with this tile here, and you'll be spitting
   out all your teeth and tongue as well.
Amphitryon: What's that, you wretch? Now you're trying
   to drive me away from my own house?
You'll stop me from knocking? Why,
   I'll tear the door right off its hinges!
Mercury: Still at it?
Amphitryon: *Yes.*
Mercury: *Take this!*
Amphitryon: *Hit your master?*
   Just wait, you wretch, till I catch you!
I'll make you the most miserable wretch
   of all men, now and forevermore.
Mercury: You must have been at the Bacchanals, old man.
Amphitryon: *What's that? What are you talking about?*
Mercury: Because you think I'm your slave.
Amphitryon: *What am I supposed to think?*
Mercury: A curse on you! The only master
   I know is Amphitryon.
Amphitryon (aside): *Have I lost my shape? Funny that Sosia*
   doesn't know me. I'll have to see.
   (aloud) *Tell me who you think I am*
   if I'm not Amphitryon.
Mercury: You? Amphitryon? Are you crazy?
   Look here, old man, I've been telling you

you're playing at Bacchanals again,
asking somebody who you are.
I warn you, old fellow, go away,
and don't you bother Amphitryon.
He's just come back from the war
and he's inside sleeping with his wife.
Amphitryon: Wife? What wife?
Mercury: *Alcmena.*
Amphitryon: *Who?*
Mercury: *How many times do I have to tell you?*
My master Amphitryon. Don't make trouble.
Amphitryon: *Who did you say he's sleeping with?*
Mercury: You'd better look out, you're in for trouble,
Making fun of me like that.
Amphitryon: Please tell me, Sosia . . .
Mercury: *That's more like it.*
He's sleeping with Alcmena, who else?
Amphitryon: In the same bed?
Mercury: *Sure, side by side.*
Amphitryon: *Oh ye gods, my goose is cooked!*
Mercury (aside): *It really is a good thing for him*
although he doesn't think it is.
Lending your wife to someone else
is like having a barren field plowed for you.
Amphitryon: Sosia . . .
Mercury: *What's that, you wretch?*
Amphitryon: *Don't you know me, you gallows-bird?*
Mercury: Sure I know you: you're the man
who won't have to look far for his lawsuits.
Amphitryon: Just once more: am I not your master
Amphitryon?
Mercury: *Why, no. You're Bacchus,*
Not Amphitryon. How many times
do I have to tell you that?
Amphitryon is in the house,
he's in bed with Alcmena, his wife.
If you keep this up, I'll fetch him out;
then you'll really get what-for.
Amphitryon: Good, do that. (aside) *I hope my reward won't be*
—after all I've done for Thebes—

to lose my home and house and country
and wife and household, along with my shape.
Mercury: All right, I'll fetch him, but in the meantime
you'd better stay away from the door.
(aside) I guess he's brought the sacrifice
to the banquet as he said he would.
(to Amphitryon)
Just you behave yourself, otherwise
I'll make a sacrifice out of you.
(Exit.)
Amphitryon: By all the gods, what madness is this
that's taken possession of my house?
What crazy things I've seen today.
Maybe it's true what the stories say:
how many Athenian men have been
transformed when in Arcadia
into wild animals and werewolves
so even their parents didn't know them.
(Enter Blepharo and Sosia.)
Blepharo: What's this, Sosia, What strange things
are these you have been telling me?
You say you found another Sosia
just like you, in front of the house?
Sosia: Yes. Since I've spawned another Sosia
and master another Amphitryon,
Maybe you've hatched another Blepharo.
Then maybe you'll believe what I say,
When you've been beat up, and your teeth knocked out,
and gone without your breakfast too.
The other Sosia—the other me—
gave this me one hell of a beating.
Blepharo: It sure is strange. But we'd better hurry
along.—Why, look, there's Amphitryon!
Amphitryon (aside): My belly is growling now from hunger.
But why should I mention foreign stories?
When, right here in Thebes, they say
Even stranger things once took place—
Cadmus, searching for Europa,
fought the monster born of Mars,

Producing enemies from dragon-seed;
*　　brother fighting against brother*
in that battle with spear and helmet—
*　　and the founder of our race,*
along with Venus' daughter, gliding,
*　　both changed to serpents in Epirus—*
thus the decrees of Jove on high
*　　and thus the Fates made it all occur.*
All the best men in our country
*　　in exchange for their noble deeds*
are punished and persecuted, like me.
*　　But still I could bear these dreadful woes*
if only . . .

Sosia:　　　　*Blepharo!*

Blepharo:　　　　　　*What's the matter?*

Sosia:　　*I don't know, but something's wrong!*

Blepharo: *How come?*

Sosia:　　　　　　*My master, like a "greeter,"*
*　　is walking in front of a door that's locked.*

Blepharo: *It's nothing. He's working up an appetite.*

Sosia:　　*All the same, it's funny he's locked*
*　　his appetite up inside the house.*

Blepharo:　　*Quit snarling!*

Sosia:　　　　　　　　*I neither snarl nor bark.*
*　　Take my word, and watch Amphitryon,*
*　　　　What's he doing by himself?*
*　　He must be figuring something out.*
*　　　　I'll just listen to what he says.*

Amphitryon (aside): *I'm afraid the gods will cheat me*
*　　of my glory won in battle.*
Everything is topsy-turvy,
*　　my whole house is in an uproar.*
My wife is an adulteress,
*　　that is what is killing me!*
And how strange about the goblet,
*　　yet the seal was still intact.*
Yes, and she knew about the battle
*　　and how I conquered Pterelas,*
killing him with my own hands . . .
*　　Aha! I begin to smell a rat,*

a rat named Sosia—he told her;
  he got there before I did.
Wait till I get my hands on him!
Sosia: That's me he means, and I wish he didn't.
  Let's not talk to him, I beg you,
    until we know what's on his mind.
Blepharo: Just as you wish.
Amphitryon (aside):   If I can only
    catch that scoundrel, he'll find out
  what it means to deceive your master
    with threats and tricks.
Sosia: Did you hear?
Blepharo: I heard.
Sosia: He'll give me a good sound thrashing.
    Well, let's talk to him anyway.
  Do you know what everyone says?
Blepharo: I don't know what you will say,
  But I can guess what you will suffer.
Sosia: The old adage: Delay and Hunger
  Fill the nostrils full of bile.
Blepharo: Anyway, let's speak to him.
  Amphitryon!
Amphitryon: I hear Blepharo.
    Now I wonder what he wants.
  Well, he's come in the nick of time
    for me to prove Alcmena's guilt.
  What do you want with me, Blepharo?
Blepharo: Have you forgotten it already?
  This morning you sent Sosia
    to the ship, inviting me to dinner.
Amphitryon: I never did. Where is the scoundrel?
Blepharo: Where is what scoundrel?
Amphitryon: Sosia.
Blepharo: Right here.
Amphitryon: Where?
Blepharo: In front of your nose.
    Don't you see?
Amphitryon: I'm so mad I can't see straight.
  He's driving me right out of my mind.
    You won't get out of this sacrifice!

    Let me, Blepharo!
Blepharo: *Listen, please!*
Amphitryon: *Go on, I'm listening—That for you!*
             (hits Sosia.)
Sosia: What for? Am I not on time?
    I couldn't have traveled any faster
    if I had the wings of Daedalus.
Blepharo: *Please leave him alone! We couldn't go*
    any faster, really we couldn't.
Amphitryon: *I don't care if he went on stilts*
    or with a tortoise' steps, he'll never
    escape my punishment today.
    —That's for the roof! That's for the tiles!
    That's for the door! That's for mocking me!
    And that's for your language!
Blepharo: *Why, what's he done?*
Amphitryon: *You want to know what he has done?*
    He locked me out of my own house
    and threw things from the roof.
Sosia: *Who, me?*
Amphitryon: Yes, you! What did you threaten me with
    if I didn't stop knocking at the door?
    Do you deny it, wretch?
Sosia: *I do!*
    Blepharo's my witness here.
    I was sent to bring him here.
Amphitryon: *Yes, but who sent you?*
Sosia: *He who asks me.*
Amphitryon: When did this happen, gallows-bird?
Sosia: *Just now—a little while ago,*
    When you and your wife were reconciled.
Amphitryon: *Bacchus must have driven you mad!*
Sosia: No Bacchus today—no Ceres either.
    You ordered the vessels cleaned for the rites,
    the sacrifice, and then you ordered
    me to summon Blepharo here
    to breakfast with you.
Amphitryon: *Blepharo,*
    May lightning strike me if I've been inside

or if I sent him. (to Sosia) *Tell me now:*
  Where did you leave me?
Sosia: *Home, with Alcmena.*
  I ran to the harbor from your house
  with your invitation to Blepharo.
  Here we are. I've not seen you before.
Amphitryon: *What's that, you wretch? My wife, you said?*
  You'll never escape a beating now.
Sosia: *Blepharo!*
Blepharo: *For my sake, leave him alone.*
  Listen to me.
Amphitryon: *Well, what is it?*
Blepharo: *He's just been saying very strange things,*
  Real miracles, in fact. Maybe
    A sorcerer or a magician
  Has cast a spell on all your household.
    Ask around and see what's happening,
  And stop torturing this poor man
    Before you really know what's what.
Amphitryon: *I guess you're right. Well, let's go in.*
  You can help me with Alcmena.

                    (Enter Jupiter from the house.)

Jupiter: *Who's been banging on my door*
  with such loud and mighty knocks?
  Who's been making all this rumpus?
    Only let me catch him, and I'll
  sacrifice him to the Teleboeans.
  Nothing is going right today.
  I left Blepharo and Sosia
  to find my kinsman Naucrates.
  Well, I haven't found him yet,
  and I've lost the other two.
  But here they come. I'll go and meet them
  and see if they have any news.
Sosia: *Here comes my master out of the house!*
  This one's a sorcerer!
Blepharo: *Oh Jupiter!*
  What's this I see? It's not Amphitryon,
    That one is! What's going on?

> They can't both be Amphitryon
> 　unless he's suddenly become twins.

Jupiter: Here's Sosia and Blepharo.
　I'll speak first. Hey, Sosia,
　Is that you at last? I'm very hungry.

Sosia:　　I told you! That one's a sorcerer.

Amphitryon: No, Thebans, I say he's the one.
　He's been in the house there with my wife
　And made her guilty of shamelessness—
　A treasure-house of adultery!

Sosia: Master, if you're really hungry,
　Here I am, chock-full of fists.

Amphitryon: Still at it, gallows-bird?

Sosia:　　　　　　　　　Go to hell,
　you sorcerer!

Amphitryon:　　Me, a sorcerer?
　Take that!

Jupiter:　　Stranger, have you gone mad?
　Why are you beating up my slave?

Amphitryon: Your slave?

Jupiter:　　　　　　　Yes, mine. You're out of your mind!

Amphitryon:　　And you're a liar.

Jupiter:　　　　　　　　　Sosia, go in.
　Make breakfast while I sacrifice him.

Sosia:　　I'm going. Amphitryon will receive
　the other Amphitryon just as nicely
　　As I, the other Sosia,
　received myself a while ago.
　　Well, while those two are having it out,
　I'll take myself into the kitchen
　and wash the dishes and drain the pots.
　　　　　　　　　　　(Exit.)

Jupiter: You dare to say that I'm a liar?

Amphitryon:　　I certainly do. You're a liar
　and corrupter of my family, too.

Jupiter:　　Just for that disgraceful speech
　I'll drag you by the scruff of the neck.

Amphitryon:　　Help!

Jupiter:　　　　　　You should have thought of that
　before.

Amphitryon: Help! Help me! Blepharo!

*Blepharo: The two of them are so alike
  that I don't know which one to help.
    Well, anyway, I'll have a try.
  Amphitryon, don't kill Amphitryon!
    Let go of his neck, I beg you!*

Jupiter: Are you calling him *Amphitryon?*

*Blepharo: Why not? He used to be one man,
  Now he's become a set of twins.
    Just because you're Amphitryon,
  doesn't mean that* he *isn't too.
    Meanwhile, let go of his neck!*

*Jupiter: I will. But tell me: does he really
    Look like Amphitryon to you?*

Blepharo: You both do.

*Amphitryon: Oh, great Jupiter,
    Why have you taken my shape away?
  Are you Amphitryon?*

Jupiter: Do you deny it?

*Amphitryon: Of course I do. There is no other
  Amphitryon but me in Thebes.*

Jupiter: No other but me *is what you mean.
  Blepharo, you be the judge.*

*Blepharo: Well, I'll see what I can do.
  You answer first.*

Amphitryon: Willingly.

*Blepharo: Before the battle with the Taphians
  What instructions did you give me?*

Amphitryon: Keep the ship ready, stick to the rudder.

Jupiter: If our men should flee, I should make for the ship.

*Amphitryon: And also to take care of the treasure
  and not let anything happen to it.*

Jupiter: What treasure?

*Blepharo: Please, you keep still.
  I'm doing the asking. How much was it?*

Jupiter: Fifty Attic talents.

*Blepharo: Exactly.
  He really knows.
    (to Amphitryon) How many Philippeans?*

Amphitryon:　　　*Two thousand.*
Jupiter:　　　　　　　　　　*And twice as many obols.*
Blepharo: You both are right. Well, one of you
　　must have been right inside that bag.
Jupiter: Listen to me. With this right hand
　　I killed the enemy Pterelas.
　I took the spoils, and in a casket
　　I took the golden goblet away
　which had been his, and gave it to
　　my wife. Then I took a bath,
　sacrificed, and went to sleep.
Amphitryon:　　　*What do I hear? Am I myself?*
　I'm awake, but dreaming, sound asleep;
　　I'm alive, but I am a dead duck.
　I am that Amphitryon
　　descended from Gorgophon, General
　of the Thebans, Creon's champion
　　against the Teleboeans. I conquered
　Taphians and Acarnanians
　　and their king with my warlike might.
　Over them I placed Cephalus,
　　son of the great Deioneus.
Jupiter: I'm the one that with armèd might
　　crushed the hostile plunderers.
　They had destroyed Electryon
　　and the brothers of my wife.
　They traversed the Ionian Sea,
　　and the Aegean and Cretan as well,
　And laid waste Achaea, Aetolia, and Phocis.
Amphitryon:　　　*Immortal gods! I don't trust myself!*
　He's telling everything that happened
　　exactly right. Listen, Blepharo . . .
Blepharo: One thing more. If you get that right,
　　then you're both Amphitryon.
Jupiter: I know what you mean. I have a scar
　　on my right arm which Pterelas
　once gave me.
Blepharo:　　　*That's exactly right.*
Amphitryon:　　　*It certainly is.*

Jupiter: *See? Here it is.*
Blepharo: Uncover and I'll look.
Jupiter: *We've uncovered.*
Blepharo: Oh, great Jupiter, there it is!
   What do I see? On both right arms,
      in exactly the same location,
   they both of them have the selfsame scar,
      reddish and livid in appearance,
   a new-made scar.—So much for judgment.
      I really don't know what I'm to do.

   (Here Plautus' ancient text resumes.)

   You'd better sort things out for yourselves.
      I'm leaving—I've got things to do.   1035
   Never in all my life have I seen
      anything as strange as this!
AMPHITRYON: Blepharo, I beg you, stand
      by me, don't leave me in the lurch!
BLEPHARO: Goodbye. How can I be of assistance
      when I don't know whom to assist?
                              (Exit.)
JUPITER: I am going inside. Alcmena's
      about to give birth.
AMPHITRYON: Oh, ye gods,
   What shall I do now? All my friends
      and my allies have deserted me.   1040
   Well, he's not going to make a fool
      of me, whoever he is, and escape!
   I'm going right straight to the king,
      I'll tell him the whole story now.
   I'll get even with that Thessalian
      wizard—just you wait and see.
   He's turned my whole house upside down.
      Why, they've all gone raving mad!
   Where has *he* gone? Heavens! I bet
      he's inside with my wife right now.
   I am the most wretched man
      in Thebes today. Now what shall I do?

Anyone can trick and fool me
    and get away with whatever they like.
I know what! I'll break the door down
    and whoever I see in there—
servant, maid, or man, or woman,
    my wife, or that adulterer,
father or grandfather—anyone
    I happen to see, I'll mow 'em down.   1050
Neither Jove nor any other
    god can stop me now, you know,
Even if they wanted to.
    Watch out in there! Now here I go;
        (Thunderclap and lightning flash;
        Amphitryon falls unconscious.)

Act V

    (Enter Bromia, a maid, from the house.)
BROMIA: Any hope I ever had
    of getting out of here alive
is gone forever. My confidence
    and hope have taken a final dive.
Land and sea and heaven too
    have all conspired to kill me dead
right here on the spot. Whatever
    shall I do? Oh, my poor head!
You've never seen such crazy things
    as there were going on inside.
Water! I feel faint . . . I'm done for.
    Where can I find a place to hide?
My head is killing me, my ears
    are ringing, and my eyes are blurred.
Nobody's more unhappy than I am
    after all that has occurred.   1060
Look what happened to Alcmena:
    she calls the gods—her time is come—
Then such a crashing, smashing, rumbling,
    grumbling noise struck everyone dumb.

Everyone dropped right in their tracks.
   Then we heard a loud voice say:
DO NOT BE AFRAID, ALCMENA.
   I TELL YOU HELP IS ON THE WAY.
THE RULER OF THE SKY HAS COME
   IN FRIENDLY SPIRIT TO YOUR AID.
SO, EVERYONE GET UP, ALL YOU
   WHO FELL BECAUSE YOU WERE AFRAID.
So then I got up on my feet.
   I thought the house was all aflame.
Alcmena called me, and in fear
   and trembling, up the stairs I came—
because, you see, I was afraid
   I was being punished for my sins.
But when I get there, what do I see?
   Alcmena's given birth to twins!   1070
—before a single one of us
   even knew or heard a sound!
But what is this? A man is lying
   right here unconscious on the ground.
He must have been struck by the lightning . . .
   he looks good and dead to me. . . .
I'd better have a look at him . . .
   Good heavens! What is this I see?
It's my master, Amphitryon.
   I'll call to him. . . .
Amphitryon!

AMPHITRYON: I'm dead.
BROMIA: Get up!
AMPHITRYON: I'm dead and gone.
BROMIA: Give me your hand.
AMPHITRYON: Who is it?
BROMIA: Your servant Bromia.
AMPHITRYON: I'm scared. Ye gods, what a thunderbolt!
   I feel just as if I'd died
   and was coming back from hell.
But you, what are you doing here?
BROMIA: We were just as afraid as you.

You never would believe the things
    we've seen there in that house of yours!   1080
I'm so dazed that I don't know
    if I'm coming or going—

AMPHITRYON: Well, tell me quickly:
Do *you* recognize me—Amphitryon,
    your master?

BROMIA: Yes.

AMPHITRYON: Look again.

BROMIA: Of course!

AMPHITRYON: You're the only one in the household
    who has any sense at all.

BROMIA: Really, you must be mistaken.

AMPHITRYON: My wife has driven me out of my mind
  with all her goings-on.

BROMIA: Oh no, Sir!
    Wait till you hear what I have to say.
You'll soon realize that your wife
    is an honest woman. It won't take long
for me to prove that point to you;
    just a few words will do the trick.
First of all, listen to this:
    Alcmena's given birth to twins.

AMPHITRYON: Twins, did you say?

BROMIA: Yes, twins.

AMPHITRYON: Heaven
    help me!

BROMIA: Let me continue, please.
    Heaven *did* help you, and Alcmena too.
    That's just what I'm trying to say.   1090

AMPHITRYON: Go on, go on.

BROMIA: Well, when the time
    had come for her to go into labor
and when the pains began, as always
    happens, she began to call
on all the gods to bring her aid,
    as is the custom, with hands washed clean
and covered head. Well, no sooner
    had she begun than we all heard

a tremendous noise of thunder. First
    we thought the house was falling down,
and then the entire house was shining
    and dazzling brightly like pure gold.
AMPHITRYON: When you're quite through telling stories,
    perhaps you will be kind enough
to tell me just what happened.
BROMIA: In all
    this time, not a sound from your wife—
no moans, no groans, not even a cry
    did any of us hear from her.
It was a painless childbirth.
AMPHITRYON: Well,
    that much is nice to know, anyway,   1100
no matter how she behaved to me.
BROMIA: Never mind about that, just listen now.
    When they were born, she told us to wash
    the babies. So we started in.
But you have never seen such a big
    strong baby as the one I bathed.
Why, we couldn't even pin
    the swaddling clothes around that child!
AMPHITRYON: Isn't that amazing! Well,
    if everything you say is true,
there's no doubt at all but that my wife
    got help from some one of the gods.
BROMIA: That's nothing! Wait till you hear the rest!
    We put him in his little crib,
when suddenly two gigantic crested
    serpents came into the pool.
Both of them raised their heads to strike . . .
AMPHITRYON: Good heavens, what are you telling me!
BROMIA: Don't be afraid.—The serpents glared
    and stared and looked around the room,   1110
but as soon as they saw the babies
    they made straightway for the crib.
I began to pull and drag
    the cradles back away from them,

frightened both for the boys and myself.
   The snakes began to follow us,
fiercer than ever. Suddenly
   that child I bathed caught sight of them.
Out he jumped from his little cradle
   and went rushing for the snakes,
and before we knew what happened,
   he'd grabbed one serpent with each hand!
AMPHITRYON: I've never heard anything as amazing
   and as terrible as that.
   I'm shivering . . . it gives me goosepimples
     just to hear you tell about it!
   Well, what happened then? Go on,
     don't stop!
BROMIA: He strangled both the snakes!
   While all this was going on,
     a loud voice called your wife by name.   1120
AMPHITRYON: Who was it?
BROMIA: Jupiter, the supreme
   and mighty ruler of gods and men.
He explained that he himself
   was the secret lover of your wife,
and that the baby—the one who strangled
   both the snakes—was his own son.
The other one, he said, was yours.
AMPHITRYON: Well, I guess I've no complaint
   if I have to share my possessions
     with the great god Jupiter.
Go inside and make the sacrificial vessels ready at once,
so I can make my offerings
   and pray to Jupiter for peace.
              (Exit Bromia.)
Then I'll call the prophet Teiresias
   and I'll ask him for advice
as to what I ought to do.
   I'll tell him about the whole affair.
             (Thunder.)
There's that awful thunder again!
   May all the gods preserve us now!   1130

JUPITER *(on the roof):*
> Take courage, Amphitryon, I'm here to help you now,
> and all your family. Don't be afraid. As for the seers,
> forget them. I will tell you all you need to know,
> both past and future, better than they, for I am Jove.
> First of all, I borrowed Alcmena for a time,
> and I conceived a child by her. She was made pregnant
> by you as well, you see, when you went out to war,
> and she has borne both of our sons with one confinement.
> The one who was begotten by my immortal seed
> shall by his deeds win immortal glory for your name.   1140
> Go to Alcmena now, and live in peace with her,
> for she has not done anything to deserve reproach.
> It was all my doing. Now I return to heaven.

AMPHITRYON: I'll do whatever you say, only
> don't forget to do your share.
> I'll go in to my wife. Never mind
> Teiresias. He's not in demand.
>> *(to the audience)*
> Now folks, for God's sake—Jove's, I mean—
> give us all a great big hand!   1146

Note on "the harbor of Persicus"

In line 402 and again in line 412 we translate *ex portu Persico* as "from the harbor of Persicus" to avoid the troublesome "from the Persian harbor"; in line 823 we omit the phrase altogether.

In line 402 Sosia says their ship arrived the night before *ex portu Persico* and in line 412 Mercury says the same. (Without a period after *Persico* the next lines may be wrongly understood as identifying the place with King Pterelas' capital in the islands to the west.) From these two passages we infer that the place was the last port of call before reaching the harbor of Thebes.

In lines 731-2, however, Amphitryon says he arrived the night before in the harbor (of Thebes), had supper there, and spent the whole night there on the ship (.. *hac noctu in portum advecti sumus; ibi cenavi atque ibi quievi in navi noctem perpetem* . . .); in 823 he asks Sosia: "Did I have dinner yesterday on board the ship (in the Persic port)?"

(*Cenavin ego in navi in portu Persico?*). Here the place must mean the harbor of Thebes—and Plautus has contradicted himself.

There is no manuscript difficulty. The commentator Festus, writing before 200 A.D., explained: "Plautus seems to mean the Euboic Gulf, since the Persian fleet is said to have anchored there, not far from Thebes." Festus was guessing. We doubt any Persian connection at all and we note that Festus would bring Amphitryon from a westward voyage to a port on the eastern coast of Greece. Festus' port would be Anthedon; see p. 31 above.

The astonishing range of conjecture about this place and about the harbor of Thebes is surveyed in D. J. Blackman's article, *Plautus and Greek Topography* in *Transactions and Proceedings of the American Philological Association*, Vol. 100 (1969), pp. 11–22. Blackman proposes an explanation from the late writer Stephen of Byzantium, who speaks of "Perseus, an Attic city and a port of the same name founded by the Athenians." We cannot locate this "Perseus," and *any* port in Attica makes nonsense of a westward voyage for Amphitryon.

It is conceivable that the *portus Persicus*, from a hypothetical Greek *limēn Persikós*, had something to do with Amphitryon's grandfather, the famous hero Perseus.

Appendix

Fragments from the lost pages of Plautus' *Amphitruo*

From the fourth century A.D. we have a work of miscellaneous information about lexicography, grammar, and antiquities, entitled *De Compendiosa Doctrina,* compiled by Nonius Marcellus. Nonius lived at Thurburiscum, now Khemissa in eastern Algeria, and was a contemporary of Saint Augustine, who was born in near-by Souk Ahras. This work often illustrates grammatical points by quotation from early authors, and to it we owe most of the following fragments from the lost pages of *Amphitruo.* Number 3 comes from the still more extensive grammatical work, *Institutiones Grammaticae,* by Priscianus, who wrote ca. 500 A.D. in Caesarea (now Cherchel), Algeria. Number 12 is quoted by both these authors, their concern being with the archaic word *scrobes.* Number 13 is cited by an unidentified commentator on *Aeneid* VIII, 127. Number 18 is some ancient scholar's gloss to a word or phrase in the text.

1. (AMPHITRYON) At ego te cruce et cruciatu mactabo, mastigia.
   But I'll offer *you* torment and torture, you whippingpost, you!
2. (MERCURY) Erus Amphitruo(st) occupatus.
   My master Amphitryon's busy.
3. (MERCURY) Abiendi nunc tibi etiam occasiost.
   You still have a chance to get away.
4. (MERCURY) Optumo iure infringatur aula cineris in caput.
   Serve you right to get a pot of ashes broken over your head.
5. (MERCURY) Ne tu postules matulam unam tibi aquai infundi in caput.
   Aren't you just begging to get a jar of water poured on your head?
6. (MERCURY) Larvatu's. edepol hominem miserum! medicum quaerita.
   You're bewitched. Poor fellow! Look for a doctor!
7. (ALCMENA) Exiurasti te mihi dixe per iocum.
   You swore you said it to me in jest.
8. (ALCMENA) Quaeso advenienti morbo medicari iube:
   tu certe aut larvatus aut cerritus es.
   Please have this sickness treated right away:
   You're either bewitched or crazy, that's for sure.
9. (ALCMENA) Nisi hoc ita factum est, proinde ut factum esse autumo,
   non caussam dico quin vero insimules probri.
   If this didn't happen just as I've said it did,
   You may justly accuse me of unchastity.
10. (AMPHITRYON) Quoius? quae me apsente corpus volgavit suom.
    Whose? Someone who prostituted herself while I was away?
11. (AMPHITRYON) Quid minitabas te facturum, si istas pepulissem fores?
    What did you threaten to do if I banged on that door?
12. (AMPHITRYON) Ibi scrobes ecfodito plus sexagenos in die.
    There you'll dig more than sixty ditches a day.
13. (AMPHITRYON) Noli pessumae *(or* pessumo*)* precari.
    Don't pray for an utter wretch.

14. (BLEPHARO) Animam comprime.
     Save your breath.
15. (JUPITER) Manufestum hunc optorto collo teneo furem flagiti.
     I have him by the neck—a flagrant thief caught right in the act!
16. (AMPHITRYON) Immo ego hunc, Thebani cives, qui domi uxorem
                                                        [meam
     impudicitia impedivit, teneo, thensaurum stupri.
     No, fellow Thebans, here he is—I've got him—
     the treasure-house of lust who disgraced my wife in my own house!
17. (AMPHITRYON) Nilne te pudet, sceleste, populi in conspectum
                                                        [ingredi?
     Aren't you even ashamed, you wretch, to be seen in public?
18. (AMPHITRYON) Clandestino.
     In secret.
19. (JUPITER or AMPHITRYON)
     Qui nequeas nostrorum uter sit Amphitruo decernere.
     You who can't decide which of us is Amphitryon.

II. FROM PLAUTUS TO MOLIÈRE

1. AN AFTERWORD TO PLAUTUS

For many centuries the twenty extant plays of Plautus and the six plays of Terence have comprised almost our entire knowledge of Roman comedy. The small number in the second instance is to be explained by Terence's death shortly after age twenty-five, perhaps in 159 B.C. There were, however, several other comic poets of the same era, not to mention a roster of tragedians, whose works are lost. At some point before 100 B.C. and while that repertory was still intact, the Romans became aware of the fact that they possessed a literary heritage and the writing of literary history was initiated. From that period we have a brief list, in verse, in which one Volcacius Sedigitus submitted his opinion of the ten best writers of comedy in the order of their excellence. "I give the palm," he says, "to Caecilius Statius" (a poet with forty-two recorded titles, whose career fell roughly between that of Plautus and that of Terence) but "Plautus as second easily surpasses the others." Terence rates only sixth place in the list. We wish we could test these judgments.

That there were revivals of Plautine plays is evident from the prologue of the *Casina,* which speaks of "a garland of poets," all of them dead now, who were living and able competitors at the time of the successful première. Through the years there also accumulated those imitations and those works by forgotten men to the point where, as Aulus Gellius relates, the scholar Varro felt obliged, around 50 B.C., to establish the twenty-one-play canon of genuine Plautus amid a hundred and thirty works loosely attributed to him.

Quite possibly it was Varro who superimposed the five-Act division upon those texts, for in his Classical era these works of two centuries earlier were looked upon as worthy but unpolished. Yet to Varro is assigned an elegiac couplet which says: "If the Muses were to speak in Latin, they would choose your meters, Plautus, and your wit." Cicero occasionally mentions Plautus respectfully, but his devotion went to Plautus' contemporary, Ennius. When Cicero complains about Plautus' odd meters, his objection is dictated by the Classical rules of prosody. It was a question of a changed climate of opinion. Horace, a generation after Cicero, is still more severely Classical. In the

Ars poetica of ca. 14 B.C. he advises literary aspirants to study the Greeks by day and by night. "But," interposes an imaginary objector, "your ancestors praised both the poetry and the wit of Plautus." To which Horace replies (lines 270–274):

> "They admired both things too tolerantly—lest I say: stupidly. —Just so you and I know how to tell uncouth from fine speech and have the skill in ears and fingers to hit the right tone."

By the time of Aulus Gellius, somewhat after 150 A.D., taste had reverted to pre-Classical Latinity, writers practiced deliberate archaism, and Plautus is termed "verborum Latinorum elegantissimus" in *Attic Nights* I, 7, 17. With the emergence of the Christians into prominence in the 300's, however, Plautus came under attack. Saint Augustine, around 400, speaks with disgust of a god like the dancing, prancing, cavorting, singing Jupiter— pretty clearly in allusion to the Jupiter of *Amphitruo*. On the other hand, his contemporary, Saint Jerome, who established himself in Bethlehem and who translated the Bible into the Latin used by the Catholic Church, writes with warm and erudite pleasure of the comedies:

> "After many sleepless nights, after the tears which the recollection of past sins tore from my vitals, I would take Plautus in hand."

At some time in the 300's or 400's the twenty-one Varronian plays were copied out anew on good parchment. In the 800's or 900's, good parchment being valuable, someone erased the entire text of that copy and wrote out portions of the Books of Kings and Chronicles on the cleaned surface. A thousand years later, in 1815, Cardinal Angelo noticed what was under the Biblical text and, after various scholars had tried to decipher the palimpsest, the German scholar Wilhelm Studemund, at the cost of his eyesight, published his Plautine transcription in 1889, which is the basis for all modern study. Our other manuscripts are all later than 900 A.D.

Through the Middle Ages Plautus was little esteemed, though Terence was sufficiently admired to be used as a Latin textbook. The lack of esteem led to the neglect of manuscripts to the point where only eight plays were actually known. One of these eight was *Amphitruo*, which, in the twelfth century, effected some curious results.

2. AMPHITRYON IN THE TWELFTH CENTURY

Probably in the early 1100's a learned man named Vitalis Blesensis (i.e. of Blois) composed a play, not for the stage but for private reading, entitled *Geta,* the source of which is either *Amphitruo* or, less probably, a hypothetical, late classical adaptation of *Amphitruo.* It begins by having Jupiter station his son Archas (= Mercury) at the entrance door in order to enjoy undisturbed the love of Alcmena. Amphitryon, however, is not returning from the wars but from a prolonged course of philosophical studies in Greece. The scenario relates to little more than Plautus' Act I, because the author's primary concern is with the slave Geta (= Sosia) who, while attending upon his master in Greece, has picked up something of the science of dialectic. Most of the text is devoted to Geta's debates, first with his lazy fellow-slave Birria, to whom he demonstrates that "something can never become nothing," and then with Archas, who has assumed the shape of Geta. Archas proves that *he,* Archas-Geta, is Geta. If so, then who is Geta? Plato, perhaps? At last Geta admits that "something"—namely himself—"has become nothing," and he swears off philosophy. Amphitryon's homecoming is hurried through. The skittish Alcmena, a good example of medieval woman as "man's confusion," deftly sidesteps difficulties, and all ends well.

The author's wit is directed against "sorcerer's apprentices" and the gist of his meaning is that "a little learning is a dangerous thing." French and Italian translations were made of this Latin *Geta* and its influence extends to John Gower's *Confessio amantis,* where a malicious Amphitryon impersonates his friend Geta in order to couple with Geta's wife "Alcmeene!"

More startling is the claim, advanced by E. Faral in *La Légende arthurienne* (1929) and repeated by Örjan Lindberger in *The Transformations of Amphitryon* (1956), to the effect that Geoffrey of Monmouth's well-known tale about the begetting of King Arthur is a wholesale adaptation of the Amphitryon story.

In Chapters 19 and 20 of Book VIII of the *Historia Regum Britanniae* (after 1135), Geoffrey tells of how Gorlois, Duke of

Cornwall, retired from court, taking his beautiful wife Igerna with him, in order to avoid the unwelcome advances made to her by King Uther Pendragon. Pursued by Uther, Gorlois placed Igerna in the safety of Castle Tintagel by the sea while he himself prepared to resist Uther at Castle Dimilioc. Then Merlin the enchanter conferred upon Uther the shape of Gorlois, and upon Uther's "familiar" Ulfin the shape of Gorlois' "familiar" Jordan, and himself making a third with these transformed persons, came to Tintagel. There Uther enjoyed Igerna without her being aware of the deception. Meanwhile at Castle Dimilioc the real Gorlois met death in battle. Yet when messengers brought this sad news to his Duchess, there was Gorlois alive and sitting beside her. Subsequently Uther married Igerna, who gave birth to the future King Arthur.

Admittedly there are parallels with the Amphitryon story, and Geoffrey was learned, wide-read, and demonstrably unscrupulous in his concoction of British "history," yet the present writer is not wholly convinced of this deliberate adaptation. Still, the idea is ingenious, especially in causing Geoffrey to exalt Arthur as a latter-day Herakles.

Professor Lindberger also reviews the claim of Jacobi's *Amphitryon in Frankreich und Deutschland* (1952) to the effect that the story of Jovianus in Chapter 59 of the *Gesta Romanorum* (before 1300) is a Christianized version of the Amphitryon story.

In sacrilegious pride the Emperor Jovianus deemed himself God. One day while he was bathing, a man who resembled him closely made off with his clothes and lived the Emperor's life, enjoying wealth, power, and the Empress. In confrontation with the latter, the real Jovianus was expelled from the palace as an impostor. Suffering and privation were his lot until he truly repented his sacrilege in Confession, after which the false Emperor revealed himself as the Guardian Angel of the real one and relinquished his role after thus goading Jovianus to repentance.

Professor Lindberger firmly rejects the Jacobi hypothesis and finds the Jovianus tale to be more plausibly derived from Near Eastern and even Hindu sources.

3. AMPHITRYON IN THE RENAISSANCE
a. *Italy*

Revival of interest in Plautus came about suddenly in 1427, when Nicolaus Cusanus discovered in Germany a manuscript of twelve long-forgotten comedies and brought it to Rome. Together with the eight known works, the twelve new ones almost completely restored the Varronian canon of twenty-one plays, and in the Rome of 1427 this was an event of immense importance. Copies were made and circulated among the international Latin-reading community of scholars, comment and debate were general, and praise was well-nigh universal.

Amid the enthusiasm for the glorious classical past now in "rebirth" it was felt that manuscript gaps should be filled, just as it was felt that mutilated statues should have their missing parts supplied, the simple theory being that a complete drama and a complete statue were more attractive than fragments of either. Thus it was that Cardinal Hermolaus Barbarus (1454–1494) came to compose the 174 lines of the *scenae suppositae* (interpolated scenes) to make up the manuscript deficiencies following line 1,034 of *Amphitruo*. It is important to realize that all editions of the play until Ritschl's mid-nineteenth century one included this Renaissance addendum without distinguishing it from the genuine Plautine context of seventeen hundred years earlier, so that all the authors to be mentioned in this section, as well as Molière and Kleist, read a longer *Amphitruo* than modern students of Latin now read.

If not brilliant, these *scenae suppositae* are competent, both dramatically and poetically, and, what is more important, they blend exceedingly well with the surrounding text. Hermolaus commanded an excellent Latin, free of both monkish naiveté and Renaissance-courtly glitter of adornment; he understood the pre-Classical metrics, and he worked obviously with loving care. His was no easy task, considering that he had to invent the climactic confrontation of Amphitryon with Jupiter-Amphitryon and that he was obliged to steer his inventive fancy to the fixed point at which the manuscript resumed, a procedure sometimes more difficult than free creation. Admittedly, as with the restora-

tion of missing arms and legs to statues, such work may be
botched or accomplished with skill. The present instance is one
of skill guided by reverence, and on the basis of those two factors
it should be judged. Classical editors may peremptorily dismiss
these 174 lines as non-ancient and therefore of no great interest;
others may carp at such subordination of creative powers to the
servile task of restoration; but, taken for what they are, these
scenae suppositae represent a product of distinguished work-
manship.

Hermolaus began by echoing the last preserved line of the
ancient text, and he deliberately echoed other foregoing lines
and motifs, apparently with the idea that that was the best way
of striking the authentic tone. He proceeded in trochaic septe-
narii (a line of seven trochees), since, happily, that was the meter
in use both before and after the manuscript lacuna. He made
plausible use of Theban background myth—Cadmus, the sowing
of the dragon-seed, etc. In the contest of the two Amphitryons
to win Blepharo's support he "doubled" and intensified the
motif of the goblet missing from the sealed box by having the
contestants recall secret military orders issued to Blepharo before
the battle, and in the matter of the treasure he named ancient
coins with antiquarian correctness—Attic talents, obols, etc. To
the baffled Amphitryon he assigned recollection of his noble
ancestry parallel to Sosia's recollection of slave parentage in Act
I. The mythology used for this purpose is freely handled material
from either "Apollodorus" or some derivative of "Apollodorus."
Cephalus son of Deioneus, for instance, is correctly named; he
was an Athenian ally of Amphitryon's in the Taphian/Teleboan
war. On the other hand, "Apollodorus" mentions a Gorgophones
as one of Alkmene's slain brothers and a Gorgophonè as an aunt
of Amphitryon's but no ancestor of Amphitryon's by that name.
—In meter, diction, allusion, and dramatic action, Hermolaus'
interpolations are so well wrought as to be almost indistinguish-
able from Plautus' own.

The enthusiasm that followed the discovery of 1427 was not
limited to scholarly editing and copying. Plautine performances
were given by amateurs to learned circles, in the original Latin
though perforce without the ancient music. With the date of

1487 there appeared a tolerably faithful translation into Italian
terza rima by Pandolfo Collenuccio. It served for the gala performance at the court of Ferrara in January of 1487 before that
eager amateur of drama, Duke Ercole I of the House of Este.
Apparently some non-Plautine spectacle was involved, because
a note has been preserved relative to that occasion which speaks
of settings that included "a paradise with stars and other machines." Four years later, in 1491, this *Anfitrione* was again produced at the court of Ferrara as part of the marriage festivities
for Alfonso d'Este and Anna Sforza. Independent mythological
scenes, dances, and a pantomime were incorporated into the performance, while Jupiter's speech announcing the birth of Hercules was expanded into an elaborate expression of hope for a
new Ercole (Hercules) to be born to the bridal couple.

To the year 1545 belongs the literary comedy—*commedia
erudita* as opposed to *commedia dell'arte*—of *The Husband*
(Il Marito) by the Venetian author Lodovico Dolce. It is a
poor work, interesting primarily because it attempted the impossible by eliminating all supernatural elements from the
plot. Once Jupiter and Mercury are reduced to contemporary mortality under the names of the nobleman Fabritio
and his servant Roscio, the magic of the old story is automatically undone. Even on the human level we are importuned to
believe that nothing more than sheer chance has provided the
town with a second master-servant pair, named Mutio and
Nespilo, physically identical to the first pair though entirely
unrelated. Jupiter-Fabritio satisfies the deceived wife, here named
Virginia, with the report of a necromancer who is able to change
people's shapes, but in order to satisfy Amphitryon-Mutio he
has recourse to a clever monk. Virginia's pregnancy, says the
monk, is the work of a prankish spirit, and when Amphitryon-
Mutio doubts this, the monk offers an alternate explanation
whereby the prankish spirit transported Mutio unawares from
the army camp to his wife's bed and back again. When Mutio
still doubts, the monk says the doubt comes of not having studied
theology. Bawdy dialogue cannot lift this silly plot out of a
slough of boredom.

b. *Spain and Portugal*

In 1525 Fernan Perez de Oliva, rector of the University of Sala-manca (and formerly of Paris), produced an extremely free adaptation of Plautus' tragicomedy under the title of *El Nascimiento de Hércules, ó Comedia de Amphitrión*. Both the additions and subtractions made by the rector were ill-advised, and religious bias made him introduce mockeries of the gods whom he was portraying. The work seems not to have been performed. Previously, however, a commendably faithful translation of the *Amphitruo* into Spanish prose had been published by court physician Francisco Lopez de Villalobos, in 1515, and this version served, in 1559, as the basis for a new adaptation called *Amphitrión* by Juan de Timoneda. A pastoral prologue opens Timoneda's prose play in ten scenes, and *canciones* are introduced both into the prologue and at the play's conclusion. These are sung by an old man named Bromio, his shepherdess daughter Pascuala, and two shepherds called Morato and Roseno. It is Roseno who takes over Mercury's old function of informing the audience about the general lines of action to come. The ten scenes are quite faithfully Plautine and the work closes with an appearance of Jupiter arrayed entirely in gold.

Perhaps through a Spanish translation the famous Portuguese poet Luiz Vaz de Camões came to compose, between 1544 and 1549, his Portuguese adaptation usually known as *Os Amphitriões*, though the earliest editions, 1587 and 1615, give the form as *Os Enfatriões*. This youthful work in eight-syllable verse called *redondilha*s may have been composed for academic performance at the University of Coimbra, but it also enjoyed success before the Lisbon public. Once again we find songs interspersed among the opening scenes. The first Act dwells somewhat over-long on lyric passages for Alcmena, for her servant Bromia, for a suitor-swain of Bromia's named Faliseo, as well as for a love-sick Jupiter. It is Mercurio who proposes the plan for impersonation, and once that plan is adopted, the scenario unfolds in Plautine fashion, though with some noteworthy differences of detail. Anfitrião is a Portuguese naval officer deeply disturbed by his wife's infidelity and the consequent offense to his honor. Alcmena herself is more sentimental than in Plautus.

By virtue of a Portuguese stage convention Sosea and Mercurio, as long as he is impersonating Sosea, speak Spanish. At the close of the work Jupiter is not seen; only his voice from inside the house proclaims the birth of Hercules, and the author does not allow Anfitrião to express any reaction to the portentous announcement. In the Iberian peninsula there was almost no reply possible for a husband in such circumstances.

c. *England*

The first English translation of *Amphitruo*, under the title of *The Birthe of Hercules,* came surprisingly late, in an undetermined year between 1600 and 1610. The unknown translator dealt very freely with the Latin text, introducing a second servant by way of foil to Sosia and adding considerable matter of his own invention. Jupiter's voice is heard at the end, speaking out of heaven, in promise of a glorious son for Amphitryon in recompense for all the trouble that has been occasioned by his pleasure-seeking in Amphitryon's household. To which the hero replies: "All rulinge Jupiter, yt shalbe as thou comandest." This may or may not have been the work performed by English actors at the court theater in Dresden on June 4, 1626, under which date the court records have the entry: "Ist eine Comoedia von Amphitrione gespielt worden." A second but less likely possibility is that the "Englische Comoedianten" played one or both parts of a two-part English drama of 1595 by one Martin Slaughter, which has been lost and whose very title is unknown, but which dealt with Hercules.

Earlier than any of these is Shakespeare's *Comedy of Errors,* usually dated 1591, which is based primarily upon Plautus' *Menaechmi* but which has at least one scene obviously imitated from that passage in *Amphitruo* where the master is denied entrance into his own house. Like *Amphitruo,* it also has two sets of doubles, where *Menaechmi* has only one pair. Since both Latin works turned on the hinge of double identities, the conflation of materials was easily managed. As stated above, no English translation of *Amphitruo* was made until after the turn of the new century, and the translation of the *Menaechmi* is dated 1595. Clearly Shakespeare must have worked from the

original Latin in both cases. Since there are no records whatsoever about Shakespeare's education, it is impossible to say
whether he ever reached those last stages of the Stratford-upon-
Avon Grammar School during which the works of Plautus were
studied, but "small Latin" he demonstrably had—doubtless not
so "small" when compared with modern students—and as a
practicing young dramatist with eyes open for potential dramatic
material it is more than likely that he would have investigated
Plautus. In Elizabethan England that would have been the logical thing to do.

The best known of the adaptations of *Amphitruo* into English
of the Elizabethan-Jacobean era is a curious item consisting of
a single Act in a large panoramic work by Thomas Heywood.
This younger contemporary of Shakespeare's set out to compose
a sequence of dramas which would survey a considerable portion
of classical mythology. The five-Act installment published in
1611 was entitled "The GOLDEN AGE or The liues of *Jupiter*
and *Saturne,* with the deifying of the Heathen Gods." In 1613
came the publication of:

> The SILVER AGE inclvding The loue of *Iupiter* to *Alcmena:*
> The birth of *Hercules.* and The Rape of PROSERPINE.
> conclvding, With the Arraignement of the Moone.

"The BRAZEN AGE," also published in 1613, devoted separate
Acts to the themes of Nessus, Meleager, Jason and Medea, "VVL-
CANS NET," and in the fifth Act canvassed the entire career
of Hercules. "The IRON AGE," which surveyed the whole Trojan War, was not published until 1632.

Within "The SILVER AGE," to cite the work by its short
title, Act I dealt with the founding of the House of Perseus,
while Act III took up miscellaneous tales about Hercules. Thus
only the space of Act II was allotted to the Amphitryon story.
This in turn has a kind of three-Act structure in miniature. After
a prologue by Homer (!), Jupiter and Ganimed (= Mercury)
arrive in the guises of Amphitrio and Socia respectively and are
welcomed by the unsuspecting Alcmena. In a supper scene Jupiter relates his victory in battle and presents the golden cup,
then he and Ganimed start back to camp. The stoppage of time

for the triple night is identified by Jupiter for the Christian
audience by saying:

> Now at this houre is fought
> By *Iosua* Duke vnto the Hebrew Nation,
> (Who are indeede the Antipodes to vs)
> His famous battle 'gainst the *Cananites,*
> And at his orison the Sunne stands still,
> That he may haue there slaughter. . . .

After this rearrangement of materials for the sake of the supper
scene with its luxurious and visual immediacy, the action proceeds
along Plautine lines until just before the dénouement. Then the
real Amphitrio and the real Socia, both woe-begone, fall asleep
side by side, while the audience beholds their "dream" of Juno
descending with Iris. (Such pageantry of descending goddesses
had apparently met with theater-goers' favor in Shakespeare's
The Tempest a year or so before.) Juno has at last discovered,
at sight of two Amphitrios in Thebes, the whereabouts of her
errant consort and in her spite she now bids Iris fetch a beldam's
tatters, for she intends to sit crosslegged like a witch at Alcmena's
threshold to prevent childbirth. Amid thunder and lightning
Jupiter emerges from the house "in his glory vnder a Raine-bow,
to whom they all kneele." Amphitrio accepts Jupiter's setting
to rights and the god announces that "Our Act thus ends." The
Ovidian matter of Juno's witch-vigil and the trick cleverly played
by the serving-maid Galantis to outwit her are deferred until
Act III, as is the birth of Alcmena's twins.

The substitution of Ganimed for Mercury is probably to be
explained by Mercury's appearance under a somewhat different
aspect of his divine nature in subsequent sections of "The
SILVER AGE." Heywood augmented the cast with minor figures,
used the typical Elizabethan-Jacobean mixtures of prose and
verse, and in general "Shakespeareanized" the script. The descending goddesses both here and in *The Tempest,* as well as
the descent of Jupiter amid thunder and lightning somewhat as
in *Cymbeline,* anticipate the grandiose effects of the Jacobean
masque. Popular in its day, Heywood's *Four Ages* now seems
more bizarrely kaleidoscopic than pleasing.

Jupiter's lines "explaining" the triple night at Thebes as

coterminous with Joshua's halted sun may be taken as symptomatic of Renaissance poets' dilemma in dealing with heathen
mythology in general and with the Amphitryon story in particular. Professor Lindberger very justly comments on the masking
over of the delicate subject matter with spectacular stage effects,
music, and dance, such as had already characterized the Ferrara
court performances a century earlier. Poets dared not take the
Amphitryon story too seriously lest they offend Christian sensi-
bilities. It was a lucky coincidence of history that preserved only
Plautus' comic version, which could be used. The fifth century
tragedies would have been too hot to handle. There were, for
instance, no Christian adaptations of Euripides' *The Bacchae*.
As late as 1807, as we shall see, Goethe professed to be shocked
by Kleist's deliberate pointing up of the parallel between
Alcmena and the Virgin Mary. That those parallels had not
escaped notice prior to 1807 is shown by a Latin school play of
1621, the *Sacri Mater Virgo* of the German provincial priest
Johannes Burmeister.

d. *Germany*

The tradition of school performances of Latin plays, to which
we have already alluded, proved pedagogically useful as well as
entertaining. In time, new plays were composed, always in Latin,
to extend the range of schoolmasters' choices. In Jesuit schools
of the post-Reformation period there was developed a considerable repertory of such new works, constituting an interesting
and much neglected sub-genre of drama. Burmeister's play of
1621, however, is quite unclassifiable. Unfortunately the text,
which was published at Lüneburg, has become so rare that even
Professor Lindberger was obliged to describe it only from second-
hand report.

Sacri Mater Virgo is nothing less than a work created so that
students might read the classics without reading the classics. Less
paradoxically expressed, it is a Christianized version of Plautus'
pagan comedy, so designed as to provide instruction in ancient
Latin simultaneously with religious edification. Alcmena has become the Virgin Mary, Jupiter is the Holy Ghost, Amphitryon
is Saint Joseph, and the infant Hercules is the Christ Child.

Mercury's prologue is assigned to the archangel Gabriel, while Mercury's more roguish lines are given to the devil of Discord, Asmodes. But this work is no adaptation in the ordinary sense of that term. Line by line within the limits of possibility, these new characters speak Plautus' text, and where the new sense made alteration imperative, Burmeister, with painful care, substituted metrically equivalent words and phrases. Where, for instance, Sosia made his unedifying remark (line 272) about Nocturnus, God of Night, being drunk:

Credo ego hac noctu Nocturnum obdormuisse ebrium,

Burmeister makes the corresponding character say:

Credo ego hac noctu Messiam promissum adfore,

(i.e. that the promised Messiah will come.) A new complication is introduced when Asmodes-Mercury makes it his business to inspire doubt in the minds of Sosia and Joseph about the Virgin Mary's chastity. When the archangel Gabriel appears in a dream to Joseph and dispels such doubt, Asmodes spreads his slander abroad, and when a priest comes to investigate the alleged adultery, Asmodes, in Sosia's shape, bars the door against him and hurls abuse. The priest later vents his wrath upon the real Sosia for this behavior. The work concludes, not with Jupiter's pronouncements about the infant Hercules, but with a Christmas scene of choiring angels and adoring shepherds.

It is worth pondering—as an index to national cultures and to stages of modernity—the fact that Burmeister's "sacred *Amphitryon*" came only eight years after Heywood's enthusiastically classical "revue" of "The SILVER AGE" and only seventeen years before Jean Rotrou sought to bring Plautus' old comedy within the limits of French Classicism.

e. *France*

Jean Rotrou turned twenty-one years of age in 1630 and as a newcomer to Paris he set boldly about making both a career and a living as a dramatic poet. At first he suffered privations in obscurity, but before long he was rescued from his unhappy plight by powerful personages who sponsored him. His first efforts were in the loose dramatic form, not so very different from Elizabethan plays, which had been established in favor by Alexandre Hardy in 1593. Next he turned to the free forms of Spanish drama, particularly of Lope de Vega. His conversion to the strict theories of French Classicism seems to have been rather sudden and it was first manifest in his play *Diane* of 1635, when he reworked one of Lope's comedies to make it conform to the famous Three Unities. In the following year, 1636—the year of Corneille's *Le Cid*—he produced his Amphitryon play under the title of *Les Sosies* (published 1638). Under the protection of Cardinal Richelieu he seems not to have had to worry about giving offense with pagan material, but he was most seriously concerned with the problem of being simultaneously true to Plautus and to those principles of dramatic composition which he now understood to be absolute. By conscientiously following both the Latin text and the rules of composition and of *bienséance* he achieved a resuscitation of the *fabula palliata*. Plautus might or might not have approved the changes, but it was in this guise or not at all that the old work was to be made to live again, and where other writers since 1427 had produced self-conscious translations or rather distorted adaptations, Rotrou brought the play into the living theatre. Having said this much, we confess the statement to have been made with the advantage of hindsight, with the knowledge that French drama was to become in the seventeenth century the European norm and the beginning of a continuous tradition, whereas the continuity of English drama, for instance, was to be seriously disrupted after 1642.

Les Sosies is a five-Act comedy in alexandrine couplets, apart from the prologue and final scenes, and it observes the unities of time, place, and action. A prologue reverent of Roman antiquity was adapted from Seneca's tragedy of *The Raging Hercules* and assigned to be spoken by the goddess Juno. Jealousy of Jupiter's latest earthly amour with Alcmena has made Juno angry, but foreknowing the future as she does, she is aware that she can prevent neither the amour itself nor its heroic by-product. She will, however, make life miserable for Hercules once he is born. None of this is strictly relevant to the comedy which is to follow, but it was apparently Rotrou's intention to balance the supernatural ending with a supernatural beginning.

Act I begins with a monologue of Mercury's in which the Moon is asked to slow her course through the skies in order to prolong Jupiter's night of pleasure with Alcmena. Social rank, Mercury observes, will oblige the chaste Moon to grant what, in lesser persons, would be vice. Gods and high aristocrats are beyond the law, apparently. In other words, Act I freely adapts the matter of Plautus' prologue.

Then for three Acts the text follows the Latin model, with only here and there a token show of independence on Rotrou's part. Plautus' maid servant Thessala, for instance, who had only a mute role, is now renamed Céphalie and given a speaking part as the confidante of Alcmène. In this way the heroine's old *canticum* about courage is now a dialogue between the two ladies. Or again, Mercury, just arriving from heaven, delivers a report on the *dolce vita* of the gods, with a side glance at Juno's jealous agitation up there. In Act IV, however, there is a significant modification of detail. Mercury-Sosia is not on the roof, nor does he pretend to be drunk, nor does he empty water down on Amphitryon; rather, he stands at a window, is perfectly sober, and delivers calculated insolence such as would befit a dignified servant dealing with a nobody. Through the stretch of the *scenae suppositae* Rotrou worked with more freedom. Three Captains now stand where once Blepharo stood alone; Amphitryon, sorely wounded in his honor, challenges Jupiter to a duel, but is disarmed by the three Captains. Here one senses the importance of the *point d'honneur* and the "nobility" of swords on stage. At the beginning of Act V Rotrou has hazarded a brief new scene, when a hungry Sosia ventures into the kitchen only to be ejected by Mercury. Amphitryon, returning with soldiers of the King's guard, is about to force his way into the house when, as in Plautus, lightning falls around him. Jupiter's final declaration is accepted by Amphitryon with submissiveness, yet with a touch of resentment, for Rotrou's audience had a Mediterranean touchiness about cuckoldry.

Devout in his allegiance to classical antiquity, Rotrou had sought to restore ancient Roman comedy to the stage. His audiences approved of his objective, tended to agree with his method, and appreciated his talent. In short, *Les Sosies* was a success. Yet for all his faithfulness to his model, his modifications had been more pervasive than he realized. Correct French alexan-

drines would alone controvert the lusty force of Plautus, but
this French Jupiter is also made to speak with that kind of
rhetorical *grandeur* that we have come to think of as peculiar to
Corneille. This Alcmène is much softer than her Roman counterpart; she is a docile *jeune dame* who bows before the will of so
great a *seigneur*. All horseplay has been toned down. The husband-wife quarrel is couched in terms of both propriety and a
certain *préciosité*. Referring to Naucrate's testimony, Amphitryon
inquires of his wife:

> Consens-tu, si sa voix convainc tes faussetés,
> A rompre le lien qui joint nos libertés?

One small detail of the venerably ancient text Rotrou felt bound
to clarify—dare we say: to correct?—namely, the confusing biology. This protracted night is Jupiter's first time with Alcmène
and it is a night of passion and Hercules is born at the end of
it—by special abrogation of the laws of Nature.

Rotrou's product is wholly French and of its own time, but,
Janus-like, it closed one era and opened another. The date of
1636 is already past the limits usually set for the Renaissance,
yet in that year *Les Sosies* achieved a Renaissance objective:
to restore Plautus' play of ca. 200 B.C. to the stage. All writers
since 1427 had sought precisely that objective, yet somehow
they had all remained subservient to the Roman writer. In a
diagram, all their works may be represented by lines projecting
from a single center: Plautus' *Amphitruo*. So too does the line
designating Rotrou. But Rotrou's method made possible Molière's *Amphitryon* in the next generation, and after Molière
the lines of *Amphitryon* development will proceed from another
center.

Such was the success of *Les Sosies* with the public that Rotrou
himself, in 1650, converted it into a grand spectacular, with
supplementary scenes and all kinds of special machines. A fourth
Act interpolation allowed Juno to make a pageant of her
jealousy in heaven before the court of the gods. From a historical
point of view, this bedizened *Naissance d'Hercule* of 1650 was
retrogression from drama back to Renaissance court entertainments, but the public delighted in it. What, one wonders, had
happened to Rotrou's neo-Classical ideals?

In 1653 we find the old drama fading away to mere panto-mime. For a court celebration on February 23rd of that year Isaac de Benserade composed an elaborate *Ballet de la Nuit,* one of the *entrées* of which was a four-Act *comédie muette* of *Amphi-tryon.* Wordless dancers now successively mimed Amphitryon's departure to the war, Jupiter's accepting of Mercury's suggestion to impersonate the absent husband, and subsequent passages from Plautus' scenario.

Clearly fad and fashion were now trifling with the old dra-matic material. But in 1668 there was to come about a new and unexpected "transformation of Amphitryon" by Molière.

4. MOLIÈRE'S AMPHITRYON

On January 13th, 1668, two days short of his forty-sixth birthday, Molière, himself playing the role of Sosia, staged the première of his new play *Amphitryon* in his own theater at the Palais-Royal. The instantaneous and extraordinary success was repeated through thirty-eight performances, the third of which was given in the Tuileries before the king on January 16th. Under the date of January 21st there is preserved the first of the glowing contemporary tributes to the work, in this case a verse-epistle by a writer named Robinet. In March the text of the drama was published, together with a dedicatory letter to the Prince de Condé—"le grand Condé," who in the interim had conquered the province of Franche-Comté (February 3rd to 19th) and was the hero of the hour. Another verse-epistle by Robinet saluted the appearance of the printed book, which he termed "le bel Amphitryon du ravissant Molière." Among the frequent revivals, that of 1685 is particularly interesting because its known distri-bution of roles to surviving members of Molière's company en-ables us to establish with fair certainty the original cast for whom the author composed. All told, 363 presentations to city and court are recorded down to 1715. In 1772 the aging Voltaire, in an article entitled *Laughter,* recalled reading the play at age eleven and almost falling over backwards from excess of mirth. It is said to have been his favorite play through all his life.

Success had been slow in coming to the merchant tapestry-worker's son, Jean-Baptiste Poquelin, who in 1643, at age twenty-one, had embarked upon a theatrical career, assuming for the purpose the stage name of "Molière." So unstable were the fortunes of his troupe, however, that the year 1645 found the young actor-manager in the Châtelet prison for debt. Followed then thirteen years of barnstorming in the southern province of Languedoc, with gratifying return to Paris in 1658 and the privilege of playing, on October 24th, before the youthful Louis XIV. Composition of literary comedies had begun in the latter phases of his provincial career, but his first major creation, L'École des femmes, was not produced until 1662. Thereafter lesser and greater plays came in rapid succession, including such memorable titles as Tartuffe (1664), Don Juan (1665), and Le Misanthrope and Le Médecin malgré lui (both in 1666). If scandal and censorship plagued him repeatedly over the first two of these, there was the compensating favor of the monarch, who had stood godfather to Molière's child in 1664 and who had conferred the title of "Troupe du roi" on Molière's company in 1665. The year 1667 marked a lull in his activity and during that lull the masterpiece of Amphitryon was composed. Its première in January of 1668 was followed by two more noteworthy pieces that same year, George Dandin in July and the coolly received L'Avare in September. Lesser and greater plays were still to be composed in the five years of life remaining to him, including Le Bourgeois Gentilhomme of 1670 and Les Femmes savantes of 1672. It was during a representation of his last play, Le Malade imaginaire, on February 17th, 1673 that the great writer and comic actor was carried off stage in dying condition in the midst of the final scene—to be buried four days later in a grave which cannot be identified.

In certain of his works, in Les Fourberies de Scapin of 1671, for example, perhaps also in L'École des maris of 1661, some elements may derive from the polished Latin comedies of Terence, but during that previously mentioned lull in 1667 the author must have been reading the older, rougher-and-readier comedies of Plautus, for Amphitryon derives from Plautus' Amphitruo as its close successor L'Avare derives from Plautus' Aulularia. Yet the impulse to composition did not come solely from Latin readings. Molière was well aware of the success enjoyed by Rotrou's Les Sosies in 1636 and afterwards, and of the success attending the same play's adaptation as a comédie-ballet, and of the welcome accorded to the *Comédie muette d'Amphi-tryon* in 1653. But the latter two were minor pieces, Rotrou's text was a little old-fashioned after thirty years, and it was fifteen years since the public had seen any Amphitryon-play. The comedy which Molière composed in the course of 1667 may be defined as a fresh adaptation directly from Plautus but with benefit of key alterations made by Rotrou. In a familiar metaphor, he achieved his high results by standing on the shoulders of both these predecessors. No other dramatic versions of *Amphitryon* seem to have been known to him.

The airy fantasy of the Prologue is of Molière's own invention, owing little to Plautus' Mercurius and nothing to Rotrou's Juno, though Pierre Bayle, in his famous *Dictionnaire historique et critique* of 1697, sought its origin in the interchange between Mercury and the Sun in the tenth of the *Dialogues of the Gods* by the Greek writer Lucian of the second century A.D. Wholly new likewise, and wholly delightful, are the several passages between Cléanthis and her husband Sosie, or between her and Mercure in the guise of Sosie. Whereas Plautus' maid-servant Bromia appeared only in the final Act and performed chiefly a messenger's function, and whereas Rotrou's Céphalie was no more than an attendant upon Alcmène, Molière chose to integrate Cléanthis into his plot of multiple pairs of double images and to give her a lively individuality of her own.

In the matter of structure, Act I follows Plautus' Act I fairly closely; Act II combines portions of Plautus' Acts II and III; while the third and final Act brings together elements of the Latin author's Acts III, IV, and V—including the *scenae suppositae,* which Molière read as integral parts of the ancient work. Rotrou, who in general followed his Latin model closely, had retained a five-Act organization, whereas Molière's instinctive taste perceived that a three-Act structure yielded a more compact form that carried his jest in three gradations straight up to its climax and dénouement. Slow beginning, steady intensification, swift conclusion: these are the principles that determined the new three-Act form.

The 1668 *Amphitryon* observes the unities of time, place, and action, which were already observed in its Roman counterpart. Except for the Prologue, all scenes take place before Amphitryon's house in Thebes, the first in pre-dawn darkness, the second at, say, mid-morning, and the third perhaps in the after-noon, of a single day. Unity of action may be said to have been even more rigorously defined by Molière than by Plautus, since the motif of the birth of Hercules, which was stressed by the Roman, is reduced to mere passing mention in the last thirty lines of the French text, thus permitting exclusive concentration on the "human" relationships of these gods and mortals. For the ancient audience, jesting at the gods was fun, yet the gods existed and therefore an admixture of seriousness made Plautus' play a tragicomedy; for the French audience these gods had no exis-tence except as characters in a work of fiction, hence the play automatically gravitates away from tragicomedy back toward the sphere of pure comedy—though we hasten to add that the human conflicts have a seriousness of their own.

About stage equipment and properties for this play we are imperfectly informed. For the Prologue we hear of a "machine" for Mercure and a chariot for the Lady Night; for the final scene, a chariot for Jupiter and presumably the "machine" for Mercure again. Complex stage machines were commonplace by the 1660's. Corneille had used them in serious drama and Ro-trou had worked them into the comédie-ballet adaptation of *Les Sosies*. What is significant in the present instance is the merely token use that Molière made of them. Actually it makes very little difference whether Jupiter and Mercure fly or step from our sight, the whole matter residing here in histrionic gesture and the spoken word. The three Acts require a house entrance with a balcony above, the place being a street in the city of Thebes; all else is at the stage manager's discretion. In the Prologue the Lady Night should appear standing in a two-wheeled chariot; her team of horses should be recognizably humans underneath horse bodies of papier-mâché. Mercure's cloud is perhaps indispensable, but the spaces of twilit sky had best not be counterfeited by the stage painter. The costumes need but suggest Greek antiquity, though in Molière's day they did not, but they should be resplendent. The two pairs of offi-cers in the final Act must, in the "classical" economy of this play, stand for crowds, but they should appear with burnished armor, helmet plumes, and scarlet cloaks, for they also have a decorative function. By two and by two they extend the series of double images which characterize the whole work.

In *Amphitryon* Molière first used what the seventeenth century termed "free verse" (vers libres), by which was meant lines
that were strictly metrical but of lengths that varied with the
poet's caprice, and with irregular rhyme patterns. There are
numerous 12/13-syllable alexandrines—the standard line of
French tragedy and of some comedies, but they are only occasionally rhymed in couplets; more often they occur in rhyme
patterns of a-b-a-b or a-b-b-a, and frequently one of the rhymes
falls in an unexpectedly shorter line. Verses of 10/11, 8/9, and
7/8 syllables are common, as are triple and quadruple rhymes.
Sosie's eight octosyllabics (813–820) interlock the triple rhymes
of: *être, connaître, maître* with the quintuple rhymes of: *doux,
jaloux, courroux, nous, coups*. To match this an English poet
would have to stand language on its head, though it is accomplished without strain in French. The translator was forced to
simplify the rhyme patterns; in prosody he followed the original
more closely, even to imitation (sometimes) of the common
alexandrine practice of combining three iambs with two anapests
(or two anapests with three iambs).

In the nineteenth century it was proposed that Molière intended royal flattery by setting Jupiter, Alcmène, and Amphitryon parallel to the real-life personages of Louis XIV, Mme de
Montespan, and M. de Montespan, and for a time the proposal
was taken seriously. On chronological grounds alone, to say
nothing of other factors, that notion is discredited. In other and
more significant ways, however, the play is a true product of
its age. Its wit and contained merriment reflect the confident
vigor of the 1660's in France, as well as the principle of "classical" restraint then so much admired. The king was in the prime
of energetic manhood; the country was at the apogee of its
fortunes; the old political struggles between crown and nobles
had been forced to a conclusion twenty years before, sufficiently
long ago for the bitterness to have waned, and the dark shadows
of another kind of strife would not begin to fall until the 1680's.
It was a propitious time, when the full and harmonious synthesis of pagan Roman splendor with modern Christian civilization seemed attainable.

If that ideal Neo-classical synthesis proved unattainable, or
at least unstable, in real life, it was achieved in this play. The
subject was unimpeachably Greco-Roman, so that Parisians

might feel at one with Athenians and Romans in taste. The author worked with full confidence in the time-honored "classical" method of *imitation,* which is to say the refashioning of an old, old story in a wholly new way, taking the "what" for granted and displaying all genius in the "how." And here, within the ancient scenario, all is new: the language, the courtliness, the refined wit, and the mental attitudes. This Jupiter is not a god but a *grand seigneur;* this Amphitryon is not a Theban warrior but a testy young nobleman of secondary, but not inferior, rank, vain, irascible, youthfully rash, aristocratically impatient; but yet upright, understandably and humanly angered and bewildered; this Alcmène is no passive human instrument for a divine will, but a virtuous young wife, tender but not lacking in mettle; this Sosie is not a slave but a gentleman's valet; this Mercure is neither a vaudeville clown nor a stooge nor a divine flunkey, but a worldly wise and slightly world-weary courtier. All of them, and the lesser characters as well, in spite of Greek names and Roman prototypes, are very French, readily identifiable types of the court and the capital. They are also universally human as they move amid this eerie array of mirror images where reality and illusion cannot be distinguished. Collectively they compose a subtle paradigm of a cosmic dilemma, yet they do so charmingly unawares. They all bear the imprint of Molière's truth and human dignity and poetic grace.

In one further respect, we feel, this play is classical—classical this time in the sense of non-Romantic—namely, in its close. To clarify this point the final lines need to be juxtaposed with the final sextet in Mozart's *Don Giovanni.* In both cases poetic illusion is not sustained to the last syllable; the stage curtain does not abruptly shut away the imaginary world from the banal reality of rows of theater seats. Rather, Sosie divides his concluding speech, addressing the larger portion of it, as previously, to the tableau of characters of which he has been a member, but, moving gradually away, he speaks his last four or five lines directly to the audience. The illusion is allowed to fade, the tableau is reduced to the stature of mere human players, and at the footlights it is no longer Sosie but the incomparable comic actor, M. de Molière, who quietly closes what the present translator considers the most nearly perfect comedy in all literature.

AMPHITRYON

A
Comedy
by
MOLIÈRE

translated by
CHARLES E. PASSAGE

ACTORS

MERCURY	Du Croisy
NIGHT	
JUPITER, in the guise of Amphitryon	La Thorillière
AMPHITRYON, General of the Thebans	La Grange
ALCMENA, wife of Amphitryon	Mlle Molière
CLEANTHIS, attendant of Alcmena and wife of Sosia	Madelaine Béjart
SOSIA, Amphitryon's valet	Molière
ARGATIPHONTIDAS	
NAUCRATES	Theban Commanders
POLIDAS	
POSICLES	

The scene is at Thebes, in front of Amphitryon's house.

NOTE. Molière, like Corneille and Racine, regularly listed the cast of
characters under the heading of "ACTORS."
The names in the right-hand column represent the hypothetical
distribution of roles among the members of Molière's troupe
on the occasion of the première on January 13, 1668 at the
Théâtre du Palais-Royal.

132

Prologue

MERCURY: One moment, lovely Night! Be so kind as to wait.
  Assistance of a certain kind is craved of you;
      I also have a word or two
      Which Jupiter would have me state.
NIGHT: Lord Mercury, I do declare!
  Who would have recognized you in that posture there?
MERCURY: Well, being tired, and just unable to comply
  With all the tasks assigned at Jupiter's behest,
  I simply sat down on this cloud to have a rest
      And wait to meet you coming by.   10
NIGHT: You cannot mean that, Mercury. You must be jesting.
  Does it befit the gods to say they're tired and resting?
MERCURY: Are we gods made of iron?
NIGHT: Of course not. Nonetheless
  One must observe decorum in divinity.
  Some words there are whose usage cannot but transgress
      Against that lofty quality,
      And which, for impropriety,
      One leaves for humans to express.
MERCURY: All very well for you to talk;
  And you, my pretty, have a chariot for your pleasure   20
  With two fine steeds, and as a lady at her leisure
  You have yourself conveyed and never need to walk.
      But my case is quite different;
  And for the poets, given my accursed fate,
      I cannot feel sufficient hate
      For being so impertinent
      As to have made, on unfair grounds,
      Rules they won't let fall in abeyance,
      Allotting each god in his rounds
      Some good vehicular conveyance,   30
      While leaving me with no way but
      To do my journeying on foot,—
Me, who, as every child knows, am, by earth and sky,
The famous envoy of the king of gods on high.

133

I am the one, beyond a doubt,
With all the errands and the bother,
Who needs, much more than any other,
The wherewithal to get about.

NIGHT: But can you alter matters, then?
Poets their willful ways profess;   40
It's not the only foolishness
Observed among those gentlemen.

And yet you wrong them, being so much vexed and ired;
They put wings on your feet because they felt your needs.

MERCURY: Yes; but is anyone less tired
For traveling at higher speeds?

NIGHT: Let us dismiss this topic, Sir,
And find out what your message is.

MERCURY: As I was saying, it is Jupiter
Who asks the favor of your cloak-of-darkness' aid.   50
It seems a new amour of his
Invites to gallant escapade.

You are, I'm sure, no stranger to his practices.
Quite often for the earth-plane he deserts the skies;
And how this master of the gods will humanize
For beauteous mortals' sakes you surely are aware,
How by a hundred tricks of his
He gets the cruelest of those fair.

He has been stricken by Alcmena's eyes,
And just now, while Amphitryon, her spouse, commands   60
The Theban troops and warrior-bands
Manoeuvering on Boeotian plains,
He has assumed his form, receiving in that guise
The recompense of all his pains
In the possession of enjoyment's sweetest prize.

The couple's situation favors his intention;
They have been married only for a few days' time,
And hence their tender love in all its youthful prime
Has prompted Jupiter to the astute invention
Of which he now makes application.   70

His stratagem has proved successful in this case;
With many lady-loves, however,
Disguise of this sort would be but a vain endeavor,

For it is not the surest way to gratification
    To have a husband's form and face.
NIGHT: I do admire Lord Jupiter, but feel misgiving
  About all these incognitos to which he's prone.
MERCURY: He likes experience at all different kinds of living;
    It's not the beastliest streak a god has shown.
Let mortals come on him in any state whatever,   80
    A sorry creature he would be
If he could never drop his fearsome majesty
And were perched on the pinnacles of sky forever.
There is, I feel, no sillier thing or more outrageous
    Than being captive of one's own sublimity;
And, most of all, to love's transports of ecstasy
    The elevated station proves disadvantageous.
Now Jupiter, who knows his pleasures very well,
Knows also how to come down from his lofty height,
    And entering into things that give delight   90
      He steps completely from his shell,
And it's no longer Jupiter that meets our sight.
NIGHT: But, granted he may stoop from that exalted station
    Down to the level of mankind,
    Accept all joys that he in human hearts may find,
      Join in their trivial conversation,
If only through all this capricious transformation
He'd stick to human nature, then I wouldn't mind.
      But seeing Jupiter as beast,
      As serpent, bull, or swan, I balk;   100
      That's not attractive in the least,
And I am not surprised if people sometimes talk.
MERCURY: Let carpers carp, they'll do no harm.
      In shifting shapes there is a charm
      To which their minds can never rise.
In present case and others this god knows what he's doing;
And in their tender passions of instinctive wooing
The beasts are not so backward as some may surmise.
NIGHT: Let us return to her whose favor he enjoys.
If by his stratagem his love has reached its goal,   110
What can he want of me? What is there I can do?
MERCURY: He wants your horses slowed down to a walk by you

To satisfy the wishes of his amorous soul.
     So that a night of such delights
     May be the longest of all nights,
With pleasure granted ampler interim,
And with postponement of the coming dawn,
     Which sooner brings return of him
     Whose place he takes while he is gone.

NIGHT: Great Jupiter undoubtedly   120
     Has a most noble task in mind,
     And fine names to it are assigned,
     This service that he asks of me.

MERCURY: In one so young this passes
     For such old-fashioned ways!
     Such work is only base
     Among the lower classes.
Once Fortune has bestowed exalted rank and station,
One may do many things that no one blames;
     Depending on one's situation,   130
     Things have a way of changing names.

NIGHT: In matters of this kind
     You're far more versed than I;
     In doing what's assigned
     It's you that I'll be guided by.

MERCURY: Ah, Lady Night, I pray you, be
     A trifle less severe and grim;
     You have among society
     A name for being not so prim.
You're *confidante* across a hundred different climes   140
     To many things at many times;
And speaking frankly of the work that we each do,
There's little to choose from between us two.

NIGHT: Enough of this contrary chaffing,
     Let us observe our true selves' rule:
     Let's not give mankind cause for laughing
     By telling truths here out of school.

MERCURY: Farewell. My mission bids me wend my downward way
And promptly put aside the form of Mercury
     To don new shape and be   150
     Amphitryon's valet.

NIGHT: I in this hemisphere with all my darkling train
           Shall linger and remain.
MERCURY: Good day, Night.   ·
NIGHT: Farewell, Mercury.   154
     (Mercury alights from his cloud upon the earth
       and Night passes on in her chariot.)

Act I

*Before the entrance gate to Amphitryon's house in Thebes.
Pre-dawn darkness. Enter Sosia with a lantern.*

SOSIA: Who goes there? Eh? With every step my fear gains power.
    I'm everybody's friend, good Sirs!
    Ah! What audacity within me stirs
    To walk abroad at such an hour!
    My master may be decked with glory,
    But he's done me a scurvy turn.   160
If feeling for his fellow man were his concern,
Would he have sent me out on any night so black?
This message now, to say that he was coming back,
    These details of his victory-story,
Why couldn't they have waited for the break of day?
    O Sosia! To what slavery
    Your life is subject anyway!
    With lords our lot is certainly
    Worse than with those of common clay.
For their sakes every creature ought to find it pleasing 170
    To sacrifice itself and die;
By day and night, hail, wind, or danger, roasting, freezing,
    The minute *they* speak, one must fly.
     Long years of service bring
     No profit in the end:
     Err in the slightest thing,
     And all their wraths descend.
    And yet our minds, for all this durance,
Cling to the empty honor of remaining loyal,
And in the fatuous notion find their reassurance 180
Of everybody's thinking we enjoy our toil.
In vain our reason calls upon us to resign,
Sometimes our irritation vainly acquiesces:
     Just seeing them so fine
     Awes us and impresses;
One hint of favor is enough to repossess us,
     And back we go in line.
    But through the dark at last my glance

Makes out our house, and all my fears are set at naught.
        For such an embassy I ought   190
        To get some speech up in advance.
I owe Alcmena's eyes a show of martial art
Portraying mighty battle where our foes were routed;
        But how to go about it
        When I did not take part?
No matter! Let's just talk away *ex tempore*
        As with eye-witness proof:
How many people tell of battles from which they
        Held cautiously aloof?
        I'll need to get my part perfected   200
        If I'm to play it at my best.
Now, here's the room to which as courier I'm directed.
        This lantern is Alcmena now,
        To whom my speech must be addressed.
(He sets the lantern on the ground and makes a bow to it.)
"Madame: Amphitryon, my master and your spouse . . .
(A good beginning!) fully mindful of your charms,
        Has sent me back here to his house
To bring you word of his successes under arms
And say he will be here as soon as time allows."
        "Ah! My poor Sosia, what a pleasure!   210
      How I rejoice to see you back again."
        "Madame, you honor me past measure,
        And I'll be envied among men."
(Well answered!) *"But how is Amphitryon reported?"*
        "As one for bravery resolved
On those occasions where his glory is involved."
        (A fine phrase, that, and well retorted!)
    "When will he come and by his sweet return
        Bring me the solace I require?"
"As soon as possible, Madame, have no concern,   220
    But later far than his heart might desire."
(Ah!) *"But how has he been affected by the war?*
What does he say? And do? Assure me with some facts."
        "Madame, he speaks less than he acts,
        And gives foes things to tremble for."
(Damn! Where is my mind getting all this cleverness?)

"What are the rebels doing? Tell me of their fate."
"Madame, they had no choice but to capitulate:
      We cut their armies up and down,
      Killed Pterelas who wore the crown,   230
Took Telebes by assault, and now the seaside town
      Rings with our feats and our success."
"O admirable! Who would have thought that such could be?
Do tell me, Sosia, all about this great event."
"Gladly, Madame; and without self-complacency
      I can describe most knowledgeably
      Exactly how the victory went.
      Madame, imagine that Telebes
        Stands here, about this way:
   (He locates the places on his hand, or on the ground.)
      It is a city, I should say,   240
      Of roughly the same size as Thebes.
        There is a river here,
        With our men on this side,
        And that space to the rear
        Our foes had occupied.
        Now this way, on a height,
        They had their infantry;
        And further to the right
        They had their cavalry.
Now once we had unto the gods uplifted prayers,   250
All orders being issued, we raised the battle shout.
The enemy formed up their horsemen in three squares,
Expecting to drive us apart and into rout.
But we soon had their ardor checked amid its course,
      And you shall see precisely how.
There was our vanguard roused to stem that tide of horse;
    There stood our own King Creon's archers now;
      And here stood our main force,
         (A slight noise is heard.)
Which first . . . But wait . . . The army's main force is afraid.
      I thought I heard a noise right near.   260
       (Enter Mercury in Sosia's form.)
      (He comes from inside Amphitryon's house.)

MERCURY: Now in his baby-face arrayed,
      Let's chase this babbler out of here:
  His coming so inopportunely might displease
      Our lovers where they sport at ease.
SOSIA *(without noticing Mercury):*
      My heart resumes its beating . . . slightly.
      I guess there wasn't anything.
    But not to risk a misadventure lightly,
    Let's finish out this interview at home.
MERCURY *(aside):*
      Improve on Mercury, you gnome,
      Or I'll see you do no such thing.   270
SOSIA *(without noticing Mercury):*
  This night exceeds all others in its length, it seems,
  My traveling time leads me to think some oversight
  Misled my lord to take the dusk for dawning light,
  Or else blond Phoebus drowses over-long in dreams
      From drinking too much wine last night.
MERCURY *(aside):*
      With what irreverence
      This lout speaks of the gods!
      My arm can teach such clods
      The price of insolence,
  And I intend to lead him on a merry chase   280
  By borrowing his name the way I did his face.
SOSIA *(catching sight of Mercury):*
      Ah! I was right, I do believe;
    All's up with me, unluckiest of creatures!
      In front of our house I perceive
      A certain man whose glowering features
      Bode ill to me without reprieve.
      To give an air of reassurance,
      I'll sing a little melody.
      (He sings, and as Mercury speaks,
        his voice trails off.)
MERCURY: Who is this rascal who so taxes my endurance
    As to go singing and annoying me?   290
  Is he inviting me to give him a sound cuff?
SOSIA *(aside):* This man does not like music; that is plain enough.

MERCURY: A whole week's gone to wrack
     Since I have broken anybody limb from limb.
     For want of exercise my arm is going slack.
                    And I yearn for a back
                    To get myself in trim.
SOSIA *(aside):*   What demon-man is here?
     I feel my soul to mortal terror giving way.
                    Why must I tremble so with fear?   300
     He might be just as scared as I am, and he may,
                    Clown that he is, be talking here
     To hide his fright from me beneath a bold display.
     Let's not have people take me for a timid hare.
     I may not be too brave, but let's show a brave face.
                    Let's pluck our courage up and dare.
     We're each alone; I'm strong; my master's of high place,
                    And our house stands right there.
MERCURY: Who goes there?
SOSIA: Me.
MERCURY: Who's me?
SOSIA: Me. *(aside)* Don't
                                             [flinch from your
                                                  goal!

MERCURY: What is your lot?
SOSIA: To be a man, and stand here talking.
MERCURY: Valet or master?   [310
SOSIA: As I choose to play my role.
MERCURY: And where might you be bound?
SOSIA: Where I choose to be
                                             [walking.

MERCURY: Ah, this I do not like.
SOSIA: And it delights my soul.
MERCURY: I want to know from you, you traitor's spawn,
                    Just what you do, of whose accord,
          What place you come from thus before the dawn,
                    Where you are going, what's your station.
SOSIA: I do both good and evil on occasion.
     I came from there; I'm going there! I serve my lord.
MERCURY: I see you're quite determined, by this show of wit   320
     To put on airs and flaunt a self-important mind.

To strike up our acquaintance I feel much inclined
  To lift my hand and slap you now with it.
SOSIA: Who? Me?
MERCURY: Yes, you. And now you know you have been hit.
      (He gives him a slap.)
SOSIA: Ouch! That one was for real!
MERCURY: No, I was only playing.
    Just giving you your own quips back.
SOSIA: By golly, friend! I don't mind saying
    It's quite a wallop that you pack.
MERCURY: That's one of my most gentle taps,
    My ordinary, weekday slaps.   330
SOSIA: If I moved in as fast as you,
    What splendid business we could do!
MERCURY: There's no cause certainly
     For discontinuation:
     The best is yet to be;
     Resume the conversation.
SOSIA: I quit. *(He starts to leave.)*
MERCURY *(stopping Sosia):*
     Where are you going now?
SOSIA: What's that to you?
MERCURY: What are you going to do?
SOSIA: I'm going in this gate.
    Why block my way? It's late.   340
MERCURY: Come near it, if you carry insolence so far,
  And on you, storms of blows will rain and hail and pour.
SOSIA: You threaten to debar
    Me from our very door?
MERCURY: What's this? Our door?
SOSIA: Yes.
MERCURY: O, what perfidy!
    You live here in this house, you claim?
SOSIA: Of course. Amphitryon's the master, isn't he?
MERCURY: He is. But why bring up his name?
SOSIA: I'm his valet.
MERCURY: You?
SOSIA: Me.
MERCURY: You're his valet?

SOSIA: That's me.
MERCURY: Amphitryon's valet?
SOSIA: Amphitryon's valet.   350
MERCURY: You name is . . . ?
SOSIA: Sosia.
MERCURY: . What!
SOSIA: Well, what else should it be?
MERCURY: You know, I have a mind to murder you today.
SOSIA: But why? What rouses you to such ferocity?
MERCURY: Just tell me where you get this fine temerity
          To take on Sosia's name this way.
SOSIA: I didn't take it; that's my name since infancy.
MERCURY: A monstrous lie! The ultimate of impudence!
     You dare assert to me that Sosia is your name?
SOSIA: Of course I do, and with good reason make the claim,
     Because the gods so willed in their omnipotence: 360
     It lies beyond my power to deny the same
          And not against myself commit offense.
                    (Mercury beats him.)
MERCURY: A thousand blows with a good cudgel lie in store
          For such unmatched effrontery.
SOSIA: Help, citizens! Help! Justice, justice, I implore.
MERCURY: What's this, you brute, you raise a shout?
SOSIA: A thousand blows to murder me,
          And you expect I won't cry out?
MERCURY: Then feel my arm . . .
SOSIA: This will not get you anywhere.
          You are the winner from the start   370
     By virtue of the lack of courage on my part,
          And your advantage is unfair.
          . It's bullying, that's what it is,
     To try and profit from the outright cowardice
          Of someone whom we are attacking.
     In beating up sure losers you besmirch your fame,
          And bravery is much to blame
          When used on those in whom it's lacking.
MERCURY: Well, are you Sosia now? Well, answer with your
                                                  [bleating!
SOSIA: Your blows have not produced a metamorphosis;   380

The only change in me so far's I notice is
  That I'm still Sosia plus a beating.
MERCURY *(threatening Sosia):*
 What? Still? A hundred more blows for this impudence.
SOSIA: O please declare a truce to blows.
MERCURY: A truce, then, to your insolence.
SOSIA: As you decide. I'll keep to silence. Goodness knows
 The battle is unequal in these arguments.
MERCURY: But tell me, are you Sosia still?
SOSIA: Alas, I'm anyone you will.
 Consign me, as you wish, to safety or disaster; 390
   Your arm makes you the master.
MERCURY: Your name was Sosia, you kept saying, all along?
SOSIA: It's true that up till now I thought that point was clear;
   But now your stick, that's master here,
   Has made me see that I was wrong.
MERCURY: It's I who am called Sosia, and all Thebes attests it,
 No other one has ever served Amphitryon.
SOSIA: You're Sosia?
MERCURY: Yes, I'm Sosia. If anyone contests it,
   He may well rue what he has done.
SOSIA *(aside):* Great gods! Must I renounce my own identity 400
 And watch a bold usurper steal my very name?
   How lucky for his game
   That I'm so cowardly!
 Except for that, I'd kill . . .
MERCURY: You're mumbling, I believe,
   And muttering something, aren't you?
SOSIA: No; but, by all the gods, I do implore your leave
   To ask about a point or two.
MERCURY: Speak.
SOSIA: But do promise me, I plead,
   I won't get beaten now.
   Let's sign a truce.
MERCURY: Agreed; 410
   This point I will allow.
SOSIA: Just tell me what has led you to this fantasy?
 Where will it get you to have made off with my name?
 And, spirit though you be, can you enforce your claim

Though I'm no longer Sosia and no longer me?
MERCURY *(raising his stick over Sosia):*
                What! You presume . . .
SOSIA: No blows!
                We called a truce to those!
MERCURY: You rascal, you impostor . . .
SOSIA: Let your insults fall
                As thickly as you choose:
                They cause but little bruise,   420
                And I don't mind at all.
MERCURY: You say you're Sosia?
SOSIA: Yes; some story quite absurd . . .
MERCURY: Stop, or I'll break our truce and cancel my pledged
                                [word.

SOSIA: No matter, I can't snuff out my identity
  And stand for talk so utterly implausible.
  For you to be who I am, is that possible?
        And can I leave off being me?
  Who ever heard of such a thing, for goodness' sake?
  And can a hundred cogent proofs be set at naught?
        Am I asleep? In bad dreams caught?   430
  Am I prone to have fits of any crazy kind?
        Am I not certainly awake?
        And am I not in my right mind?
  And did my noble lord Amphitryon not please
  To send me to his wife Alcmena at this place?
  Am I not duty-bound, while speaking his love's praise,
  To chronicle his feats against our enemies?
  Have I not just arrived up here straight from the port?
        Do I not hold a lantern in my hand?
  And don't I find you here right in our entrance court?   440
  Don't I talk human speech so you may understand?
  Are you not stronger for the courage that I lack
        By keeping me from our own door?
  Have you not vented all your fury on my back?
        Have you not beat me till I'm sore?
        Ah! All of this is only far too true;
        Would Heaven it were not, indeed!
  So stop abusing one poor man the way you do,

And let me now discharge my duties with all speed.
MERCURY: Stop! or my righteous anger on your back will wreak
   A storm that will make you dissolve and decompose   [450
        For, every single word you speak
        Applies to me, except the blows.
SOSIA: How I this morning left the ship, this lantern knows:[1] 453a
   With terror in my soul. And surely it was I   453b
   Amphitryon then as his message-bearer chose   453c
   To send here to his wife Alcmena?
MERCURY: There you lie!   } 453d
   It's I Amphitryon back to Alcmena sent,
   Who from the Persic port have just come hurriedly.
   It's I who now report the glorious event
   Whereby his arm achieved the total victory
   And down into the dust our foemen's leader bent.
   And Sosia is my name, with utter certitude,
        The son of Davos, skilled in shepherd arts,   460
   The brother of young Harpax, deceased in foreign parts,
        The spouse of Cleanthis the prude
        Whose whims will make me lose my mind.
   In Thebes I have received hard blows of every kind
        Of which I never breathed a mention,
   And once, in public, I was branded here behind
        For being too good of intention.
SOSIA (softly, aside):
        He's right. He's Sosia. Who else could invent
        All these things he is saying, and which fit?
   My soul is overwhelmed with sheer astonishment.   470
   I find myself beginning to believe in it.
   In fact, now that I look him over, I observe
   In form and face and gesture he is just like me.
        Let's ask some question that may serve
        To shed light on this mystery.
(aloud)
   Of all the booty taken from the enemy,
   What did Amphitryon select for his own part?

---

[1] Lines numbered 453a–d appeared in the editions of 1682 and 1734, but not in the first edition of March 1668. They may be a substitute for Sosia's long speech just preceding.

MERCURY: A brooch with five huge diamonds mounted splendidly
    Worn by their chieftain, and a rarest work of art.
SOSIA: To whom does he intend to give so rich a present?   480
MERCURY: He means it for his wife; it well befits her charms.
SOSIA: But for safe carrying, where is this brooch at present?
MERCURY: Inside a casket, sealed up with my master's arms.
SOSIA *(softly, aside):*
    There's not a word of any statement where he's lying
    And now I really do begin to doubt I'm me.
    Right here, by force, he's Sosia; that, there's no denying;
    And he may well be so in actuality.
    Yet when I touch myself, and when I think about it,
            It seems that I am really me.
    Where can I find some light of certitude undoubted   490
            To clear up all these things I see?
    The things I did when there was no one standing by,
    Now short of being me, no one could know about.
    I'll question him on those and startle him, no doubt.
    It's something to confound him with, and worth a try.
    (aloud)
    While battle raged, what were you doing in our tent
            Where you were keeping out of sight?
MERCURY: There was a ham . . .
SOSIA *(softly, aside):*   He knows! . . . that I had
MERCURY: [brought to light;
  I cut myself two slices that were succulent
            And munched on them with great delight.   500
    There was some wine—the kind they hide; I had a cup:
    Delighting to the taste, and to the eyes delighting.
            It got my courage up
            For our men who were fighting.
SOSIA *(softly, aside):*
            Here's proof without a peer
            For his side; and I ask:
            What can be added here,
            Unless he hid inside the flask?
    (aloud)
    I simply can't deny, with all the proofs you summon,

That you are Sosia; I am ready to agree.   510
But if you are, then who am I supposed to be?
For, after all, I really can't help being someone.
MERCURY: When I am through with being he,
          You may be Sosia: well and granted.
But while I am still he, I'll see you dead and planted
          If you attempt that fantasy.
SOSIA: I find this whole dilemma baffling, all the same,
          And reason is itself in odd estrangement.
But we must settle, after all, on some arrangement;
The easiest way for me would be to play your game.   520
MERCURY: So, gallows-bird, you've come to like the *bastinado*?
SOSIA *(beaten by Mercury):*
What's this? Great gods! His theme is louder and *marcato*.
My back will need a month to live this beating down.
Let's leave this demon-man and go back into town.
O what a herald I have been, ye gods above!
MERCURY *(alone):* At last I've sent him packing! My severity
Well suited many actions he was guilty of.
But I see Jupiter escorting gallantly
          Alcmena in her radiant love.
     Enter Jupiter (in the form of Amphitryon), Alcmena,
                    and Cleanthis.
JUPITER: Forbid the torches, dear Alcmena, to come out.   530
They offer me the pleasure of beholding you,
But at the same time they betray my visit too,
          Which no one had best know about.
My love, entrammeled in the duties which my station
Imposed upon me by the glory of our arms,
Has stolen moments from my heavy obligation
          And here bestowed them on your charms.
This theft, which to your beauty I have dedicated,
Might find that general opinion would abhor it;
          I want no witness implicated   540
          Save one who might be grateful for it.
ALCMENA: The glory of your exploits casts its light on me,
And in your fame, Amphitryon, I have my part;
          The brilliance of your victory

Affects the tenderest recesses of my heart;
    But when I see that fateful honor stealing
        The one I love away from me,
I cannot help, in my extreme of tender feeling,
        But hold it in hostility
And set my wishes up against the cruel dealing   550
    That makes you bear the Theban captaincy.
How sweet it is, when he has been victorious,
To see one whom one loves exalted in renown;
And yet things fraught with peril mingle with the glorious,
And soon enough some grievous blow has struck us down.
How many are the terrors that afflict the soul
    At hearing news about the slightest fray!
Amid the horrors of such thoughts, what can allay,
        Or what can possibly console
        The dread that stands within harm's way?   560
No matter what the wreath upon a victor's head,
Or in supremest honor have whatever part,
Is it worth what it costs in sufferings of the heart
That must, for a beloved's sake, still live in dread?
JUPITER: There is no thing about you but enraptures me.
    Each signifies to me a heart on fire with love;
    And it is, I confess, enchanting utterly
    To find such in the one I am enamoured of.
    And yet one scruple does torment me, I admit,
    Amid the tender feeling that you manifest;   570
    And to enjoy that, dear Alcmena, at its best,
    I wish no sense of duty entered into it.
    The favors I receive from you, O let me owe them
    To nothing but your ardor and what my love gives,
    And let it not be conjugal prerogatives
        Alone that cause you to bestow them.
ALCMENA: Yet those prerogatives alone confer permission
        To yield myself to my desire;
    I do not understand this sudden inhibition
        That checks the ardor of your fire.   580
JUPITER: Toward you I have a passion and a tenderness
        Transcending what a husband feels,
    And at so sweet a moment you can never guess
        The delicacy that it conceals.

Ah! You can not imagine how a heart's distress
Will scrutinize a hundred trifles, each in turn,
     Or how it feels a deep concern
     About the form of happiness.
     In me, Alcmena fair, today
A husband and a lover both in one you see;   590
But frankly, nothing but the lover interests me,
And here the lover finds the husband in his way,
The lover is extremely jealous of your vows,
Your heart's surrender to himself alone he wants,
     And in his passion disallows
     Anything the husband grants.
He craves to have your ardor drawn from purest fonts,
Wants nothing held by matrimonial constraint;
He will not countenance a tiresome obligation
Wherefrom our hearts are kept in constant perturbation   600
     And sweetest favors take a taint.
To satisfy his delicacy, his wish contends
That on this point, which now has brought him to despair,
You should remove him from a thing that so offends,
That you confine your virtue to the husband's share,
And that your heart, in all the goodness it possesses,
Should give the lover its full fund of tendernesses.
ALCMENA: Amphitryon, I must protest
     You mock yourself by speaking thus in jest,
     And people might, I fear, think you absurd   610
     If they were standing by and overheard.
JUPITER: The things I say contain more reason,
     Alcmena, than you think they do.
But staying longer now might be construed as treason,
And for my getting back the moments are too few.
Farewell: my duty calls for such barbarities
     As wrenching me away from you;
But, fair Alcmena, when you see your husband, please
     Be mindful of the lover too.
ALCMENA: I shall not put asunder what the gods unite;   620
Husband and lover both are precious in my sight.
CLEANTHIS (aside):
     O gods above! what fond caresses
     A consort dearly loved bestows!

      While my wretch of a husband knows
      Nothing of such tendernesses!

MERCURY *(aside):*
      The Lady Night I'll now apprise
      She need but fold these veils and vanish;
      These stars the mounting Sun will banish,
   If he will kindly now but leave his couch and rise.
      (Cleanthis and Mercury are left alone.)
      (Mercury starts to leave.)

CLEANTHIS: What? Would you leave me thus forlorn?   630

MERCURY: Why not? You wouldn't want me shirking
      The duty to which I am sworn?
   I must go with Amphitryon, for whom I'm working.

CLEANTHIS: But leaving so abruptly now!

MERCURY: You traitor! I'll remember this!
      O what a time to start a row!
   There's so much time to be together, as it is.

CLEANTHIS: But to leave me this way with such brutality,
   Without a single kindly word to say to me!

MERCURY: Now where the devil would I scare up   640
      Sweet nothings I could talk about?
   With fifteen years of marriage words are all used up,
   And everything we had to say has been talked out.

CLEANTHIS: Look, traitor, at Amphitryon;
   See how Alcmena is the passion of his life;
   Then blush to think how little ardor you waste on
      The woman whom you call your wife.

MERCURY: Good lord, Cleanthis! They're still lovers in their prime
      All things pass at a certain age;
   And what for them is seemly as they start their climb   650
   Would ill fit us old married people at our stage.
   How silly we would be to stand here and commence
      To fetch forth gallant eloquence!

CLEATHIS: What? Monster, am I past all love-experience
      And past the age of sighing after?

MERCURY: You're not, as I don't mind admitting.
   But sighs from me at my age would be so unfitting
      As to cause sides to split with laughter.

CLEANTHIS: Do you deserve, you rogue, good fortune's highest
                            [favor:

A wife whose honor never yet was known to waver?   660
MERCURY: Great god! You're proper to excess:
          And all this honor is a waste.
          I wish you'd be less prim and chaste
          And try my nerves a little less.
CLEANTHIS: What's this? Because I am too upright, you find fault?
MERCURY: A woman's gentleness is what holds charms for me.
          And you make virtue both assault
          And never-ending battery.
CLEANTHIS: What you need is the hearts full of false tendernesses
     Possessed by women of such fine and noble talents   670
     That they can overwhelm their husbands with caresses
     And make them swallow their indulgences with gallants.
MERCURY: Just let me tell you, if you please,
     A rumored evil touches none but stupid fools;
          And I would make the first of rules:
          "Less honor and a lot more peace."
CLEANTHIS: What? Do you mean to say you wouldn't turn a hair
     If I should carry on an open love affair?
MERCURY: Yes, if from scenes and tantrums it entailed remission,
     And if it changed your methods and your disposition.   680
          I much prefer convenient vice
          To virtue that is over-nice.
          Farewell, my darling Cleanthis,
          Amphitryon has need of me.
                    (He leaves.)
CLEANTHIS *(alone):* Why is my courage so remiss
     In punishing this wretch for all his infamy?
          Oh! It is maddening to be
          An honest woman at times like this!   688

Act II

Amphitryon, Sosia.

AMPHITRYON:

   Come here, you rogue, come here. You realize, you cheat, you,

   That what you tell me warrants thrashing you today,   690

   And that for me to deal with you the proper way

         I only lack a stick to beat you.

SOSIA: Sir, if you take things in that key,

         There's nothing left for me to say.

         And you'll be right, undoubtedly.

AMPHITRYON: Do you think you'll pass off as actuality

   Tales I can see are wildest flights of fantasy?

SOSIA: No, you're the master, Sir, and I a mere valet;

   And nothing shall be other than as you now say.

AMPHITRYON: Ah! I must bring my furious rage within control,

   The entire story of your mission must be heard.   [700

         Before I meet my wife, my goal

   Must be to clear up just exactly what occurred.

   So gather all your wits, reflect within your soul,

   And answer each and every question, word for word.

SOSIA: But so as to avoid offense,

         Tell me beforehand, if you please,

   Precisely how you wish to have me treat this matter.

   Am I to speak, Sir, by my conscience's decrees,

   Or in the manner used with men of consequence?   710

         Must truth be told at all events,

         Or should I be discreet and flatter?

AMPHITRYON: No, I impose no obligation

   Except to state what happened clearly and precisely.

SOSIA: Good, I'll oblige you very nicely;

         Proceed with your interrogation.

AMPHITRYON:

   About that order issued and which you demur to. . . .

SOSIA: I set out while the skies were veiled in deepest black,

   And, for the nuisance, cursing you behind your back,

   With twenty curses on the order you refer to.   720

AMPHITRYON: What, rascal?

SOSIA: Sir, you need but speak, if you
                                                    [prefer to,
          And I'll switch to a lying tack.

AMPHITRYON: Ah! This is how a servant shows us his devotion.
     But never mind. What happened as you went your ways?

SOSIA: Sheer terror had me in commotion
          At everything that met my gaze.

AMPHITRYON: Poltroon!

SOSIA: When Nature formed us, she
                                          [indulged caprices;
          To different tendencies she has us each incline:
          In danger some men find that their delight increases,
                While staying alive increases mine.   730

AMPHITRYON: Arriving then before the house . . . ?

SOSIA: Outside the
                                                    [gate,
          I thought I'd just rehearse delivery of my story
                And try out how I would relate
          The winning of the battle in its total glory.

AMPHITRYON: And then?

SOSIA: Someone appeared and started
                                          [bothering me.

AMPHITRYON: Who?

SOSIA: Me, a Sosia who obeys you jealously,
          Whom you sent to Alcmena from the port, that's who,
          A second me who knows our secrets to a T,
                Just like the me that's telling you.

AMPHITRYON: What nonsense!

SOSIA: No, Sir, it is absolutely true.   740
          This me had gotten to our house ahead of me;
                And there I was, I swear to you,
                Before I possibly could be.

AMPHITRYON: This cursed stuff that you are saying,
                What reason for it can there be?
                Is this a dream? Have wits gone straying?
                Or is it wine? Or lunacy?
                Or some bad joke someone is playing?

SOSIA: No, this is really what occurred,
          These are no idle fantasies.   750
  I am a man of honor, and I pledge my word,
          And you'll believe me, if you please,—
  Supposing no one else was Sosia but me,
          There I get home and find I'm two;
  And of the two me's there, both piqued with jealousy,
  One is inside the house, the other is with you.
  The me now standing here, with all his travel stains,
  There found the other me of fresh and dapper kind,
          With nothing further on his mind
          Than battering backs and beating brains.   760
AMPHITRYON: I must be tolerant enough,
  My temper must be gentle, moderate, and sage,
  To stand for servants' rambling with such silly stuff.
SOSIA: Sir, if you fly up in a rage,
          We'll have no interview at all:
          I stop at once, as you recall.
AMPHITRYON: No, I will hear you. After all, I said I would,
  And hold my temper too. But tell me seriously:
  In this fresh mystery you come reeling off to me,
          Is there a shade of likelihood?   770
SOSIA: No, you're quite right. The thing appears ridiculous,
          Past anything belief would claim,
          A thing that no one comprehends,
  A wild, fantastic tale, absurd, preposterous,
          And shocking to our common sense:
          And yet it happened, all the same.
AMPHITRYON: Could anyone believe it, short of going mad?
SOSIA: *I* didn't quite believe it, till the pain got bad.
  My pride was hurt at finding two of me abroad,
  And for a time I called the other one a fraud.   780
  But finally he forced me to acknowledge him;
  I saw that he was me, with no deceptive whim.
  From head to toe he was identical with me,
  With charming manners, handsome bearing, noble pride;
          Two drops of water side by side
          Would not match so identically.
  If he just swung his fists with less ferocity,
          I would be wholly satisfied.

AMPHITRYON: What patience I must have while I expostulate!
But finally you did succeed in getting past? 790
SOSIA: Get past? Would you have me tempt fate?
Was I to go on flouting reason to the last?
And didn't I forbid myself to pass the gate?
AMPHITRYON: How so?
SOSIA: A stick beat fierce and fast:
My back still bears the bruises of its painful weight.
AMPHITRYON: A stick?
SOSIA: Yes,
AMPHITRYON: Whose stick?
SOSIA: Mine.
AMPHITRYON: You beat yourself?
[What for?
SOSIA: Yes, mine; but not the me you see.
It was the me at home, who has the strength of four.
AMPHITRYON: May all the gods confound you in your idiocy!
SOSIA: These are no trivialities. 800
The me I met has qualities
The present me must say are vastly advantageous;
His arm is strong, his spirit high,
Of that I have firm guarantees;
That demon-me so thrashed me that my head's awry,
His mad-cap temper is outrageous.
AMPHITRYON: But did you see my wife, I ask you?
SOSIA: No.
AMPHITRYON: Why not?
SOSIA: There was a very cogent reason.
AMPHITRYON: And who prevented you? Explain yourself, you sot.
SOSIA: I've told you that; must it be twenty times repeated? 810
The me with whom I ignominiously competed,
The me who seized possession of our gate by treason,
Who made me play the humble act,
Who claims to be the only me,
Who bears the real me jealousy,
The valiant me who there attacked
And raged against the coward me,
The me who's at our house, in fact,
Who showed himself so masterfully
The master as he whacked and thwacked. 820

AMPHITRYON:
　He must have had too much to drink and lost his head,
　　And now he's talking through his hat.
SOSIA: If I drank anything but water, strike me dead,
　　And you may have my oath on that.
AMPHITRYON:
　Then sleep misled your senses into strange confusions,
　Or else a troubled dream, amid its mysteries,
　　　Has made you see all these delusions,
　　　Which you now call true histories.
SOSIA: No, not that either. Not one moment did I drowse,
　　Nor do I now feel so inclined.　　　　　　　　　　　830
　　　I'm wide awake right now, I find;
　And I was wide awake this morning at our house.
　So was the other Sosia when he beat me blind,
　　Awake and of a murderous mind.
AMPHITRYON:　　Be silent now and follow me;
　　　My brain is tired out and balks.
　I must be mad to have stood here so patiently
　And listen to the nonsense that a servant talks.
SOSIA (aside):　　No speech is credited with sense
　　　If some obscure man authors it:　　　　　　　　840
　　　These would be words of choicest wit
　　　If said by one of consequence.
AMPHITRYON:　　Let us go in, and no more tarry.
　But here Alcmena comes in all her loveliness.
　My presence here she surely won't so much as guess.
　　　I'll speak to her while she's unwary.
　　　　　(Enter Alcmena and Cleanthis.)
ALCMENA (without seeing Amphitryon):
　Let us, Cleanthis, go and to the gods address
　　　Our prayers and worship for my spouse,
　And render thanks for all the glorious success
　Which by his hand redounds on Thebes and on our house.　850
　　　　　(catching sight of Amphitryon)
　O gods!
AMPHITRYON:　　Please heaven now, as victor in the strife,
　　　I may be met with pleasure by my wife,
　　　And that this day auspicious for my passion

Return you to my sight in just as loving fashion:
     Let me find ardor equalling
     The love that I in my soul bring!
ALCMENA: What! Back so soon?
AMPHITRYON: Why, yes! I have returned, of
                                       [course!
I must say your devotion bears me sorry witness,
     And this "What! Back so soon?" of yours
I find on this occasion hardly of a fitness   860
     For one whose heart in love endures.
     I had imagined with concern
    That I had stayed perhaps too long away.
The expectation of a much desired return
Lends monstrous length to every moment of delay,
     And absences, brief though they be,
Of loved ones seem to last for an eternity.
ALCMENA: But I don't . . .
AMPHITRYON: No Alcmena, one's impatience is,
At times like this, the measurer of time's amount;
     And you count moments of my absences   870
     As those who know not love might count.
     When someone loves with all his being
     All absences are murderous,
     And one we're truly fond of seeing
     Can not come back too soon for us.
     Your recent greeting, I confess,
Leaves me with strong cause for complaining of;
     And I expected from your love
Quite different shows of joy and tenderness.
ALCMENA: I can't imagine what might be   880
The basis for the allegations offered by you;
     And if you have complaints of me,
     I do not know, quite honestly,
     What it would take to satisfy you;
Last night, upon your glad return, as I recall,
An amply tender joy was witnessed on my part,
     And to your love's need I gave all
The ministrations you could look for from my heart.
AMPHITRYON: What's that?

ALCMENA: Did I not then display before your
                                                   [gaze
The quick emotions of a total eagerness?   890
Can heart's delight express itself in better ways
To a returning husband loved with tenderness?
AMPHITRYON: What are you saying?
ALCMENA: What is more, you did display,
At seeing me, a joy and rapture past believing;
And since you left me only at the break of day,
      Then why should my surprise cause you dismay
          At your return just after leaving?
AMPHITRYON: Can it be my return, in its precipitancy,
    Inspired a dream last night, Alcmena, in your heart,
      Foreshowing actuality?   900
And that, perhaps while sleeping, you so treated me
         That now you feel you've done your part
         For my love's sake substantially?
ALCMENA: Or might some vapor with a fine malignancy,
         Have blurred the actuality
Of your return last night, my husband, in your heart?
And from my loving welcome granted loyally
         You now deny me any part
         Of my love's gracious courtesy?
AMPHITRYON: This vapor you propose would be, at best,   910
      It seems to me, a trifle strange.
ALCMENA: It will serve as a fair exchange
      For such a dream as you suggest.
AMPHITRYON: Unless it was a dream, no one can find
   A plausible excuse for what your lips report.
ALCMENA: Unless it was a vapor which upset your mind,
   No one can credit stories to which you resort.
AMPHITRYON: Alcmena, shall we let this vapor rest?
ALCMENA: Then let's dismiss this dream, Amphitryon.
AMPHITRYON: In matters such as this, it's a rare jest   920
   That is not carried to extremes and overdone.
ALCMENA: Quite so. To prove it, I, for one,
   Begin to feel annoyance rising in my breast.
AMPHITRYON: Is this the way you fancy you will make amends
   For the reception I complained about before?

ALCMENA: Is it by such tricks you set store
                   To have some fun at my expense?
AMPHITRYON: Let's end this frivolousness, Alcmena, if you please,
                   And let us talk more seriously.
ALCMENA: Amphitryon, enough of whimsicality;   930
                   This bantering should really cease.
AMPHITRYON: You go so far as tell me to my face
          That I was here before this present moment now?
ALCMENA: And would you be so bold as disavow
          That yesterday, toward evening, you came to this place?
AMPHITRYON: That I came here?
ALCMENA: Most certainly; and furthermore
                   You left again before the dawn.
AMPHITRYON (aside):
          Who ever heard an argument like this before?
          And who would not be baffled at conclusions drawn?
          Well, Sosia?
SOSIA: Why, she needs six grains of hellebore;   940
                   It's clear, my lord, her wits are gone.
AMPHITRYON: Alcmena, by the gods on high!
                   This talk is odd and most dismaying.
                   Collect your wits that are awry,
                   And do consider what you're saying.
ALCMENA: I have been thinking all this through,
          Your coming was observed by all beneath this roof.
          Your reasons I don't know for acting as you do,
          But if this matter stood in any need of proof:—
          Suppose this failure to remember were the case;   950
          How then could I have heard the news, except from you,
                   Of your last battle that took place?
          And what about King Pterelas' five diamonds too,
                   The king who fell before your might
                   Down into everlasting night?
          Could anyone want proof more certain or more fair?
AMPHITRYON: What? I've already given you
          The diamond brooch that fell to my allotted share,
                   And which I took with you in view?
ALCMENA: Of course. It isn't hard to make that plain   960
          By final evidence.

AMPHITRYON: How so?

ALCMENA: Why, here it is.

AMPHITRYON: Sosia!

SOSIA *(drawing a jewel box from his pocket):*
                     She's joking, Sir; I have it here in this.
           Her claiming otherwise is vain.

AMPHITRYON *(looking at the jewel box):*
     The seal is still unbroken?

ALCMENA *(presenting the diamond brooch to Amphitryon):*
                               Is this a delusion?
     Well, then, you find this proof has cogency enough?

AMPHITRYON: O heaven! Righteous heaven!

ALCMENA: Amphitryon, you see,
           You are absurd with all this silly stuff,
     And you should feel ashamed and thrown into confusion.

AMPHITRYON: Quick! Break that seal!

SOSIA *(opening the jewel box):*
                          My word! There's nothing
                                          [here inside.

     There was some magic used to get it out of there;   970
     Or else it flew here by itself, without a guide,
     With previous knowledge that she wanted it to wear.

AMPHITRYON *(aside):*
     Ye gods whose powers over mortal things preside,
       What strange adventures! And the omens that they bear
           All woe unto my love betide!

SOSIA *(to Amphitryon):*
     If what she says is true, we share a single fate;
     And just like me, you find that you, Sir, have been doubled.

AMPHITRYON: Shut up.

ALCMENA: What makes you look so desperate,
           And why are you so deeply troubled?

AMPHITRYON *(aside):* O heaven! What a strange dissension!   980
     I glimpse events that fall outside of nature's sphere;
           My honor dreads some misadventure here
                That goes beyond my comprehension.

ALCMENA: With this proof positive, are you still meditating
     Denial of the facts? Do you need more persuasion?

AMPHITRYON: No; but, if possible, would you now mind relating
           Just what occurred on that occasion?

ALCMENA: By asking me for an account of what took place,
    You still imply that you were not the one who came.
AMPHITRYON: Forgive me; I have reasons in this case   990
    For asking you to tell about it just the same.
ALCMENA: Are you beset with worries of such seriousness
    That recollection has so soon deserted you?
AMPHITRYON:
    Perhaps; but it would please me greatly nonetheless
        To hear you tell it all anew.
ALCMENA: The story is no very lengthy one to tell.
        I met you with surprise and pleasure,
        I kissed you tenderly as well,
    And gave my joy expression in the fullest measure.
AMPHITRYON (to himself):
    To think I missed a greeting I'd have liked so well!   1000
ALCMENA: You first gave me this gift of prime significance,
    Which you had destined for me from the booty seized.
        Your heart, with vehemence,
    Revealed its fires to me in all their violence,
    The tiresome burden of its heavy obligation,
    Its pangs of absence, which at sight of me were eased,
        Its fretful waiting and anticipation
            Until the time came for returning.
    And never did your love, in such a situation,
    Seem more affectionate, more passionately burning.   1010
AMPHITRYON (to himself):
    Could anyone devise a worse assassination?
ALCMENA: And all that rapture, all that tenderness,
    Believe me, did not find disfavor in my sight;
        And if you want me to confess,
    My heart, Amphitryon, found them a sheer delight.
AMPHITRYON: Continue, please.
ALCMENA: We spoke whatever came to mind,
    Kept interrupting, telling other news instead.
    Then food was served. Together tête-à-tête we dined;
    And once the meal was over, we went off to bed.
AMPHITRYON: Together?
ALCMENA: Why, of course. Your question is
                    [absurd.   1020

AMPHITRYON (aside):
    Ah! There's the cruelest blow in all that I have heard,
    The one my jealousy most feared to find was true.
ALCMENA: What makes you flush so red at mention of that word?
    Did I do something wrong in going to bed with you?
AMPHITRYON: No, I was not the one, to my immense chagrin,
    And anyone who says that I came here last night
                Is telling lies; in fact, the height
                Of all lies that have ever been.
ALCMENA: Amphitryon!
AMPHITRYON: You traitress!
ALCMENA: What a state you're in!
AMPHITRYON: Why bother to be gentle now, and why assuage   1030
    Such a reverse as this undoes my self-control;
    And at this moment nothing breathes within my soul
                Except revenge and frantic rage.
ALCMENA: Revenge on whom, I ask? And what makes you deny
            All faith in me and say I am to blame?
AMPHITRYON: That, I don't know; it surely wasn't I;
    I might do anything in my despair and shame.
ALCMENA: The facts speak for themselves; this is a monstrous lie,
                Husband unworthy of the name!
                You go too far when you accuse me   1040
    Of infidelity without fair testimony.
    If this is all by pretext that you so abuse me,
    A pretext to dissolve the bonds of matrimony
                Which tie me to you as if caught,
                Then subterfuge is all for naught,
                And I stand ready, come what may,
    To see these marriage bonds dissolved this very day.
AMPHITRYON: Considering the monstrous insult done to me,
    That's probably the step for which you should prepare.
    It is the least that I could do, and it may be   1050
                The matter won't end even there.
    I see dishonor certain, misfortune without fail,
    And love will try in vain now to becloud the matter.
    But I am still in doubt about the strict detail.
    And my just wrath intends to clarify this latter.
    Your brother can with full assurance verify

That till this morning I was with him constantly.
I'll go and fetch him now, and he will give the lie
To this untrue return that you impute to me.
Then to this mystery's center we shall force a path;   1060
    Strange as it is, it won't evade me.
And in the agitation of a righteous wrath
    Woe unto him who has betrayed me!

SOSIA: Sir . . .

AMPHITRYON: You are not to follow me.
    Just wait right here and be at call.
        (Exit.)

CLEANTHIS *(to Alcmena):*   Shall I . . . ?

ALCMENA: Leave me to privacy.
I cannot listen now to anything at all.
        (Exit.)

CLEANTHIS *(aside):*
His brain must be upset by one thing or another;
    But soon, as like as not,
    They'll make peace through her brother.   1070

SOSIA *(aside):* This was a pretty nasty blow my master got,
    And he is in an awful dither.
I also fear there's something brewing for my lot,
And I must try to reach an understanding with her.

CLEANTHIS *(aside):*
Let's see if he will come and so much as address me!
But I'll be careful not to let my interest show.

SOSIA *(aside):*
Sometimes the worst thing is to find out and to know,
    And questions to her now distress me.
But wouldn't it be better not to risk the chance
    And not know trouble in advance?   1080
    But, what the deuce, I have to see,
    I couldn't keep myself from trying,
    It's human nature, satisfying
    The pique of curiosity
    In things that better were left lying.
God keep you now, Cleanthis!

CLEANTHIS: So you've got around,
    You traitor, to approach us here!

SOSIA: My goodness! What's the matter? Always angry found,
       You take offense at nothing, dear.
CLEANTHIS: What do you mean by nothing?
SOSIA: Nothing, I suppose,
   Means nothing, whether one is speaking verse or prose.   [1090
        And nothing, as you know quite well,
        Means nothing, or not much to tell.
CLEANTHIS: I don't know what is keeping me,
       You wretch, from scratching out your eyes
 And showing you just what a woman's rage can be.
SOSIA: Oh my! What is it now that makes your temper rise?
CLEANTHIS: That little scene you played a while ago was meant,
       Perhaps, as nothing, should I say?
SOSIA: What scene?
CLEANTHIS: So you play innocent?   1100
       You follow out your master's bent,
  Pretending that you never came back here today?
SOSIA: No; claims of that sort I'll make none.
       But I'm not trying to be smart.
    We drank some curious wine before our start,
  So I've forgotten just what all I may have done.
CLEANTHIS: You think that such excuses still will get . . . ?
SOSIA: No, honestly. But you can bet
  In my condition I may well have played some prank
       Or done things I would now regret,   1110
       But now my mind's a total blank.
CLEANTHIS: You mean you don't remember how you came along
  And treated me so vilely, just back up from port?
SOSIA: Not the least little thing. Give me the full report.
       I'm fair, I'm just, my will is strong,
  And I'll pass sentence on myself if I did wrong.
CLEANTHIS: Why, when Amphitryon's arrival gave the clue,
  I would not go to bed, but waited up for you.
  But never have I seen such coldness in my life:
  I had to jog your memory that you had a wife.   1120
       And when I was about to kiss you,
  You turned your head round to the ear, so I would miss you.
SOSIA: Good!
CLEANTHIS: Good?

SOSIA: Cleanthis, you don't see just what is leading
                My words to take the form they do.
        I'd eaten garlic, and, like any man of breeding,
        I tried to keep unpleasant breath away from you.
CLEANTHIS: I mentioned all the tendernesses of my heart,
        Yet all I said just left you like a block of wood,
                And not one word of kindness could
                You bring yourself to on your part.   1130
SOSIA (aside): Cheer up!
CLEANTHIS: In vain I let my passion's flame burn high,
        My chaste affection found you icy cold instead;
        At such a glad homecoming you would not comply,
        Refusing so much as to take the place in bed
        Which by the laws of marriage you must occupy.
SOSIA: I would not come to bed . . . ?
CLEANTHIS: No, coward.
SOSIA: Can that be?
CLEANTHIS: You certainly refused, you traitor.
        Of all affronts that is the one that is most painful.
        And then this morning, far from making up with me,
                As you and I were parting later,   1140
        You said some things to me that were outright disdainful.
SOSIA (aside): Hurrah for Sosia!
CLEANTHIS: How do you treat my complaint?
                You laugh at your fine enterprise?
SOSIA: Oh, am I satisfied with me!
CLEANTHIS: Is this how you repent for an atrocity?
SOSIA: I never would have thought that I had been so wise.
CLEANTHIS: Far from condemning your malicious perfidy,
        You let your joy show on your face without restraint?
SOSIA: Don't carry on so! Goodness! If I seem so sprightly,
        Believe me, I had reasons of the strongest sort;   1150
        Without a thought about it, I never did so rightly
        As when I treated you the way that you report.
CLEANTHIS: You're mocking me! How do you dare?
SOSIA: No, No! Quite honestly I say it.
        The way my mind was running, I had quite a scare,
        But what you've told me does a great deal to allay it.

You had me worried, and I was afraid I might
    Have done a foolish thing last night.

CLEANTHIS:
    What is this fear of yours? What is it you are thinking?

SOSIA: The doctors say that when a man's been drinking.   1160
    He'd best observe avoidance of his wife;
With union while in that condition there's a linking,
They say, with dullard offspring who are short of life.
Just see how right my heart was to be cold and shrinking:
I could have caused all sorts of endless woes and strife.

CLEANTHIS: The doctors are a silly lot,
    With all their tedious arguments.
    Why don't they treat the sick, and not
Try managing the lives of those with health and sense?
    They meddle in too many things,   1170
When to our chaste desires they issue yea's and nay's;
    Then too concerning dog-star days
They come along with all their rules and hectorings,
    All nonsense of their idle ways.

SOSIA: Now, now!

CLEANTHIS: No, I maintain that harm will come of this.
The heads that reasoned out those reasons must be muddled.
There's neither wine nor season that can be amiss
For duty to the conjugal observances,
    And all those doctors are befuddled.

SOSIA: Your animus toward them I urge you to forget;   1180
    They're honest fellows really, despite what people say.

CLEANTHIS:
    Don't eat your humble pie too soon; you're not through yet.
The weak excuse you offer isn't worth a thing,
And soon or late I'll have my vengeance for the way
I see myself mistreated every single day.
I still recall our recent talk and feel its sting.
There are some means, you traitor, that I have devised
To use the liberty your heart has authorized.

SOSIA: What?

CLEANTHIS: You just finished saying I was free to take
    A lover now, for all you care.   1190

SOSIA: Oh, but I was mistaken there.

I now unsay that; there's too much at stake.
Don't act upon my hasty word; beware!
CLEANTHIS: If I can bring myself to do,
    However, what you have proposed . . .
SOSIA: Let us break off this interview:
  Here comes Amphitryon, and he seems well disposed.
        (Enter Jupiter.)

JUPITER *(aside):*
  I've come back here to find Alcmena and appease her,
  To banish cares that keep her heart in irritation,
  And give my ardent love, which guides me here to please her,
    The sweet delight of reconciliation.   [1200
        (to Cleanthis)
    Alcmena's home now, I presume?
CLEANTHIS: Yes, filled with a disquietude
    Which only longs for solitude
  And which denies me any access to her room.
JUPITER: Whatever her command may be,
    She won't deny herself to me.
CLEANTHIS: Her mood, as far as I could see,
    Required a sudden privacy.
        (Exit Jupiter.)
SOSIA: How is his happy manner to be understood,   1210
    Cleanthis, after all his rage?
CLEANTHIS: It means: if we did as we should,
  We women would pack men off to the devil's cage;
    The best of them are still no good.
SOSIA: You speak in anger, don't deny it.
  But you are far too much attached to men to do it;
  And all of you would be, I fancy, hard put to it,
    If once the devil were to try it.
CLEANTHIS: In fact . . .
SOSIA: They're coming. Let's be quiet.
      (Enter Jupiter with Alcmena.)
JUPITER: But would you leave me desperate?   1220
    Alas! Wait, fair Alcmena, wait!
ALCMENA: No, with the author of my pain
    I am unable to remain.
JUPITER: I beg you . . .

ALCMENA: Leave me.
JUPITER: What . . . ?
ALCMENA: Again I say it:
                                                         [Leave me.

JUPITER *(softly, aside):*
  My soul is saddened, and her tears of sorrow grieve me.
  (aloud): But do permit my heart . . .
ALCMENA: No, do not follow me.
JUPITER: Where do you mean to go?
ALCMENA: Wherever you won't be.
JUPITER: There your attempt will fail directly.
  Your beauty links me to you by a bond too strong
  For me to do without you for one moment long;   1230
            Where you are, there you may expect me.
ALCMENA: And I shall flee from you directly.
JUPITER: Am I so very horrifying?
ALCMENA: Beyond all words so, in my eyes.
            I see you as a monster, terrifying,
            Whose very presence petrifies,
            Ferocious, cruel, scarifying,
            From whom to any place one flies.
  At sight of you I feel the anguish of the dying,
            I writhe in torment, agonize,   1240
            And I see naught beneath the skies
            That I so loathe and so despise
  But, more than you, I'd find it gratifying.
JUPITER: These are, alas! harsh sentiments your lips pronounce.
ALCMENA: Within my heart are many more;
  And my heart rankles that, to sum up all the counts,
            Words are in insufficient store . . .
JUPITER: How could my love cause you such pain
  That I should seem to be a monster in your sight?
ALCMENA: Just heaven! Can he ask, when it is all so plain!   1250
            And isn't it enough to slay outright?
JUPITER: Ah! in a gentler tone, I pray . . .
ALCMENA: No, neither sight nor sound of you can be allowed.
JUPITER: You really have the heart to treat me in this way?
            Is this the tender love you vowed
  Would last forever when I came here yesterday?

ALCMENA: No, that love is no more; your coarse brutalities
    Have bidden it be otherwise.
 That tender, ardent love has suffered its demise;
 Gashed with a hundred cruelly smarting injuries,   1260
    Slain here within my heart it lies.
 Its place is filled by anger quite inflexible,
 By fierce resentment equally inexorable,
 And by despair which wanton murder justifies.
 My heart shall hate you for a deed so execrable;
 To the degree I loved you once my hate shall rise,
    And that is hate as much as possible.
JUPITER: Alas! your love would seem to have had little force
 If it can fade and die of anything so small!
 Should what was done in simple jest cause a divorce?   1270
 And should mere raillery turn love to bitter gall?
ALCMENA: Ah! that is just what gives the most offense,
  The very point my anger can't excuse.
 Had honest jealousy incited your abuse,
    My torment would be less intense.
  True jealousy has certain manifestations
  The force of which can sweep us past our goal;
 But souls of greater prudence will, on such occasions,
   Though with some effort on the whole,
   Keep their emotions in control.   1280
 A fit of passion in a heart that once has erred
 Can still win back the soul to whom it gave offense;
  And in the love for which the lapse occurred
 It finds at least, in spite of all its violence,
   The grounds for a forgiving word.
Such outbursts find the thing that first caused them to be,
The best excuse against resentment in a soul,
   And one grants pardon readily
   For what was not in one's control.
   But that, from sheerest frivolousness,   1290
One should fly into fury in highest degree,
That one should injure, and with such ferocity,
   The honor and the kindliness
   Of one who loves us tenderly,
  That in itself is cruel to excess,
  And it will never quit my memory.

JUPITER: Yes, you are right, Alcmena, and to you I bow.
  This was indeed a crime, an odious offense;
    Defending it is futile now.
  Yet grant my heart the right to plead its own defense   1300
    And to declare the culprit's name
    Who for this outrage is to blame,
   For I say if the final truth be known,
  Your husband bears the guilt, Alcmena, he alone,
  And guilty you must find him also in your view.
  In all this outrage here the lover had no part,
  Offense against you bursts the limits of his heart;
  That heart has far too much respect and love for you
    To think of doing such a thing,
  And if it were inclined through weakness so to do,   1310
    He would his vengeance on it bring,
 He would snatch up a sword and pierce it through and through.
  The husband here exceeded that devout submission
    One must forever feel for you;
  Harsh actions showed the husband when he found permission
  From marriage laws for anything he chose to do.
  Yes, he's the culprit in this case beyond a doubt,
  He used your lovely self with criminal intent;
    Abhor that husband, cast him out,
    He's yours to deal with, I consent.   1320
  But, sweet Alcmena, spare the lover punishment
    Which from your anger might accrue;
    Don't make the lover suffer too,
    Divide him from the guilty one;
    And if you wish full justice done,
  Chastise him not at all for what he did not do.
ALCMENA: Oh! all these subtleties appear
    To have the flimsiest excuse,
    And to an angry mind, I fear,
  Your words are poorly timed and of but little use.   1330
  Your subterfuge I find preposterously lame,
  I make no fine distinctions as to the offense,
    And on my anger both have equal claim;
    Before its righteous vehemence
  The husband and the lover are the same.

As far as I'm concerned, they are identical,
My wounded soul sees them as painted equally
      In colors of iniquity;
Both have offended me, and both are criminal,
      And both are odious to me.   1340
JUPITER: Ah, well, since you will have it so,
      Then you must charge me with the crime.
Yes, you are acting rightly when you bid me go
To immolation for your anger at this time.
You stand beneath a justified resentment's sway,
And all the mighty wrath of which you make display
Subjects me to a torment I deserve to know.
      Quite rightly my approach drives you away,
        And rightly you propose to flee
        From any place where I may be.   1350
     To you I must be something to despise,
And you must wish me harm beyond the hope of change.
There is no horror which my crime does not outrange
      In its offense to your fair eyes.
To gods and men alike the heinous action cries,
And my audacity deserves to have you use
      Against me every fiercest-raging dart
        Your hate can send into my heart,
        But my heart for forgiveness sues.
To ask you such, I throw myself upon my knees,   1360
      I beg you for it in the name
Of the most tender love and the most ardent flame
      That ever burned in ecstasies.
      And if your heart denies this boon,
Which, beautiful Alcmena, I seek to procure,
      May some blow fall upon me soon
      And by quick death give me relief
      From this harsh misery and grief
      Which I no longer can endure.
      Yes, I despair, as things now are;   1370
      Alcmena, do not go so far
As think that, loving your celestial charms this way,
I could survive your anger for a single day.
The barbarous length of these dread moments with you wreaks

   Such mortal blows and buffeting
   That my poor heart is perishing;
The cruel wounds torn by a thousand vultures' beaks
Have nothing comparable to my fierce suffering.
Alcmena, you have but to hand your verdict down,
And if there is no hope of pardon from your frown,   1380
This sword shall instantly deliver one strong blow
And in your sight transpierce a heart of utter woe,
This heart, this traitor-heart, that so deserves to perish
For having angered someone only fit to cherish.
Descending to the shadowy realm, it will be glad
If my death can allay your wrath, however late,
And leave within your soul, after a day so sad,
   No slightest memory of hate
   When you recall the love we had!
This is the sovereign favor I dare ask of Fate.   1390

ALCMENA: Ah! cruel husband!
JUPITER: Make your final judgment plain.
ALCMENA: Must I still kindly feelings toward you entertain
 And see you heap me with indignity and pain?
JUPITER: No matter what resentment follows from our crimes,
 Can it withstand repentance in a heart on fire?
ALCMENA: A heart filled full of love will die a thousand times
 Before it will offend its object of desire.
JUPITER: The more one loves, the easier to exonerate . . .
ALCMENA: No, do not talk about it. You deserve my hate.
JUPITER: You hate me, then?
ALCMENA: To that end I bend all my strength,
 And I am vexed to find that my heart cannot force,   [1400
 For all that your offense does merit such a course,
   Its vengeance to that proper length.
JUPITER: But why this fierce exasperation,
 When I have offered you my death in expiation?
 Say but the word, and on the spot I shall comply.
ALCMENA: Can one who cannot hate still want someone to die?
JUPITER: But I can not continue living any more
   Unless your anger has subsided,
 Until on pardon you have graciously decided,   1410
   Which at your feet I here implore.
    (Sosia and Cleanthis also kneel.)

Decide for one alternative:
For punishment or absolution.

ALCMENA: Alas! with either resolution
I give more than I want to give!
By keeping up my anger to which I was driven,
My heart has found itself betrayed;
By saying that I cannot hate,
Have I already not forgiven?

JUPITER: Ah! fair Alcmena, at this peak of happiness ...   1420

ALCMENA: Enough! My too great weakness fills me with distress.

JUPITER: Go, Sosia, hurry now and see,
While my soul tarries in this realm of ecstasy,
How many of the army's officers are free,
And bid them come to dinner here with me.

(softly aside)
While he is absent, Mercury
Shall fill his place quite admirably.

(Exeunt Jupiter and Alcmena.)

SOSIA: Thus they, Cleanthis, end their differences.
Shall we take their example now
And make some peace between the two of us somehow,   1430
A little mending of our fences?

CLEANTHIS: To please you, I suppose, and bury your offenses?

SOSIA: What? You don't want to?

CLEANTHIS: No.

SOSIA: Oh well, then, never mind.
I'll leave.

CLEANTHIS: No, no! Come back, you lout.

SOSIA: No, I'll do nothing of the kind.
It's my turn to be angry and to pout.

(Exit.)

CLEANTHIS: Go on, then, dog! Leave me behind.
Being an honest woman sometimes wears me out.   1438

Act III

AMPHITRYON: Yes, Fate is hiding him deliberately from me,
  And I am weary after making every round.   1440
  I cannot think of a more cruel destiny:
  I could not find, no matter where my steps were bound,
      The man I'm seeking desperately,—
  Yet all of those I did not care to find, I found.
  A thousand tedious bores, who fancy they are none,
  Came flocking up to talk about the feats we'd done,
  Although they hardly knew me, driving me to madness.
  Amid the cruel worries now afflicting me,
  Their glad embraces and their joviality
  Were burdens added to my anxious weight of sadness.   1450
      In vain I try to slip away
      And flee their tiresome adulations:
  Their killing friendship everywhere holds me at bay,
  And while I give their warmth of eager salutations
      A nod confirming what they say,
  I softly curse them with a hundred imprecations.
  How little one is pleased with honors and with praise
  And all that mighty victory can ever earn,
  When on the suffering soul a grievous sorrow weighs!
  How gladly one would give that glory in return   1460
      For peace of soul and carefree days!
      My jealousy at every turn
      The depth of my disgrace surveys;
      The more I make it my concern,
  The less sense can I make out of its wretched maze.
  I am not too astonished at the diamond-theft:
  Seals can be broken after men are out of sight;
  But it's the gift they claim I brought myself last night
  That makes the sharp embarrassment in which I'm left.
  Nature does sometimes produce resemblances   1470
  And some impostors have abused them on occasion;
  But that a man as husband finds acceptance is,
  I find, incredible in such a situation.

176

On every count there are a thousand differences,
Each bound to strike a woman's shrewd evaluation.
      The magic spells of Thessaly
Are credited with strange effects since times of old,
But all the famous tales about them ever told
Have always struck my mind as sheer inanity;
And I would feel the threads of Fate were oddly crossed,   1480
      If after victory in battle
      I had to trust such silly prattle,
      And at the price of honor lost.
I'll sound her out once more about this mystery
And see if it is not some vain hallucination
That holds her troubled mind in weird captivity.
      Ah! righteous heaven grant this thought
      May prove the proper explanation,
And that, for my sake now, her mind is overwrought.

              Enter Mercury.[1]

MERCURY: As long as love in this place offers me no pleasure,   1490
  I shall at least create some of another kind:
  I'm going to try and liven up my serious leisure
  And drive this man Amphitryon out of his mind.
  I know that in a god that's not true charity,
  But, then, such isn't just exactly my concern:
      My planet rather gives the turn
      For mischief and for deviltry.

AMPHITRYON *(without seeing Mercury):*
  Why should this gate be closed at such an hour as this?
MERCURY: Hey! Easy there! Who's knocking?
AMPHITRYON: Me.
MERCURY: And who is
                           ["me?"

AMPHITRYON: Ah! Open up!
MERCURY: What? Open? And who may you be,
  To speak in such a tone and make disturbances?   [1500
AMPHITRYON: What? Don't you recognize me?
MERCURY: No,
    Nor do I want to in the least.

---

[1] The 1734 edition adds the words: *on the balcony of Amphitryon's house, without being seen or heard by Amphitryon.*

AMPHITRYON *(aside):* Can rationality be everywhere deceased?
  Is it an epidemic?
                (aloud) Sosia! Sosia! Ho!
MERCURY: Yes, Sosia is my name, that's so;
    What do you take me for? A beast?
AMPHITRYON: Do you see me?
MERCURY: Quite well. Your fist has quite a
                                          [flair
    For racket-making. What's occurred?
    What is it that you want down there?   1510
AMPHITRYON: What do I want, you gallows-bird?
MERCURY: What is it? Don't just stand and stare.
    Speak up, if you want to be heard.
AMPHITRYON: If I come up there with a stick,
    You'll understand me pretty quick.
    I'll also teach you properly
    What tone of voice to use to me.
MERCURY: If you so much as move to batter down that gate,
  I'll send you down some messengers that won't be pleasant.
AMPHITRYON: Did ever anyone see insolence so great?   1520
  Who'd ever dream it from a servant, from a peasant?
MERCURY: Well, then! What is it? Do you have me all reviewed?
  Have you inspected me enough with those round eyes?
  How he does stretch them open in his wild surprise!
    If looks could bite, I would be chewed
    Already into morsel size.
AMPHITRYON: I am myself aghast at what is now accruing
    From such an impudent attack.
  What monstrous tempests for yourself you now are brewing!
  What storms of blows are going to break across your back!   1530
MERCURY: Fellow, if from this place you don't soon disappear,
  You're likely to acquire some bruise or some contusion.
AMPHITRYON:
  And you, you blockhead, will find out to your confusion
  What comes to servants who attack their masters here!
MERCURY: My master? You?
AMPHITRYON: You dare allege not knowing me?
MERCURY: I recognize no other than Amphitryon.
AMPHITRYON: I am Amphitryon! Now who else could I be?

MERCURY: Amphitryon?
AMPHITRYON: Of course.
MERCURY: Now there's a funny one!
    What tavern were you in to make your face so red
            And get this tipsy look on you?   1540
AMPHITRYON: Still more?
MERCURY: Was it a wine fit for a banquet spread?
AMPHITRYON: Gods!
MERCURY: Which kind was it: old or new?
AMPHITRYON: How many blows!
MERCURY: The new kind goes right to your
                                                        [head
            Unless you add some water too.
AMPHITRYON:
    Oh! I'll tear out that tongue of yours before I'm through.
MERCURY: Just go along, good fellow, please.
            You might be overheard out here.
    I have respect for wine: be off now, disappear,
    And let Amphitryon enjoy himself in peace.
AMPHITRYON: Amphitryon is there inside the house?
MERCURY: Of course.
    The laurels of his total triumph wreathe his brow,   [1550
            And he's with fair Alcmena now,
    Enjoying the delights of amiable discourse.
    They've patched their lovers' quarrel up with compromise
    And now they know the joy that comes when two agree.
    Beware of how you trouble their sweet privacy,
            Unless you want him to chastise
            Your over-great temerity.
                        (Exit)
AMPHITRYON: Ah! what a cruel blow unto my soul he deals!
    What fierce dismay he casts into my troubled mind!   1560
    If things stand as this traitor says, my spirit reels
    To think of where I may my love and honor find.
    For what decision would I opt, if reason chose?
            Does speech or silence make the better claim?
    And must I, in my anger, hush up or expose
            This great dishonor to my name?
    Must I deliberate in an affront so vile?

Redress is futile and there's nothing to defend;
    All my anxiety meanwhile
    Should seek revenge as its one end.   1570
(Enter Sosia with Naucrates and Polidas.)[1]
SOSIA *(to Amphitryon):*
  Sir, try as I might try, the most that I could do
  Was to invite and bring these gentlemen you see.
AMPHITRYON: Ah! there you are?
SOSIA: Sir?
AMPHITRYON: Impudent! And reckless
                                       [too!

SOSIA: What?
AMPHITRYON: Now I'll teach you to show disrespect to me.
SOSIA: Why, what's the matter?
AMPHITRYON *(putting his hand on his sword):*
                    What's the matter, wretched one?
SOSIA *(to Naucrates and Polidas):*
            Protect me, Sirs! Oh come and save me!
NAUCRATES: Oh, I entreat you, stay your hand.
SOSIA: What have I
                                      [done?

AMPHITRYON: You ask that, block-head? Still you brave me?
                (to Naucrates)
  O let me satisfy my righteous wrath this time.
SOSIA:
  When someone's hanged, he should be told the reason why. 1580
NAUCRATES *(to Amphitryon):*
  But deign at least to state the nature of his crime.
SOSIA: Hold firm, Sirs, please! Don't let him by!
AMPHITRYON: He's just had the audacity
          To close my own door in my face,
          Then in the bargain threaten me
          In language that was foul and base.
  Ah, rascal! *(putting his hand on his sword)*
SOSIA *(falling to his knees):* I'm a dead man.
NAUCRATES: *(to Amphitryon):* Calm your wrath, I pray.
SOSIA: O Sirs!

---

1 The 1734 edition adds: *from the rear of the stage.*

POLIDAS: What is it?
SOSIA: Has he hit me?
AMPHITRYON: No, no, I'm going to make him pay
  For words he used a little while ago to twit me.   1590
SOSIA: But how can such a thing be true
  If at your own instructions I was elsewhere then?
  The evidence is here with these two gentlemen
  Whom I went and invited home to dine with you.
NAUCRATES: He did just bring that message to us, it is true,
          And has not left our sight since then.
AMPHITRYON: Who issued those instructions?
SOSIA: You did.
AMPHITRYON: And when?
SOSIA: Why, after peace was made
  And you were all in raptures at the truce concluded,   1600
      Whereby Alcmena's anger was allayed.
              (Sosia stands up.)
AMPHITRYON: O heaven! Every step today
  Adds something further to my cruel martyrdom!
          To such an impasse have I come,
      I don't know what to think or what to say.
NAUCRATES: All these things he has told us have been happening
          Are none of Nature's operation;
  Before you lose your temper and do anything,
  This strange adventure should be brought to explanation.
AMPHITRYON: Come! You can second my attempts at any rate;
  Heaven has sent you here most expeditiously.   1610
  Let us find out what Fortune holds in store for me,
  Let's plumb this mystery, and let us know our fate.
      I long to know it, yet I hold my breath
          Because I fear it more than death.
      (Amphitryon knocks at the door of the house.)
              (Enter Jupiter.)
JUPITER: What noise of tumult strikes my ear?
          Who knocks as master at my door?
AMPHITRYON: Just gods! What do I see?
NAUCRATES: What marvel have we
                                                      [here?

  What? Two Amphitryons where there was one before?

AMPHITRYON *(aside):*   My soul is paralyzed with fear,
  The episode concludes, and I approach my fall;   1620
        My destiny has been made clear,
        And what I now see tells me all.
NAUCRATES: The more my gaze inspects, the more I am surprised
  At how their features in a single pattern run.
SOSIA *(going over to Jupiter):* Sirs, this is the authentic one;
  The other's an impostor and should be chastised.
POLIDAS: Their sameness is so marvelous
        That judgment here must be withheld.
AMPHITRYON: The wretched trickster then has far outwitted us:
  This sword of mine will have his magic soon dispelled.   1630
NAUCRATES *(to Amphitryon, who has drawn his sword):*
        Stop!
AMPHITRYON: Let me go.
NAUCRATES: Gods! What are you about to do?
AMPHITRYON:
  Chastise this bold impostor for his shameless treasons.
JUPITER: One moment! Temper is of no avail to you;
  And anger of this sort will lead some to construe
  Your action as based on the weakest kind of reasons.
SOSIA: Yes, he has talismans to pass, by wizardry,
        As head of every household where he goes.
AMPHITRYON: I'll make you feel a thousand blows
  For saying things that are so utterly outrageous.
SOSIA: My master's known to be courageous,   1640
  And he won't have his servants beaten wantonly.
AMPHITRYON: Let me assuage my anger at its swollen flood
  And wash away this insult in a scoundrel's blood.
NAUCRATES *(holding Amphitryon back):*
  We will not stand for seeing such strange combat done,
        Amphitryon against Amphitryon.
AMPHITRYON: Is this all that my honor can expect from friends?
  That each supports a rascal, each his cause defends?
  Instead of being first to bolster up my wrath,
  They set up obstacles themselves to block my path?
NAUCRATES: How can we possibly decide   1650
        A way to have this quarrel ended,
        When two Amphitryons divide

Our eager zeal and hold it in mid-air suspended?
In manifesting our support of you today
We might mistake you and go wrong, we gravely fear.
In you we see Amphitryon indeed appear,
The Thebans' rescuer and glorious mainstay;
But then we also see him standing over here,
And which one is the real one, we are loath to say.
   Our stand is no wise dubious,   1660
We'll make the false one bite the dust before we're through,
But now he's hidden by the likeness of you two;
   And it would be too hazardous
   To act before we rightly knew.
   Once let us see with our own eyes
  On whose part this deceitful trick may be,
And once we have untangled this whole mystery,
No one will need to tell us where our duty lies.
JUPITER: Yes, you are right; the striking likeness must confuse you
And understandably you waver in debate.   1670
I take no umbrage, seeing you thus hesitate,
I am more reasonable, and readily excuse you.
Between us there's no difference that can be perceived,
And I can see how anyone could be deceived.
You witness no display of frantic rage from me,
   No drawing of my sword today;
That would not help much to resolve this mystery,
And I can find a gentler and a surer way.
   One of us is Amphitryon,
Though at the present time we each appear as he.   1680
On me the task devolves to end this consternation.
I shall reveal myself so well to everyone
That in his full awareness of who I may be,
Each man concurs as to what blood engendered me,
And that for further talk there will be no occasion.
Upon the Theban citizens I soon shall call
To hear the truth disclosed to fullest cognizance.
The matter surely is of such a consequence
   To warrant the high circumstance
   Of clarifying it to all.   1690
Such public evidence Alcmena now expects.

Her virtue, which this strife dishonorably affects,
Asks to be guaranteed, and this I undertake.
My love to her has pledged her full exoneration;
The noblest heads I summon now in convocation
To hear such statements for her name's and glory's sake.
While waiting for these witnesses to come, once more
    I pray you, of your courtesy,
    To come inside and dine with me,
    As Sosia asked you to before.   1700

SOSIA: I made no error, Sirs! Past doubt here stands the winner.
    His words end all uncertainty:
    The true Amphitryon is he
    Who has us in and serves us dinner.

AMPHITRYON: O heaven! Can I sink to any worse disgrace?
  Must I stand like a martyr listening helplessly
  To all that this impostor tells me to my face,
  And in the fury which his statements rouse in me
    Discover that my hands are bound?

NAUCRATES *(to Amphitryon):*
  Your protest is ill made. Permit us to await   1710
    What explanation he will state
    To give these grievances their due.
      I don't know if he's lying,
      But there's just no denying
      What he says does ring true.

AMPHITRYON:
  Go, luke-warm friends, and fawn upon this arrant cheat.
  Thebes holds for me friends of a different sort from you,
  And I shall find some who will lend their hands and treat
  This insult as their own because they feel it too.

JUPITER: I shall await their coming, and adjudicate   1720
    The matter in their common view.

AMPHITRYON:
  That way you think, knave, you'll escape your present strait,
  But from my vengeance nothing can deliver you.

JUPITER: I shall not at the present stage
      Reply to your insulting charge,
      But I shall soon confound this rage
      With a mere word, to all at large.

AMPHITRYON:
> Not heaven's very self could save you from my wrath,
> And I shall track you to the very depths of hell.

JUPITER: You will not need to take that path;   1730
> I shall not flee, as all shall soon see very well.

AMPHITRYON *(aside)*:
> Come on, before he's finished with his banquet's course,
> Let's gather friends who'll follow where my anger goes,
>> And break into my house by force
>> And slay him with a thousand blows.

JUPITER: Without ado, then, follow me
> Inside the house and we'll commence.

NAUCRATES: This whole adventure certainly
> Counfounds all reason and all sense.

SOSIA: A truce, Sirs, now to all amazement. Here are treats   1740
> To keep us all at table till tomorrow very well.
> *(alone):*
> I'm going to get my fill, and will I ever dwell
>> Upon the story of our feats!
>> I long to get down to those eats,
>> I'm hungrier than I can tell.

> [*While Amphitryon sets off alone to find other supporters for his cause, Jupiter takes Naucrates and Polidas in to dinner. Sosia, having lingered a moment, is about to follow the host when he is suddenly confronted by Mercury, who bars his way.*]

MERCURY: Stop! So you're sticking in your nose again, disgusting
> Little food-and-kitchen scenter?

SOSIA: Oh please now, let me by!

MERCURY: And still you try to enter?
> I see your backbone needs adjusting.

SOSIA: Have mercy, brave and generous me,   1750
>> Restrain your anger, I implore.
>> Please don't beat Sosia any more,
> Don't deign to beat your very self so murderously.

MERCURY: At impudence you're very quick.
>> Who gave you leave to use that name?
> When I forbade expressly any use of same
> Unless you want a thousand blows from my good stick?

SOSIA: The name serves, as it happens, both of us at once,
          So our one master has a pair,
    And everyone knows me as Sosia everywhere.   1760
              I'll gladly let you use it too,
              But you should let me have my share.
              Let's let the two Amphitryons
              Show jealousy the way they do,
              And while they have their arguments,
    Why don't we Sosias make a truce between us two?
MERCURY: No. One is quite enough, and I will not permit
              Creation of a subdivision.
SOSIA: But I'll concede you the superior position;
    I'll take the junior, you the senior grade of it.   1770
MERCURY: No. Brothers are a nuisance. This is not for me,
              I want to be the only son.
SOSIA: O heart of barbarous tyranny!
    Then let me be at least your shadow.
MERCURY: I want none.
SOSIA: Let pity humanize a soul so pitiless;
    Just let me be with you in that capacity.
              As shadow I will serve with such submissiveness
                    That you'll be satisfied with me.
MERCURY: No quarter. That's a law that will not change.
    If you so much as set foot in that door again,   1780
              A thousand blows will beat your skin.
SOSIA: Alas! poor Sosia, what a strange
              And weird predicament you're in.
MERCURY: What! do your lips still make so bold
    To take upon yourself a name that I forbid?
SOSIA: I didn't mean this self of mine,
              I meant the Sosia who of old
              Lived right here when my parents did,
              And who most cruelly was told
    He had to stay outside when it was time to dine.   1790
MERCURY: Take care you don't relapse into your fit again,
    If you want to continue life with living men.
SOSIA (aside):
    How I would thrash you if my courage could be stirred,
    You double whoreson bastard puffed up in your pride.

MERCURY: What are you saying?
SOSIA: Nothing.
MERCURY:
                                      But I caught a word.
SOSIA: Just ask if I so much as sighed.
MERCURY: What I heard had a certain ring
               Like "whoreson bastard" in my ear,
                   As sure as anything.
SOSIA: The weather must have set some parrot talking here.   1800
MERCURY: Farewell. If you should have an itching back to scour,
               My residence is here, of course.
                   [*Mercury goes back inside the house.*]
SOSIA (*alone*):   O heaven, but the dinner hour
    Is an accursed time to be turned out-of-doors!
    But then, in our affliction let us yield to fate
    And go along today with sightless fantasy.
                   We may as well affiliate
                   Amphitryon in misery
                   With Sosia for his misery-mate.
    I see him coming now in worthy company.   1810
           [*Sosia remains in a corner of the stage, without
       being seen. Enter Amphitryon accompanied by
       Argatiphontidas and Posicles.*]
AMPHITRYON:
    Stop here, Sirs. Let us space ourselves somewhat apart
               And don't all rush in at the start
               But wait till there is urgent need.
POSICLES: I understand this blow must deeply touch your heart.
AMPHITRYON: Ah! mortal is my grief in every way indeed.
                   I suffer for my love
                   As much as for my name.
POSICLES: If this resemblance is as great as you tell of,
               Alcmena might not be to blame . . .
AMPHITRYON: Ah, in this matter it's assumed   1820
    The simple error is a crime and brings me shame,
    And, even if unwitting, innocence is doomed.
    Such errors, set them in whatever light you will,
               Touch points of utmost delicacy;
           If reason sometimes grants them pardon, still,
    Honor and love refuse to do so stubbornly.

ARGATIPHONTIDAS:
   I won't have my thoughts tangled in these arguments;
   I hate your gentlemen who are so loath to move;
   It is a habit at which I take deep offense,
   And one which men of spirit never will approve.   1830
   Once someone has engaged us, duty bids us serve
         No cause but his, and never swerve.
   Argatiphontidas rejects all compromises.
   To listen while a friend holds truce and interview
   Is something men of honor will not stoop to do.
   The voice of vengeance is the only voice he prizes.
         The process holds no charm for me.
   The only way to start when someone angers you
         Is to forget all mystery
         And draw your sword and run him through.   1840
         Yes, you will see, come what come may,
   Argatiphontidas will march and never falter;
         And you must promise me today
         This gallows-bird will get his halter
         From my hand and no other way.

AMPHITRYON: Then forward!

SOSIA: Sir, I come, and at your knees I sue
   For punishment of my accursed audacity.
   Please go ahead and hit me, beat me black-and-blue,
         Even kill me in your anger too:
         That's what I merit thoroughly,   1850
   And never will I say a word of blame to you.

AMPHITRYON: Get up. What's happening?

SOSIA: They drove me right away;
   As I was joining them to have the fun of eating,
         I never dreamed that I would stay
         Outside to give myself a beating.
   The other me, the servant of the other you,
         Has played his devil-tricks anew.
         We both are being victimized,
         Sir, and we're equally ill-fated:
         I find myself de-Sosia-ized   1860
         And you've been dis-Amphitryon-ated,

AMPHITRYON:
   Come on.

SOSIA: But shouldn't we first see who might be near?
              [*Enter Cleanthis, Naucrates, and Polidas
                        from the house.*]
CLEANTHIS: O heaven!
AMPHITRYON: What puts you in this flurry?
              And why do I inspire such fear?
CLEANTHIS:Why, you're upstairs in there, and yet I see you here.
NAUCRATES (*to Amphitryon*):
              He is at hand, you needn't worry,
    To give us all the explanations we are seeking,
    And if one may believe the things that he's been speaking,
    He will deliver us from all distress and worry.
                     [*Enter Mercury.*]
MERCURY: Yes, you shall all behold him with your very eyes: 1870
              He is the chief of gods above,
    Whom, in the semblance that she cherished most in love,
    Alcmena caused to come down from the highest skies.
              And as for me, I'm Mercury.
    For lack of things to do, I did beat up a bit
              The man whose shape I tried for size.
    But let him be assured that he'll get over it,
              For there is honor in the rod
              That deals a beating from a god.
SOSIA: I must say, Master God, I'm much obliged for this.   1880
    I could have done without your marks of courtesy.
MERCURY: Herewith I give him back the right of being Sosia.
    I'm tired of wearing such an ugly face as his,
    And once back in the sky I'll take me some ambrosia
              And wash his features off of me.
                 (*He flies up into the sky.*)
SOSIA: May heaven spoil your appetite for further strife!
    You beat like mad in every fit of rage you threw.
              I never saw in all my life
              A god more devil-like than you.
                 (*Enter Jupiter on a cloud.*)
              [*on his eagle, armed with his thunderbolt,
                  amid thunder and lightning.*][1]
JUPITER: Behold, Amphitryon, who your impostor is,   1890

[1] Words in brackets are from the 1682 edition.

See Jupiter emerge from your resemblances.
By signs like these you recognize him readily.
Here is, I think, sufficient to provide the balm
        To make your heart as it should be
And in your being reestablish peace and calm.
My name, unceasingly adored throughout the earth,
Suppresses scandal which might otherwise occur.
        A portion shared with Jupiter
        In no wise lessens human worth.
It is a glory rather, a glory by all odds,   1900
To be the rival of the sovereign of the gods.
Your love, as I see, has no reason to complain.
        In this adventure I am due,
Although I am a god, to feel the jealous pain.
Alcmena is entirely yours, do what one may,
And there must be great comfort, from your point of view,
In that, to win her heart, there is no other way
        Except by seeming to be you,
That in all his immortal glory Jupiter
In his own person could not shake her loyalty,   1910
        And all that he received from her
Was given to you alone in her true constancy.
SOSIA: Lord Jupiter knows how to sugar-coat a pill.
JUPITER: Let all the black vexations of your heart now cease,
    And let the seething wrath that burns you now, be still.
    To your house shall be born a son whose feats shall fill
    The universe, and his name shall be Hercules.
    The splendor of a fortune rich in everything
    My favor and support of you will demonstrate;
        The whole world I shall bring   1920
        To envy your high fate.
        Put all your trust for future time
        In such assurances as these.
        To doubt them is a grievous crime.
        The words of Jupiter sublime
        Are the decrees of destinies.
        (He vanishes among the clouds.)
NAUCRATES: I am delighted with these brilliant indications. . . .
SOSIA: Would you be willing, Sirs, to hear advice from me?

Do not embark too hastily
   On flattering congratulations;   1930
   There's danger in such embarkations;
On either party's side the compliment may be
   Beset with awkward complications.
The great god Jupiter has honored us so much,
His kindness toward us doubtless is without a second;
   He promises unfailing luck, and such
   A fortune as is rich in everything,
And, for our house, birth of a mighty son is reckoned:
   All this is very flattering.
   But let us cut discussion short,   1940
And let us each go home and quietly to bed.
   Always, in matters of this sort,
   We're best off when the least is said.   (1943)

III. FROM MOLIÈRE TO KLEIST

1. DRYDEN'S *Amphitryon*

In October of 1690 there was published in London John Dryden's *Amphitryon, or The Two Socias, a Comedy, with the Musick of the Songs compos'd by Mr. Henry Purcel.* The fifty-nine-year-old dramatist and poet was still widely admired, even though religious and political reasons had recently debarred him from the Poet Laureateship which he had held since 1670, and his new play was a success on the stage, both immediately and in revivals for over a century. In his Epistle Dedicatory to Sir William Gower the author speaks of indebtedness to Plautus and Molière, "the two greatest Names of Ancient and Modern Comedy," and declares that he has made additions and alterations only as "the difference of our Stage from the *Roman* and the *French* did so require it." A reviewer of 1691 named Langbaine said that Mr. Dryden had

> "... more closely followed the *French,* than the *Latin* Poet: but however it must with Justice be allowed, that what he borrowed, he has improv'd throughout; and Molliere is as much exceeded by Mr. *Dryden,* as *Rotrou* is outdone by *Molliere*."

Montague Summers, the 1932 editor of Dryden's works, warmly seconds the 1691 reviewer, saying that Dryden "has ample acknowledgment of such hints as he took from Plautus and Molière, upon both of whom he has so vastly improved." Mr. Summers further endorses Sir Walter Scott's description of the play as "one of the happiest effusions of Dryden's comic muse."

Relatively small circles of London's high society dictated the character of much of Dryden's dramatic production, so it is no mystery that this *Amphitryon* should have found favor with the group for whom it was written. Aristocratic audiences kept it alive for a century or more. Sir Walter's cordial endorsement is a little more surprising, and Mr. Summers as an ardent admirer surely speaks for a minority in the twentieth century.

"Mercury and Phoebus descend in several Machines" to open the play with a discussion of Jupiter's intentions in summoning the latter. Jupiter, likewise via a machine, descends to clarify his intentions, which are, of course, to possess Alcmena. Mercury inquires whether he "wou'd fornicate in the Shape of a Bull, or a Ram, or an Eagle, or a Swan," and when Phoebus remarks, half aside, "Any disguise to hide the King of Gods," Jupiter replies:

> I know your Malice, *Phoebus,* you wou'd say
> That when a Monarch sins it shou'd be secret,
> To keep exterior show of Sanctity,
> Maintain Respect, and cover bad Example:
> For Kings and Priests are in a manner bound
> For Reverence sake to be close Hypocrites.
>   . . . . .
> I love, because 'twas in the Fates I shou'd.
>   . . . . .
> Fate is, what I
> By vertue of Omnipotence have made it:
> And pow'r Omnipotent can do no wrong.

Indeed, Jupiter earmarked Amphitryon's wife for his own pleasure when he created her and tonight he means to collect the outstanding debt of that pleasure. Mercury's observations to his father's face are politically daring and theologically devastating, as when he finds that Jupiter fore-created evils expressly to justify procreating Hercules to overcome them.—One can only wonder what was in the heart of hearts of Dryden, who in youth had admired Cromwell and the Puritans, who had in subsequent years supported Charles II and the Church of England, and who still later forfeited public offices by converting to Catholicism.

When Mercury tarries behind the other two in order to talk to Madame Night we find ourselves suddenly confronted with a prose paraphrase of Molière's prologue. Here she is "Old Night" and a bawd, protesting but compliant. The second scene is devoted to Jupiter-Amphitryon's arrival in Alcmena's presence. Thereafter, Acts II, III, and IV follow Molière's scenario fairly faithfully, now in prose and now in verse, sometimes in almost word-for-word translation, more often in a form considerably expanded. Of specifically Plautine passages there are very few. However, a sub-plot has been added to the matter taken from

Molière, centering upon Alcmena's voraciously greedy attendant lady Phaedra and the unscrupulous Judge Gripus. The latter's entrance is put off until late in Act III. Although Bromia, Socia's wife, is retained in the cast of characters, she is merely a shrewish caricature and a foil to Phaedra, while Phaedra is allowed to flirt with both the real Socia and with Mercury-Socia. The latter bribes her with a golden goblet which he has stolen from Judge Gripus, only to have the lady retire to bed with the goblet rather than with him. At the close of Act IV Phaedra is astonished to come into the presence of both Socias simultaneously, whereupon Mercury-Socia half-reveals his godhood to her, first by seeing through her clothes—to the extent of naming every item in her pockets, then by stamping his foot—the regular signal for the stage trapdoor to open and admit a corps de ballet from the cellar. Dryden's songs, set to Purcell's music, alternate with dances by mythological figures to close Act IV, just as the third Act had concluded with Jupiter-Amphitryon's serenade to Alcmena on the balcony and with ballet dances. Purcell also contributed an overture and nine incidental pieces in all, chiefly dances, so that this *Amphitryon,* though subtitled a comedy, came close to what the late seventeenth century English public termed an opera, i.e. a play with incidental music, singing, dancing, and spectacle. Purcell's scores were popular enough to be printed at the end of the quarto edition of the play, a most unusual practice.

Much of the fifth Act is unavoidably occupied with winding up the sub-plot about Phaedra and Judge Gripus, so that the dénouement of the main story fills barely the two final pages of text. Two peals of thunder herald Jupiter's approach in a machine, whence he addresses a stage full of characters with the proclamation of the future birth of Hercules. Amphitryon and Alcmena stand speechless as the work concludes with remarks by Socia and by Mercury. Whereupon Mrs. Mountfort, stepping forth from her *persona* of Phaedra, spoke an epilogue about "how sweet a time those Heathen Ladies had" in the days when adultery was no sin, and about how Jove, "when he usurp'd the Husband's name, . . . civilly . . . saved the Ladies fame."

With the overture, incidental music, ballet dances, second plot, and expanded speeches in the main plot, Dryden's *Amphi-*

tryon would require twice the time needed for Molière's spare comedy. There was "something for everyone," and audiences might well be gratified. What is more, the work contains skillful and witty writing and, occasionally, striking turns of poetic phrase that are almost Elizabethan in quality. The modern reader, however, comes away saddened at such high talents squandered for the mere diversion of *monde* and *demimonde*. To say that Dryden was ruined as a dramatic poet by his public is not to say anything very new, but the pity of such a waste is none the less deplorable. If Alcmena comes off tolerably well, and if Amphitryon is not the worst of men, the two of them together cannot offset a stageful of distasteful persons that range from the unprincipled scoundrel of a Jupiter to the unprincipled Harpy of a Phaedra. What the plays lacks is humanity. And if the author's purpose was the castigation of vice by merciless depiction of vice, then the Amphitryon scenario was not the proper vehicle for his purpose. The vices of gods in whom neither the author nor the audience believed cannot make for effective satire.

2. *Amphitryon* IN THE EIGHTEENTH CENTURY

On December 15, 1756 Dryden's play appeared at the Drury Lane Theatre in a form considerably modified by one Dr. Hawkesworth, whose "Occasional Prologue" claimed:

> The scenes which *Plautus* drew, to-night we shew
> Touch'd by Molière, by Dryden taught to glow.

This version held the stage through the lifetime of the actor Woodward and in 1777, the year of his death, was published as "A Comedy, Altered from Dryden, by Mr. Woodward," though the version was really that of Hawkesworth plus a few stage variants. On October 27, 1781 a ballad opera called *Jupiter and Alcmena* and based on Dryden was given at Covent Garden, but with such lack of success that the text was not published. A two-Act version, emphasizing the farcical elements, ran for eight performances in 1826, while in 1872 a three-Act adaptation by John Oxenford drew high praise. The program announced that "both adapter and management have approached Dryden with

diffidence and reverence," a statement that betokens the self-conscious revival of a classic. Literary folk might enjoy it, but bourgeois and Romantic taste could no longer cherish the work.
Dryden's *Amphitryon* is stranded in the aristocratic era.

On the continent meanwhile, Molière's version held the stage
without a rival, not only in its native France but in other countries as well, where it might be read as part of the general European training of the upper classes in French language and literature and where it might be occasionally performed in French,
either by traveling French troupes or by amateurs, for particular
circles.

At this point it is necessary to outline very briefly a sub-chapter
of Amphitryon history devoted to versions of the story in the
form of opera, ballet, vaudeville, and a few versions in dramatic
form. The time span of this sub-chapter is about a hundred
years, from the 1680's to the 1780's, and the sheer number of
these musical and semi-musical treatments must compensate for
the fact that, rightly or wrongly, they are all forgotten works. In
listing them we follow L. R. Shero's article: *Alcmena and Amphitryon in Ancient and Modern Drama* in *Transactions and Proceedings of the American Philological Association,* LXXXVII
(1956), pp. 192–238.

From the last two decades of the seventeenth century Professor
Shero mentions an *Amphitryon* by Pierre Beauchamps, 1680,
a ballet with singing, performed "à l'hôtel de Condé;" a musical
Amphitryon of 1681, composer and librettist unknown, which
is described as "un petit opéra de la comédie d'Amphitryon
avec des entr'actes en musique;" a German opera of *Jupiter und
Alcmene,* composer and librettist unknown, performed in Dresden in 1696 and in 1704; and a three-Act "ballet héro-comique"
by Venard de la Jonchère of uncertain date and of uncertain
title.

After the beginning of the eighteenth century Professor Shero's
list continues with: an Italian opera of *Anfitrione,* librettist
unknown, music by Gasparini Francesco, performed in Rome,
1707; a French parody-vaudeville by François Raguenet, performed at Lille in 1713; an unpublished three-Act French vaudeville by l'abbé Pellegrini, performed at the Saint-Germain fair
in 1714; an Italian opera libretto by Pietro Pariati, composer

of the music unknown, used perhaps in Munich or Vienna between 1720 and 1725 with the title of *Anfitrione;* a Lisbon performance in 1736 of a Portuguese opera called *Amphitryão, ou
Jupiter, e Alcmena* by the Brazilian-born converted Jew, An-
tonio José da Silva (1705–1739), who was burned at the stake as
a heretic by the Inquisition. (Actually, this "opera" is an elaborate spectacle play in prose and verse with vocal numbers for
chorus and soloists.) Professor Shero's list continues with an
elaborate Spanish verse play subtitled a "melodrama musical,"
performed by an enormous cast for King Philip V around 1740;
the author was José de Cañizares and the full title is *Amor es
todo invención: Jupiter, y Amphitrion.* Next comes that *rara
avis,* an English opera. Report has it that this *Amphitryon* of
1764 was withdrawn after a few performances at the Drury Lane
Theater because the libretto by Richard Holt was dull rather
than because the music by Michael Arne and Jonathan Battishill
was not good. In Paris an *opéra comique* of *Amphitryon* failed
in 1786 despite a libretto by Charles Sedaine and music by the
leading French composer of his day, André-Erneste-Modeste
Grétry. Sedaine did not even include the libretto in his collected
works. To this list, already strikingly international in its scope,
should be added an item from 1787, discussed by Professor Lindberger, namely a performance at the Drottingholm Court
Theater in Sweden of Molière's comedy augmented by "Quatre
Intermèdes" allegedly written by Swedish King Gustavus III and
with special music composed by the conductor of the royal
orchestra. If the king did not actually write the French verses of
the "Intermèdes" himself, he inspired the comédie-ballet organization after models he had admired in France and he was not
adverse to the homage of the final "Intermède," which addressed
him as victor in war and lover of peace.

In examining the works of the Danish comedy writer and
essayist Ludvig Holberg, Professor Lindberger notes a somewhat
cool attitude toward Molière at the beginning of Holberg's
career in the 1720's, growing to a strong admiration in the
1750's. *Epistle 190* of 1750, for instance, sharply observes:

> "No one should or can criticize me for preferring Molière's judg-
> ment to that of the entire University of Paris. One notes that great
> writers of comedy have tried first and foremost to imitate Plautus

and have not conformed to the criticism of learned men. One notes
that of all the ancient pieces which Molière undertook to translate
and rewrite, all are by Plautus and none are by Terence. It is not
too much to say that Plautus' *Amphitryon, Aulularia,* and *Menechmi*
still are the greatest comedies that we have."

(P. M. Mitchell: *Selected Essays of Ludvig Holberg,*
translation, University of Kansas Press, 1955)

Yet only muted echoes of either *Amphitruo* or of *Amphitryon*
are to be heard in Holberg's comedies *Kildereisen* and *Henrik
og Pernille,* both of 1724, and only a slight influence from
Sosia's lines may be observed in the speeches of the title-hero of
the famous *Jeppe paa Bjerget* (Jeppe of the Hill) of 1722.

To round out this brief summary of late seventeenth century
and eighteenth century proliferation of the Amphitryon theme
we mention three further items from Professor Shero's article:
a 1678 *Amphitryo* of unknown authorship performed in Dresden, apparently with conspicuous roles for Juno and Iris in its
latter portion; an *Anfitrion* by Santos Diez Gonzalez of an unknown date in the eighteenth century; and a play in German,
dated 1716, by an unidentified Austrian author, which is reported
in some detail by Lady Mary Wortley Montagu in a letter of
September 14, 1716 to Alexander Pope.

3. THE *Amphitryon* OF JOHANN DANIEL FALK

Belatedly eighteenth century despite its date of 1804 is the *Amphitryon* of Johann Daniel Falk, a comedy in blank verse which
paraphrased much of Molière's text but enormously increased its
length and its cast of characters. In his preface, Falk explained
that he wished to present a gallery of types of persons from the
world of Menander and Philemon. Thus we meet, in addition to
the usual personages, Alcmena's father Electryon, Amphitryon's
housekeeper Damokleia and his cook Doriskus, a soldier named
Thraso, two parasites named Licht and Schatten, several fishermen, several slaves, and several representatives of different occu-
pations. Of new episodes, there is one in which Sosia is punished
by Amphitryon by being tied in a sack and handed over to two
fishermen to be drowned; but he was rescued by being brought
up in the fishing net of a second pair of fishermen. Under the

spell of Weimar classicism in general and of Goethe's *Iphigenie auf Tauris* in particular, Falk brought his play to conclusion by having a Thoas-like Jupiter refrain from disrupting a happy marriage and having him bestow a country estate upon Amphitryon in token of his immense esteem for the young husband. The use of blank verse, the god's exalted veneration for Alkmene, and touches of lyric pantheism (expressed partly in phrases caught from Goethe), are marks of this earnest amateur's drama which will be duplicated in Kleist's *Amphitryon* of 1807, whether by coincidence or by design is not clear. The concept of an *Amphitryon* diverted to the ideals of Weimarian *humanitas* was ingenious and not without merit, however poor might be the execution of the idea. It would be like Kleist to catch a hint from such an amateur and to combine it with other ideas to highest advantage.

4. KLEIST'S *Amphitryon*

The astounding literary career of Heinrich von Kleist was entirely contained in a single decade, from some point in the year 1801 to his suicide on November 21, 1811. Several non-essential careers, before and during the essential one, were in succession enthusiastically begun and abruptly terminated. From age fifteen until age twenty-two (1792–1799) he served in the Prussian army, his family having been militarily illustrious for three centuries, yet when he resigned his Lieutenancy in 1799 he characterized the army, in a private letter, as "a monument of tyranny." Briefly, in the spring of 1802, he rented an island cottage in Switzerland with the intention of becoming an idyllic farmer. Under family pressure he agreed, in June of 1804, to enter the Prussian civil service. Restless travels occupied some of the intervals between these employments. At one point philosophy, at another point science, seemed to him the paramount concern of his life, and then again literature. By 1805 he had published his distinguished first play, *Die Familie Schoffenstein,* destroyed a second, *Robert Guiskard*—the reconstructed 524 opening lines of which are accounted one of his finest achievements, and composed some part of a third, the comedy called *The Broken Jug* (Der zerbrochene Krug). After satisfactory work as a civil servant

in Berlin, he was transferred to an office in Königsberg in May
of 1805, where, for twenty months he continued his duties in
apparent contentment. These same twenty months saw the creation of two admirable prose narratives, *The Marquise of O.*
(Die Marquise von O.) and *The Earthquake in Chile* (Das Erd-
beben in Chili), and the first work on the inimitable Novelle,
Michael Kohlhaas, as well as preliminary composition of the
long one-Act drama *Penthesilea* and the total composition of the
five-Act drama *Amphitryon.* Such a quantity of creative writing
is surprising under the circumstances, but the originality of the
ideas and the sureness of their execution are nothing less than
staggering.

At our remove of distance we need to recall how extraordinary
and how independent a choice Kleist made in dealing with
Molière's *Amphitryon,* which was begun as a translation and
then continued with such radical changes as to become a wholly
new drama. Molière's play was an established masterpiece of
the old, established political, social, and esthetic order. It represented one of the glories of that "Versailles culture" against
which the Romantiker were in full tilt of protest. August Wilhelm Schlegel, it is true, singled out the French work for special
praise, but Romantic doctrine recommended seeking inspiration
almost anywhere except in French literature of the era since
"Malherbe came." Kleist, however, followed or did not follow
German Romantic doctrine as he chose, and on two counts:
selecting a French classical model and selecting a subject from
Greco-Roman antiquity, he flew in the face of that doctrine.
Hence the need to point out that Kleist was *not* a German
Romanticist, especially in *Amphitryon,* but he was, of course,
a Romanticist in the broader international sense of the term.
With caution thus observed relative to the troublesome word
"Romantic," we define this German *Amphitryon* as Molière's
play infused with new Romantic content.

The subtitle reads: "a comedy after Molière" (ein Lustspiel
nach Molière). There is no doubt but that it was undertaken as
a straightforward translation from the French, the exquisite
"free verse" yielding place to the blank verse which Lessing,
Goethe, and Schiller had made the standard external form of
German high drama through the previous quarter-century. Kleist

made no attempt to collate different versions of the Amphitryon
story, but when his hero bends down his helmet crest as a sign
to distinguish himself from his rival (line 2125), there is the suggestion that Plautus' Latin comedy was familiar to the translator-
adapter. The junction of comic and serious elements in the new
work is likewise nearer to the Latin tragicomedy than to the
pure comedy of the French master.

Whether Kleist translated and then abandoned Molière's Prologue, is unknown. In any case, its gist could be reduced to a
mere six lines in Mercury's entrance-speech, perhaps because
audiences could be counted on to know it in a general way.
Minor changes were made, some purposefully, some apparently
at random, but collectively they alter the tone of the whole. Why
king Ptérélas became King Labdacus, it is hard to say, since the
names are metrically identical, except that Kleist knew that
other Theban story about Oedipus, grandson of Labdacus. From
Lessing's *Hamburgische Dramaturgie,* 55th article, with its discussion of tragicomedy and of Plautus' *Amphitruo,* must have
come the Hellenized form: Sosías, which we have brought back
to the usual Sósia in the present translation. The enemy capital
of Telebes, deduced by Rotrou from "the Teleboans" probably
for convenience of rhyme with Thebes and retained by Molière,
was supplanted by the no less imaginary Pharissa, without alter-
ing the fanciful geography. Bits of academic lore were introduced: in Homeric fashion Mercury, as a god, swears "by the
Styx" (line 101), but *Latin* phrases were put into the mouth of
Sosia (lines 81, 642)! The language used by Charis and her husband or supposed husband is earthier, deliberately, than in the
French: Charis does the washing and helps with the hay-making
(line 562), as Cleanthis did not. Yet Act I, free though it may be
as a translation, is still faithful, by and large, to Molière.

So is Act II, up to Molière's line 1198 (Scene IV of the French
scene divisions) and Kleist's line 1106. Then comes different
matter.

The French Jupiter had presented Alcmène with dead King
Ptérélas' five diamonds arranged in a cluster as an ornament of
dress; in Plautus the token was King Pterelaus' golden drinking
goblet. Kleist, applying one of those bits of academic lore, made
the object an authentic headband of Greek antiquity: a ribbon

which passed across the forehead, circled the head, tied in a bow behind, with the long streamer-ends left to fall forward over the shoulders and chest; this particular headband had an uncommonly large diamond attached to it, worn in the middle of King Ptérélas-Labdacus' forehead. Without detaching the jewel, Alcmena may wear the headband as a girdle, with the jewel at her waist, or perhaps from shoulder to hip as a baldric (lines 952–3 and 1392). In receiving the gift, she had noticed a monogram engraved in gold upon the diamond and had assumed, without careful inspection, that the engraved initial letter was an "A"—for "Amphitryon." At the point where the German text diverges from its French source, Alcmena comes in distress to discuss with Charis the frightening, just-discovered evidence that the monogram is not an "A" but a "J"—for "Jupiter." Thus the passive token itself is made to hover between illusion and reality like most of the events in the drama.

When Jupiter enters (line 1236) upon the ladies' troubled colloquy it is for a scene quite unlike the ideal husband's suit to the offended wife that we found in Molière. Before this Jupiter this Alcmena falls abjectly to her knees imploring a decision as to whether the jewel was or was not his and imploring death if it was not.

With subtle ambiguities Jupiter replies that no other *man* could have come to her, or, if so, it made no difference, since all who come to her take on Amphitryon's form in her eyes. This statement she takes to be her husband's benign excuse for her own improper conduct and she starts to leave in horror, but he restrains her, saying that if the comer were a *devil* out of hell her purity is still untainted and that the devil must now be suffering unspeakable torment of unrequited love. When she is not convinced by his sophistry, he passes gradually over into speech in first person as king of the gods, first with the phrase "Were I Zeus" (line 1314) as a qualifier, then (line 1333 ff.) with the outright statement: "By power innate in me," concluding with the assertion that it was the *god* who came to her last night. The "innate power" she accepts as a husband's innate power, but she is scandalized at "Amphitryon's" blasphemy. Jupiter declares that he desires to ascend among the gods even if she does not; moreover he wants heroic sons. Alcmena counters this "divine hypothesis" by saying it could not have been Jupiter last night, else she would now be dead from contact with divinity. Whereat Jupiter rebukes her for presuming to know the godhead's will; as a reverent "man," *he* will not be so presumptuous. Again she concludes that her husband is making generous but extravagant excuse for her fault. Then he claims that Zeus did come, but, since even Zeus assumed Amphitryon's form—as King of the Gods he was surely not obligated to do so—the deception was a supreme tribute to her husband. The supreme compliment to her husband momentarily reassures Alcmena.

No sooner is she calmed than Jupiter deliberately proposes a new cause for agitation, for in this "temptation scene" there is used refined psychological cruelty to probe the most secret recesses of conscience. What, he asks, if Zeus practiced this deceit only because she had neglected him even in her prayers, worshiping her husband when she should have been adoring the god? Alcmena denies such idolatrous neglect, but Jupiter reminds her that she discerned the letter "A" even in the configuration of the god's forked lightning. "How do you know that?!" she cries in startled anguish. He ignores her question, insisting that she conceives even of godhead in the shape of her husband. To which she retorts with an argument older than Christianity, that a worshiper needs a statue or painting, an image, on which to concentrate attention during prayer. Jupiter returns to the assertion that Zeus's coming to her was a punishment for her neglect of him even in prayer. Still, Zeus will be lenient if, in the future, she will concentrate on him alone while at her prayers—and specifically rehearse each detail of the love night. And if her husband distracts her while she is at her prayers, she must ask him to leave her for an hour to herself. She promises such solitary prayer for the first hour of every morning, and once again she is calm.

Again Jupiter presses new agitating questions. What, he asks, if Jupiter came to her right now? If he did, Alcmena would know ecstasy beyond anything her mortal husband ever inspired. The troubled lady answers by saying that, if only she could live this last day backwards, she would forgo even the one vision of the god that she has had. In exasperation Jupiter curses the "illusion"—that is the illusion of being loved for himself—that brought him down from the skies in the first place. Perceiving that her "husband" is upset, she cries out, "Have I hurt you?" Jupiter, following his own train of thought, confesses celestial loneliness and celestial ardor and inquires whether she would even now—"if chosen by fate to pay the gratitude of many millions"—commit celestial adultery to the extent of a single smile in order to rejoice the loneliness of the god. Humbly she replies, "May my creator rule and govern me!" He forces the issue: *Would* she? And humbly she replies that she would do so in a divided way, she would give all her reverence to the god and all her love to her husband.

Urgently he proposes: "What if I *were* the god?"—and adds: "to you." Terror-stricken anew, she begs him to declare categorically whether he is Amphitryon or Jupiter in disguise as Amphitryon. To which he answers, "I am Amphitryon—to you," and returns to his urgent question, "What if I were this god— to you: what would you do?" Humbly Alcmena says she would follow him even unto death. "Yes," says Jupiter, "you would follow me *if* Amphitryon were not standing by; but what if he stepped in just as Jupiter was holding you in his arms?"—"If that were to happen," she replies,

". . . . . . I would then be sad, and I would wish
That he were then the god, and that you would
Remain Amphitryon, as you surely are."

Marvelling at her fidelity to her husband in even that ultimate test, Jupiter terms her the nearest to perfection of all creatures he has created with his hands "in many eons." Aghast at his speaking like the Creator Himself, she cries protestingly, "Amphitryon!" And he with rapture starts to leave her, promising to reveal the total truth

". . . . before the starry hosts have danced
Their way across the silent fields of night."

With his bidding Sosia to summon to a feast "All guests that you find anywhere in camp," we return to Molière's scenario.

Kleist, who was fond of interrogation scenes, here outdid himself in subtleties by interweaving Christian theological concepts into the basic pattern of classical mythology. What we have arranged as the first paragraph in the above summary is already difficult, but the subsequent paragraphs offer greater difficulties still. An audience must realize that this Jupiter sees our most secret thoughts as classical divinities did not, even to the degree of knowing Alcmena's secret perception of the forked lightning as a great capital letter "A." The Commandment against graven images underlies his charge of her outward conformity while actually adoring the "idol" of Amphitryon in her heart. In our third paragraph Alcmena is challenged with the *choice* of union with the godhead, as subtly testing a proposal as any Satan ever made to Jesus in the desert. The Virgin Mary, who was also selected "by fate" from among many millions, was offered no such choice by the Archangel Gabriel; it was the Son of God who *chose* to become flesh. Yet Alcmena's humble responses on this occasion seem to echo those made by Mary to the Annunciation—as Kleist's friend Adam Müller, who arranged for the publication of this play, publicly maintained in the summer of 1807 that they did, though critics have not all agreed. The god's enunciation of cosmic loneliness, on the other hand, is neither classical nor truly Christian, but rather is voiced in terms of Romantic Pantheism, and the speaker anticipates such Romantic figures as Byron's heroes, Vigny's Moses, and Lermontov's Demon.

An audience may be counted on to relish the lover's stratagems and the utter purity of the lady, and they will not fail to see that even the King of the Gods must take on the form of her husband in order to come near her. Nor will they miss the point that here is a Romantic apotheosis of the constant wife—quite possibly the bachelor author's ideal. In this sense the scene is wholly stageworthy. But to follow the ultra-subtle arguments in detail is another matter, requiring reflective thought, and here we must concur in the frequent judgment of the work as "closet drama" —not in the meaning of unplayable fantasy but in the meaning of intellectual weight.

As Act II concludes with a Sosia-Charis interchange parallel to Molière's but more rudely farcical, we perceive that Kleist intended a "stretching" of his model's noble characters upward, so to speak, and of his model's lower characters downward, in deliberate Romantic disharmony as opposed to Neo-classical harmony. Goethe with distaste noted the classical Sosia juxtaposed with a "modern" Jupiter, just as he condemned the play for its willful "confusion of emotion."

We may feel free to disagree with Goethe, yet, coming to Act III, which returns to a discreetly free paraphrase of Molière, we may honestly ask whether the subject matter is now possible after what we have just been through. There is a disparity of artistic matter and artistic manner that puts the total work out of focus. Moreover, a Shakespearean quality intrudes upon this last Act. Not only does Kleist have one "Commander" too many, but he clearly intended a stage crowd for the finale of his play. In the last pages Amphitryon is put through a spiritual ordeal exceeding anything envisaged by Molière, until he matches his wife's devotion by denying his very identity in order to justify her preference for Jupiter over him. At that sign of his total submission, this Jehovah-Jupiter finds him worthy of such a wife and rewards his humility by declaring the truth. There has been a very Christian trial of proud hearts here. And yet, for all his filial surrender to this father-god, Amphitryon sturdily asks for sons "great like the sons of Tyndarus"—Tyndarus being that other by-passed husband, and heaven-achieving Hercules is vouchsafed to him. The "machines" of 1668, whatever they may have been, are now replaced by operatic stage illusion as the clouds part behind Jupiter and reveal "the summit of Olympus where the Olympians are assembled." Wagner admired this work and we here discern the future Rainbow Bridge spanning to the golden ramparts of Valhalla at the end of *Das Rheingold*.

Alcmena, meanwhile, has collapsed beneath the blow of her manifest error and lies unconscious amid the divine leave-taking. She has conceived of her husband as a god to the point where the divine impersonator had seemed to her more like her husband than her husband himself; she had

> ". . needed the bright splendor of the sunlight
> To tell the venal body of a lout (Amphitryon)
> From the high glory of these regal limbs, (Jupiter)
> To tell the bullock from the royal stag!"

Under her revealed blasphemy she fainted. Amphitryon in the last line of the text calls to her, and the final syllable of the text is her answering "Ah!" Depending on the inflection of that syllable and its accompanying gesture, an actress can turn this

entire work at the very last second into a shattering tragedy or
into a conciliatory comedy. Surely the author intended the latter.
Romantic tension has held the illusion to the moment of the
quickly falling curtain, the exact opposite of Molière's procedure.

Kleist's *Amphitryon* is a problematic work. It is easy to see
why no performance worthy of the name was attempted until
1902 at the Vienna Burgtheater and why its stage history has
been a brief chronicle. It is artistically an imperfect jointure of
disparates; one is almost tempted to say a Romantic experiment
that nobly failed. It is also an intellectual and emotional tour
de force, unique, gripping, and even dazzling, never to be forgotten by the heart and mind that have once explored it.

AMPHITRYON

A Comedy after Molière

by

HEINRICH VON KLEIST

translated by

CHARLES E. PASSAGE

JUPITER, in the form of Amphitryon
MERCURY, in the form of Sosia
AMPHITRYON, Commander-in-chief of the Thebans
SOSIA, his servant
ALCMENA, wife of Amphitryon
CHARIS, wife of Sosia
Army Officers

Time: An indeterminate but remote period of Greek history.
Place: Before the entrance to Amphitryon's palace in Thebes.

Act I

It is night. Enter Sosia with a lantern.

SOSIA: Hey! Who's that sneaking by there? Ho!—If day
    Would break, I wouldn't mind; the night is . . . What?
    I'm friendly, gentlemen! We share one road. . . .
    You've come across the truest fellow, by
    My faith, the sun has ever shone upon—
    Or rather I should say right now: the moon. . . .
    They're either rascals, arrant coward knaves
    That haven't got the stomach to attack me,
    Or else the wind was rustling through the leaves.
    Each sound is shrieking noise here in these hills.—   10
    Go easy! Take it slow!—But if I don't
    Soon bump my head against the gate of Thebes,
    I'll travel down into the dark of Orcus.
    Oh! Devil take it! Testing me to see
    If I have courage, if I'm a man of spirit,
    My master could have tried a different way.
    Fame crowns him, so the whole world says, and honor,
    But sending me out in the dead of night
    Was what I'd call a pretty low-down trick.
    A bit of feeling, love of fellow-man,   20
    Would suit me better than the wedge of virtues
    He drives to split the ranks of enemies.
    "Sosia," said he, "bestir yourself, my servant;
    You shall proclaim my victory in Thebes
    And make announcement to my tender lady
    Of my arrival, which will follow soon."
    But if that couldn't wait until tomorrow
    I'll be a horse—a saddled horse at that!
    But look! There stands, I do believe, our house!
    Hurrah! You're at your destination, Sosia,   30
    And to all enemies shall be forgiveness.
    Now, friend, you must be thinking of your errand.
    You will be solemnly brought to the princess,

Alcmena, and to her you then will owe
A full report composed with rhetoric
Of the engagement that Amphitryon
Has fought to victory for the fatherland.
—But how the devil can I do that when
I wasn't present? Damn! I do wish I
Had peeped out of the tent from time to time   40
While both the armies were in combat there.
Oh, well! I'll talk away of hacks and thrusts
And won't come off one bit worse than some others
Who never heard a whizzing arrow either.
It wouldn't hurt, though, to rehearse the part.
A good idea, Sosia! Try it out.
Let this spot be the audience hall, and let
This lantern be Alcmena waiting on her throne.
            (He sets the lantern on the ground.)
Serenest Highness! From Amphitryon,
My gracious master and your noble spouse,   50
I come to bring you joyous tidings of
His triumph over the Athenians.
—(A good beginning!)—*"Truly, dearest Sosia,
I cannot moderate my joy, now that
I see you once again."*—Most excellent lady,
Your kindness shames me, though it surely would
Cause any other man to swell with pride.
—(See! That's not too bad either!)—*"And the dearly
Beloved of my soul, Amhpitryon,
How is he?*—Gracious lady, I'll be brief: 60
Like any man of spirit on the field of glory!
—(O clever fellow!)—*"When will he be coming?"*
No later than his duties will allow,
Though not so soon as he perhaps might like.
—(Damnation take me!)—*"Was there nothing else
He bade you tell me, Sosia?*—He says little,
Does much, and all earth trembles when his name is heard.
—(By damn! Where am I getting all this wit?)
"They're in retreat, you say, the Athenians?"
—They are; and Labdacus is dead, their leader;   70
Pharissa's fallen; and wherever there

Are hills, they echo with our shout of triumph.—
"O dearest Sosia, you must tell me all
About it to the very last detail."
—My gracious lady, I am at your service.
About this victory I can, I flatter
Myself, provide you with a full report.
Imagine, then, if you will be so kind,
Pharissa standing over on this side—

       (He indicates the places on his hand.)

That is a city, you must realize,   80
In area as large as, *praeter propter,*
With no exaggeration, if not larger,
Than Thebes. Here runs the river. Our men are
In battle order here upon a hill;
And thronging in the valley are the foe.
And now when they have offered up their vows to heaven
So that the region of the clouds resounded,
And all appropriate orders being issued,
They pour forth toward us like the streams in flood.
But we, no whit less brave than they, showed them   90
The road for home—and you shall see just how.
First they came up against our vanguard here;
It broke. Then they came up against our archers there;
They yielded ground. Emboldened now, they moved against
The body of our slingers; these ceded them the field.
Now as they recklessly approached our main contingent,
The latter plunged—Wait! Something's wrong with that.
I think I hear a noise from over there.

      (Mercury, in Sosia's form, steps out of
        Amphitryon's house.)

MERCURY *(aside):* If I don't get that uninvited rascal
Out there away from this house pretty soon,   100
Then, by the Styx, endangered stands the pleasure
Of the embraces in Alcmena's arms
For which Zeus the Olympian today
Took on Amphitryon's form and came to earth.
SOSIA *(without seeing Mercury):*
I guess it's nothing, and my fear is gone.
But just in order to avoid adventures,

I think I'll now complete the journey home
And there acquit myself of my commission.
MERCURY *(aside):* You'll have to outwit me, my friend, or else
    I'll find some method of preventing that.   110
SOSIA: But this night surely is of endless length.
    If I have not been five hours on the road,
    Five hours by the sundial there in Thebes,
    I'll shoot that sundial piecemeal off the tower.
    Either my master, in the drunkenness
    Of victory, mistook the evening for the morning,
    Or else the wanton Phoebus slumbers on
    From last night's too deep gazing into bottles.
MERCURY: The disrespect with which that rascal there
    Speaks of the gods! But have a little patience: 120
    This arm will soon be teaching him respect.
SOSIA *(catching sight of Mercury):*
    Oh! By the gods of night, now I am lost!
    Around the house there stalks a prowling thief
    That soon or late I'll see upon the gallows.
    —I must be bold about it, self-assured.
                (He whistles.)
MERCURY *(aloud):* Who might that lout be over there, that takes
    The liberty, as if he were at home,
    Of dinning in my ears with whistling now?
    Is my stick maybe meant to dance the tune?
SOSIA: He doesn't seem to be a friend to music.   130
MERCURY: It is a week now since I've found a man
    Whose bones I've had a chance of smashing up.
    My arm is getting stiff, I feel, from resting,
    And some back just about the breadth of yours
    Is what I'm looking for to get in practice.
SOSIA: Now who the devil sired that fellow yonder?
    I feel a deathly pallor seizing me
    That stops the breath inside of me.
    If hell itself had spewed him up,
    The sight of him could not so rob me of my wits.   140
    —But maybe this clown feels the way I feel
    And he's just trying out the role of fire-eater
    To scare the living daylights out of me.

Hold on, lout! I can do that too. What's more,
I'm here alone; so's he; I've got two fists;
He's got the same; and if good luck's against me,
I've got a sure retreat right there. So: forward!

(Mercury blocks his way.)

MERCURY: Halt there! Who goes there?

SOSIA: Me.

MERCURY: What kind of me?

SOSIA: My own, so please you. And I think my me
   Goes toll-free like another. Courage, Sosia!   150

MERCURY: Halt! You won't get away so easily.
   What kind of standing have you?

SOSIA: Kind of standing?
   Why, I stand on two feet, as you can see.

MERCURY: I mean, are you a master or a servant?

SOSIA: That all depends on how you look at me.
   I may be master or I may be man.

MERCURY: Good. I don't like you.

SOSIA: Well, now, that's too bad.

MERCURY: In one word, traitor, I am asking you,
   You good-for-nothing street-and-corner-lounger,
   Who you may be, where you are coming from   160
   And going to, and why you're loitering here?

SOSIA: To all these questions I can give no answer
   But this: I am a man, I come from that way,
   I'm going this way, and I have before me
   Something that is beginning to annoy me.

MERCURY: I see that you are witty, and that you
   Are of a mind to shrug me off. But still
   I feel a hankering to prolong acquaintance.
   And so, to start off our involvement, I
   Now lift this hand of mine to box your ears.   170

SOSIA: Who? Me?

MERCURY: Yes, you. And now you know for sure.
   Now what conclusion do you draw?

SOSIA: Damnation!
   You deal a mighty blow there, my good man.

MERCURY: A blow of medium-gauge. Sometimes I hit
   Still harder.

SOSIA: If I were in the same mood,
  We could start in and have a lovely fight.
MERCURY: I'd like that. I enjoy that sort of thing.
SOSIA: But business forces me to take my leave.
                    (He starts to go.
                    Mercury blocks his way.)
MERCURY: Where?
SOSIA: What the devil's that to you?
MERCURY: I want to know.
  Where are you off to?
SOSIA: Through that gate there, which   180
  I'm going to have them open. Let me pass.
MERCURY: If you are impudent enough to go
  Up to that castle gate there, on your head
  A tempest and a storm of blows will pour.
SOSIA: What? I am not to enter my own house?
MERCURY: Your house? Say that again.
SOSIA: Why, yes: my house.
MERCURY: You mean to say that you are of this household?
SOSIA: Why not? Is it Amphitryon's house or not?
MERCURY: Is this Amphitryon's house? Of course it is,
  You dolt. Of course this is Amphitryon's house,   190
  The mansion of the Captain of the Thebans.
  So what do you conclude?
SOSIA: What I conclude
  Is that I'm going in. I am his servant.
MERCURY: His serv . . .
SOSIA: His servant.
MERCURY: You?
SOSIA: Yes, me.
MERCURY: Amphitryon's
                                               [servant?
SOSIA: Amphitryon's servant, the Theban Captain's servant.
MERCURY: Your name is . . . ?
SOSIA: Sosia.
MERCURY: Sos . . .
SOSIA: My name is Sosia.
MERCURY: Listen, I'm going to smash your every bone.
SOSIA: What? Are you crazy?

MERCURY: Who gave you the right,
  You shameless wretch, of taking Sosia's name?

SOSIA: I didn't take it, it was given to me.   200
  My father can account to you for it.

MERCURY: Who ever heard of impudence like this?
  You dare to tell me, rascal, to my face
  That you are Sosia?

SOSIA: Yes, of course I do.
  And on the very best of grounds: because
  The great gods will it so; because it is
  Not in my power to contend against them
  And claim to be some other than I am;
  Because I must be me, Amphitryon's servant,
  Though I might ten times rather be Amphitryon   210
  Himself, his cousin, or his brother-in-law.

MERCURY: Just wait! I'll try to change you into something.

SOSIA: Help, citizens! Help, Thebans! Murder! Thieves!

MERCURY: What, good-for-nothing, you cry out yet?

SOSIA: What?
  You beat me, and I'm not supposed to shout?

MERCURY: Don't you know it is night-time, sleeping-time,
  And that inside this castle here Alcmena,
  Amphitryon's spouse, is sleeping?

SOSIA: Devil take you now!
  I have to come off worst because you see
  I have no stick at hand the way you do.   220
  But dealing blows without sustaining any,
  That's no heroic act. I'm telling you:
  It's wrong to flaunt your courage against people
  Who are compelled by Fate to hide their own.

MERCURY: So, to the point: who are you?

SOSIA (aside):   If I do
  Escape this man, I'll offer half a bottle
  Of wine and pour it out upon the ground.

MERCURY: Are you still Sosia?

SOSIA: Oh, please let me go.
  Your stick will make me cease to be at all,
  But not cease to be me, because I am.   230
  The only difference is that I now feel

That I'm the Sosia who has had a beating.
MERCURY: Look here, you cur, I'm going to knock you cold.
                    (He threatens him.)
SOSIA: Stop your molesting me!
MERCURY: No, I won't stop
    Until you stop . . .
SOSIA: All right, then I will stop.
    Not one word will I say. You shall be right,
    Whatever you propose, I'll say "Yes!" to it.
MERCURY: Are you still Sosia now, you traitor?
SOSIA: Ah!
    I'm what you say I am. Command what I
    Must do; your stick makes you the master of my life.   240
MERCURY: You did say Sosia used to be the name you had?
SOSIA: It's true that up until the present moment I
    Believed that that was how the matter stood.
    But stress has now convinced me of your reasons,
    And now I see that I was in the wrong.
MERCURY: I am the one whose name is Sosia.
SOSIA: Sosia. . . . ?
    You?
MERCURY: Sosia, yes. And anyone who adds
    A gloss to that should watch out for this stick.
SOSIA (aside): O ye eternal gods up there! Must I
    Renounce my very self now, let myself   250
    Be robbed of my own name by an impostor?
MERCURY: You're muttering between your teeth, I hear?
SOSIA: Oh, nothing that has much to do with you.
    But I implore you though, by all the gods
    In Greece that hold sway over you and me,
    Allow me for a single moment's time
    To speak with you in frank and open discourse.
MERCURY: Speak.
SOSIA: But your stick will play a silent role?
    Not take part in the conversation? Promise
    Me now that we shall make a truce.
MERCURY: So be it.   260
    This point I will allow.
SOSIA: Well, tell me then:

How did you ever get this unheard-of
Idea: making off thus with my name?
Now, if it were my cloak, or if it were
My supper . . . But my name! Why, can you wear it?
Or can you eat it? Drink it? Mortgage it?
How can this act of thievery profit you?
MERCURY: What! You—presume—
SOSIA: Now stop, now stop, I say!
We did conclude a truce.
MERCURY: What impudence!
You good-for-nothing!
SOSIA: There I won't protest.   270
Abuse I can put up with. Bargaining
Can still go on.
MERCURY: You say your name is Sosia?
SOSIA: Yes, I admit, an unconfirmed
Report did reach my ears. . . .
MERCURY: Enough. The truce
Is off, and here I take the floor again.
SOSIA: To hell with you! I can't annihilate
Myself, transform myself, slough off my skin
And hang my skin around your shoulders. Since
The world began, was there the likes of this?
Can I be dreaming? Did I overdo   280
My morning dram of fortifying tonic?
Or can it be that I'm not fully conscious?
And did Amphitryon not send me here
To bring the princess news of his return?
Am I not charged with telling her how he
Gained victory and how Pharissa fell?
And didn't I just recently arrive?
Do I not hold this lantern? Did I not
Find you hanging around here by this gate,
And when I started to come near this entrance   290
Did you not take your stick and thrash my back
Inhumanly till it was black and blue,
Maintaining to my face it was not I
But rather you who was Amphitryon's servant?
All this, I feel, alas! is but too true;

Would that the gods had rather deigned to have me mad!
MERCURY: Look, dolt! My anger will come pouring down
   On you again like hail at any moment.
   All you have just been saying, point for point,
   Applies to me—except, of course, the beating.   300
SOSIA: To you?—Now by the gods, this lantern here
   Is witness . . .
MERCURY: That's a lie, I say, you traitor.
   I was the one Amphitryon sent here.
   And yesterday the Captain of the Thebans,
   When covered with the dust of battle still
   He left Mars' shrine where he had sacrificed,
   Charged me to tell his victory in Thebes
   And how the foe's commander, Labdacus,
   Had perished at his hands in the engagement;
   Because, I tell you, I am Sosia,   310
   His servant, son of doughty shepherd Davus,
   Born here, and brother to that Harpagon
   Who died abroad, and husband of that Charis
   Who drives me frantic with her moods and whims;
   The Sosia who was recently in jail
   And who got fifty counted on his rear
   For having carried honesty too far.
SOSIA (aside): He's right! And short of being Sosia
   Himself, there's no one who could be aware
   Of all the things he seems to know about.   320
   You can't help but believe in him a bit.
   Besides, now that I look him in the eye,
   He has my shape and size, he has my bearing,
   And my own rascally expression too.
   —I'll put a couple of good questions to him
   To get this matter straight. (aloud) About the booty
   That was discovered in the enemy camp,
   Will you tell me what was Amphitryon's
   Intention and what share of it was his?
MERCURY: His share was Labdacus's jeweled head-band
   Which was discovered in that monarch's tent.
SOSIA: And what was done then to that jeweled head-band?   330
MERCURY: Amphitryon's monogram was then engraved

In gleaming strokes upon its golden brow.
SOSIA: Presumably he wears it now himself?
MERCURY: It's destined for Alcmena. She will wear
Its jewel at her breast in memory of
The victory.
SOSIA: And from the camp this gift
Will be sent to her . . . ?
MERCURY: In a golden casket
On which Amphitryon's coat of arms is stamped. 340
SOSIA *(aside):* Why, he knows all about it.—Thunderation!
I really now begin to doubt myself.
By impudence he was already Sosia,
And by his stick; and now—that's all I need—
He's getting to be so by valid reasons.
Yet when I pinch myself I still would swear
This body's Sosia's body yet.
—How will I get out of this labyrinth?
The things I did when I was all alone,
The things that no one saw, no one can know, 350
Unless *he*'s really me, as well as *I* am.
—Good! Here's a question that will shed some light.
Why not? We'll see now if this catches him.
(aloud)
When both the armies there were locked in combat,
What were you doing in among the tents,
I ask you, where you hid so cleverly?
MERCURY: There was a ham—
SOSIA *(aside):* Can this man be possessed?
MERCURY: —that I found in a corner of the tent;
I sliced myself a juicy center cut,
And then I neatly broached a case of bottles 360
To get a bit of cheer and spirit for
The battle that was being fought outside.
SOSIA *(aside):* I'm done for now. It would make no difference
If earth were to engulf me on the spot,
For no one drinks out of a bottle-case
Unless he accidentally found the key
That fits it, in the sack, the way I did.
(aloud)

I see, old friend, quite clearly now that you
Embody all the share of Sosia that
Could ever be of use upon this earth.   370
Beyond this I find all superfluous.
And far be it from me to importune;
I gladly yield precedence to you. But do have
The kindness, if you please, to make it clear,
As long as I'm not Sosia, *who* I am.
Because, you will admit, I must be *something*.
MERCURY: When I get through with being Sosia, you
Have my permission to be he; I grant this.
But just as long as I am he, you risk
Your neck by taking up that shameless notion.   380
SOSIA: All right, all right. My head begins to swim.
I see now, by my soul, how matters stand,
Though I can't say I fully understand it.
But somehow this thing must come to an end.
The wisest thing, to bring it to conclusion,
Would be for me to go my way.—Farewell.
                    (He starts toward the house. Mercury
                         thrusts him back.)
MERCURY: What's this, you gallows-bird! Must I be forced
To smash your every bone?
                    (He beats him.)
SOSIA: Just gods above!
Where is you care of me? My back won't heal
In weeks, not even if Amphitryon   390
Withholds *his* stick. All right! I'll just get out
Of this fiend's way and go back down to camp
For all this hellish night may blackly stare.
Some glorious embassy I've made of it!
But what reception will your master give you, Sosia?
                    (Exit.)
MERCURY: Well, finally! Couldn't you have scampered sooner?
You might have spared yourself some nasty blows.
This clown has no idea of the honor
Of having had a thrashing from a god;
I hit him like the best of jailers, too.   400
But that's no matter. He has sinned enough

And merits beating—maybe not today,
But if not, then he's part-paid in advance.
I only hope the rascal with his yelling
As if he had been skewered for the grill
Did not wake up the lovers!—But, as I live!
Here comes Zeus now, the father of the gods,
And tenderly Alcmena gives him escort
As if he were her dear Amphitryon.

(Enter Jupiter in Amphitryon's shape,
accompanied by Alcmena and Charis. Torches.)

JUPITER: Command the torches, dear Alcmena, to   410
Withdraw. They cast a radiance, to be sure,
Upon the loveliest charm that blooms on earth
And no Olympian has seen one more fair.
And yet—how shall I say it? They betray
Him who was lured here by that charm, beloved,
And it had best remain our little secret
That your Amphitryon has been in Thebes.
They have been stolen from the war, these moments
That I have spent in sacrifice to love;
The world might misconstrue this act of theft,   420
And I would gladly do without all other
Witness than the one who thanks me for it.

ALCMENA: Amphitryon! Oh, must you go? Oh, what
A burden so much glory is, my dearest!
How gladly would I change the head-band
That you have won, for a bouquet of violets
That had been gathered by a lowly cottage.
What do we need besides ourselves? Why must
So many alien things be forced upon you,
A crown and the commanding general's staff,   430
For, when the people cheer you and their rapture
Expends itself in every glorious name,
The thought is very sweet that you belong to me;
But can that fleeting charm make up for what
I feel whenever in the thick of combat
An arrow is aimed at this cherished breast?
How empty is this house when you are gone!
How dull without you is the merry dance

Of hours that should escort me up the day!
Ah! What the country robs me of, I did   440
Not feel, Amphitryon, until today
When I possessed you for two rapid hours.
JUPITER: How you delight me, my beloved! But
    You do cause me concern on one count, which,
    As trivial as it is, I still must mention.
    You know there is a law of marriage, and
    A duty, and that anyone denied
    In love can yet before a judge demand it.
    This law upsets my fairest happiness.
    To *you,* my dearest, to your heart, I long   450
    To owe all favors, and I would not like
    Compliance with a mere formality,
    Which you may look on as an obligation.
    How soon you could dispel this trifling doubt!
    Disclose your inmost heart and tell me whether
    It was your legal spouse whom you received
    Today or whether it was your beloved.
ALCMENA: My spouse and my beloved! What are you saying?
    Is it not that most sacred bond alone
    That justifies receiving you at all?   460
    How can a social law distress you so,
    Which, far from operating for restriction,
    Most fortunately rather opens wide
    All barriers opposed to bold desires?
JUPITER: Alcmena dearest, what I feel for you
    Outsoars, you see, as far as to the sun,
    What any husband owes you. Disaccustom
    Yourself, beloved, to your spouse,
    Make a distinction between me and him.
    It pains me so, this odious confusion;   470
    I find the thought intolerable that you
    Have merely granted access to a puppy
    That coldly fancies he has rights on you.
    My own desire, my sweetest light,
    Is to have seemed a being quite unique,
    Your conqueror because the mighty gods
    Taught me the art of conquest over you.

But why drag in the vain Commander of
The Thebans who for his exalted house
Wooed recently and won a wealthy princess?   480
What do you say? I would so like to leave
Your virtue all to him, that public coxcomb,
And keep your love entirely for myself.
ALCMENA: Amphitryon! You jest. If the people here
Should hear you thus revile Amphitryon,
They could not help but think you someone else,
I don't know whom. It was not I who dropped
Remarks this cheerful night about distinctions
That can be made between husband and lover.
But since the gods conjoined one and the other   490
In you for my sake, I forgive the latter
For any wrong the former may have done.
JUPITER: Then promise me that this glad festival
That we have celebrated in reunion
Shall never fade out of your memory,
And that the godlike day that we have spent,
My best beloved, shall not be confused
With humdrum days of further married life.
O promise me that you will think of me
When once Amphitryon returns from war . . .   500
ALCMENA: Why, surely. What else should I say?
JUPITER: O thank you!
It has more sense and meaning than you think.
Farewell. My duty calls me.
ALCMENA: Must you go?
And not, beloved, finish this brief night
With me as it flees on ten thousand pinions?
JUPITER: Have you found this night shorter than the others?
ALCMENA: Ah!
JUPITER: But, sweet child, Aurora could not do
More for our happiness than she has done.
Farewell. I shall see to it that the others
Shall last no longer than the earth requires.   510
ALCMENA: He's drunk, I do believe. And so am I.
                         (Exeunt.)
CHARIS (aside): I call that tenderness! And loyalty!

A pretty festival, when married people
Meet once again after long separation!
But that oaf over there who's wed to me—
A log would have the tenderness that he has.
MERCURY *(aside):* Now I must hurry and remind Dame Night
So that the universe does not become disordered.
That good match-making goddess now has tarried
For more than seventeen hours over Thebes.   520
She may proceed now in her way and cast
Her veil upon still other fine adventures.
CHARIS *(aloud):* See that unfeeling creature! Off he goes.
MERCURY: Well, mustn't I go with Amphitryon?
If he is going to bed, should I not also
Go and stretch out upon my bear-skin too?
CHARIS: You could say something.
MERCURY: Time enough for that.
What you were asking, you already know,
And that's enough. On that score I'm laconic.
CHARIS: You're just a blockhead. You should say: "Dear wife,   530
Be fond of me, don't cry," and other things.
MERCURY: Now, what the devil's getting into you?
Should I spend time here making faces for you?
Eleven married years kill conversation,
And it's a dog's age since I was talked out.
CHARIS: Look at Amphitryon, you traitor, how
He can be tender, like the simplest people,
And stand in shame that in submission to
His wife and in his matrimonial love
A lord in the great world surpasses you.   540
MERCURY: Why, child, he still is on his honeymoon.
There is an age at which all things are charming.
What's right for that young couple, I would want
To watch from far away, if we should do it.
But two old donkeys like ourselves would look
Quite silly tossing sweet nothings around.
CHARIS: Unfeeling boor! What kind of talk is that?
Am I no longer able . . . ?
MERCURY: I didn't say that.
Your obvious decline can be ignored,

And when it's dark, you look quite grey. But out   550
Here in the open it would cause a riot
If I should start to fool around with you.
CHARIS: Did I not go and wash as soon as you
    Arrived? Did I not comb my hair, you traitor?
    And did I not put on fresh change of clothes?
    And all for nothing but to be abused?
MERCURY: What is the use of changing clothes? If you
    Could doff the garb bestowed on you by Nature,
    I'd find your dirty apron good enough.
CHARIS: When you were courting me you seemed to like it.   560
    I should have put it on while in the kitchen,
    While washing, and while helping with the hay.
    Can I help things if time has left its mark?
MERCURY: No, dearest wife. But I can't mend them either.
CHARIS: You rascal, you just don't deserve a wife
    Of upright character and conduct such as mine.
MERCURY: I wish you were a trifle less the wife
    Of character and didn't wear my ears
    Out with your everlasting bickering.
CHARIS: Oho! So you mislike my having always   570
    Maintained my honor and my good repute?
MERCURY: Heaven forfend I should! Maintain your virtue,
    But just don't drive it jingling through the streets
    And to the market like a horse with sleighbells.
CHARIS: You ought to have a wife, the kind they have
    In Thebes: deceitful, full of sly intrigue,
    A wife who'd drown you in her honeyed words
    To make you swallow your own cuckolding.
MERCURY: As far as that's concerned, I'll tell you frankly:
    Imagined evils torment none but fools.   580
    And I feel sorry for the man whose friend
    Advances his connubial pay: that man
    Grows old and lives up all his children's lives.[1]
CHARIS: Are you so shameless as to egg me on?
    So impudent as to incite me outright

---

[1] The "friend's" advance spares him the expenditure of vital strength in begetting his own children.

To take up with the friendly Theban who
Lurks in the evenings on my every path?
MERCURY: The devil take me, yes! Provided only
That you will spare me the reports of it.
Complaisant sin, I find, is worth as much   590
As tedious virtue; and my motto is:
Not so much honor and more peace in Thebes.
Farewell, now, Charis darling. I must go.
Amphitryon must be in camp by now.
                (Exit.)
CHARIS: Oh, why must I lack the determination
To punish this contemptible poltroon
By clear and overt action, O ye gods!
How I regret the fact now that the world
Takes me as being such an upright woman!   599

Act II

It is daylight. Amphitryon. Sosia.

AMPHITRYON: Answer me, you thieving vagabond,   600
   You cursed clown! Do you know, good-for-nothing,
   Your chatter's going to bring you to the gallows?
   And that to deal with you as you deserve
   My anger needs no more than a good stick?
SOSIA: If that's the way you take it, I'll keep still.
   Command—and I was dreaming, or I'm drunk.
AMPHITRYON: To palm off such a fairy tale on me!
   The kind of stories that our nurses murmur
   Into the ears of children in the evening.—
   Do you imagine I'll believe such nonsense?   610
SOSIA: O never! You're the master, I'm the servant,
   And you will do or not do, as you choose.
AMPHITRYON: So be it. I shall now repress my wrath,
   Constrain myself to patience, and once more
   Hear the entire occurrence told anew.
   —I must unsnarl this devil's riddle and
   I won't set foot in that house till I do.
   —Now gather all your wits together once
   And answer me on each and every point.
SOSIA: But, Sir, from fear—forgive me—of offending,   620
   If I request before we start this topic
   That you should set the tone of the discussion:
   Am I to speak from my sincere convictions,
   —An honest fellow, you may be assured—
   Or talk with you the way they do at court?
   Should I come straight out with the truth, or should I
   Comport myself like one of proper breeding?
AMPHITRYON: No nonsense now. What I require of you
   Is a report with nothing kept from me.
SOSIA: Good. Let me do that now. You shall be served.   630
   All you need do is toss the questions at me.
AMPHITRYON: With orders that I issued you . . .
SOSIA: I went

Through an infernal darkness, as if day
Had been submerged ten thousand fathoms deep,
Consigning to all devils you, the errand,
The road to Thebes, and the whole royal palace.

AMPHITRYON:
What's that you're saying, knave?

SOSIA: Sir, that's the truth.

AMPHITRYON: Good. Further. As you made your way along . . .

SOSIA: I steadily put one foot down ahead of
The other, and I left my tracks behind me.   640

AMPHITRYON: I'm asking whether anything occurred!

SOSIA: No, nothing, Sir, except that *salva venia*
I did have fright and terror in my soul.

AMPHITRYON: And on arrival here . . . ?

SOSIA: I did a bit
Of practice on the speech I had to make
And wittily pretended that the lantern
Would represent for me your spouse the princess.

AMPHITRYON: That being done . . . ?

SOSIA: I was disturbed. It came.

AMPHITRYON:
Disturbed? By what? Who then disturbed you?

SOSIA: Sosia.

AMPHITRYON:
What do you mean by that?

SOSIA: What do I mean by that?   650
My goodness! There you're asking me too much.
While practicing, I was disturbed by Sosia.

AMPHITRYON: By Sosia! What Sosia? What sort
Of gallows-bird or lout then of a Sosia,
Apart from you, that bears that name in Thebes
Disturbed you while you're at your practicing?

SOSIA: What Sosia? Why, the one that's in your service,
Whom yesterday you sent out from the camp
To tell of your arrival at the palace.

AMPHITRYON: What? You?

SOSIA: Yes, me. A me that is informed   660
Of all our secret acts and private matters,
Who knows about the casket with the diamonds,

Exactly like the me now talking with you.
AMPHITRYON: What fairy tales!
SOSIA: This fairy tale is real.
  I hope to die, Sir, if I'm telling lies.
  And that me had arrived ahead of me,
  So I was here, in that case, by my soul,
  Before I ever had arrived.
AMPHITRYON: Where are you getting all this crazy stuff?
  This mish-mash? Out of dreams? Or drunkenness?   670
  Your unhinged brain? Or could it be a joke?
SOSIA: I'm absolutely serious, Sir, and you
  Will grant me credence, on my word of honor,
  If you will be so kind. I swear to you
  That I, who set out single from the camp,
  Arrived at Thebes and destination double;
  That here I met myself and stared at me;
  That here the me that stands before you now,
  Exhausted then with weariness and hunger,
  Found the other one, who came from inside   680
  The house, all fresh, a devil of a fellow;
  And that that pair of rascals, each one jealous
  About the carrying out of your commission,
  Got straightway in an argument, and I
  Was forced to scamper back to camp again
  For having been unreasonable about it.
AMPHITRYON: I must be of a gentle disposition,
  And peaceable by nature, self-effacing,
  To stand for having any servant talk like this.
SOSIA: Sir, if you are annoyed, I will be silent   690
  And we will talk about some other topic.
AMPHITRYON: All right. Go on. I'll hold my temper down,
  You see, and hear your story out with patience.
  But tell me now upon your conscience whether
  The things that you propound to me as true
  Convey the faintest plausibility.
  Can anyone make sense of them? Or grasp it?
SOSIA: Far from it! But who's asking that of you?
  I'd send off to the madhouse any man
  Who claims he understands a bit of this.   700

There simply is no rhyme or reason to it,
It's wizardry, as in a fairy tale,
And yet it's there, like sunlight, just the same.
AMPHITRYON: Yet how can one in his right mind believe it?
SOSIA: My goodness! It cost me the utmost pain,
  Just as with you, before I did believe it.
  I thought I was possessed when I discovered
  Myself ensconced and raving on the spot,
  And for some time I called myself a swindler.
  But finally I recognized, was forced   710
  To recognize both this me and the other.
  He stood, as if the air had formed a mirror,
  In front of me—appearance just like mine,
  Of just my bearing—see?—and just my figure;
  Two drops of water could not be more like.
  If he had only been more sociable,
  Not such a surly brute, I could, upon
  My honor, have been very pleased with him.
AMPHITRYON: O, to what self-restraint I am condemned!
  —But did you finally get in the house?   720
SOSIA: Get in the house! What! You're a good one! How?
  Would I permit it? Listen to reason? Did I
  Not stubbornly forbid myself the door?
AMPHITRYON: How, in the devil's name?
SOSIA: How? with a stick,
  The marks of which are still upon my back.
AMPHITRYON:
  So someone thrashed you?
SOSIA: Soundly.
AMPHITRYON: Who? Who thrashed you?
  Who dared to do that?
SOSIA: Me.
AMPHITRYON: You thrashed yourself?
SOSIA: Yes, I did. Not the me now standing here,
  But that accursed me outside the house
  That beats a man like five good oarsmen.   730
AMPHITRYON: Misfortune come to you for talking so to me!
SOSIA: Sir, I can prove it, if you want me to.
  My witness, and a most trustworthy one,

Is my companion in bad luck: my back.
—The me that chased me out of here had great
Advantage over me: he had his courage
And two trained arms, just like a gladiator's.
AMPHITRYON: Well, to conclude, then. Did you see my wife?
SOSIA: No.
AMPHITRYON: No? Why not?
SOSIA: Ah! For the best of reasons.
AMPHITRYON: And who, you traitor, was the cause of failure   740
   To do your duty? Good-for-nothing dog!
SOSIA: Must I repeat it ten and ten times over?
   Me, as I told you, me, that devil-me
   That had acquired possession of the entrance,
   The me that claims to be the only me,
   The me there in the house, the me that has
   The stick, the me that beat me half to death.
AMPHITRYON: This animal must have been drinking and
   Completely lost what little brains he had.
SOSIA: The devil take me if I've had a drop   750
   To drink today above my proper portion.
   You can believe me on my oath, my goodness.
AMPHITRYON: —Well, maybe you have overdone the matter
   Of sleeping?—Maybe you had some bad dream
   In which you saw this crazy happening
   That you are telling me as actual fact . . . ?
SOSIA: No, it's not that. I did not sleep last night
   And didn't feel like sleeping in the woods there;
   And I was wide awake when I arrived here;
   The other Sosia too was wide awake   760
   And lively when he cudgeled me so soundly.
AMPHITRYON: Stop. Why should I exhaust my brain? I will
   Myself go crazy listening to such drivel.
   Useless, spineless, rattle-headed creature
   With no sense in you, no intelligence.
   Come on.
SOSIA (aside):   That's how it is. Because it's my mouth says it,
   It's silly stuff and not worth listening to.
   But let a great man thrash himself that way,
   And everyone cries: Miracle!

AMPHITRYON: Go, have them open up the gate for me. 770
  —But what is this I see? Here comes Alcmena.
  She'll be surprised; she's not expecting me.
                   (Enter Alcmena and Charis.)
ALCMENA: Come, my Charis. Let us gratefully
  Lay offering on the altar for the gods.
  Let me implore their sacred, high protection
  To be continued for the best of husbands.
                (catching sight of Amphitryon)
  O heaven! Amphitryon!
AMPHITRYON: May heaven grant
  My wife may not be frightened by me now!
  I shall not fear that after our brief parting
  Alcmena will receive less tenderly 780
  Than her Amphitryon returns to her.
ALCMENA: What? Back so soon?
AMPHITRYON: This exclamation
  I find to be a really dubious omen
  Of whether the gods will fulfill that wish.
  This "Back so soon?" does not sound like the greeting—
  By heaven, no!—of true and ardent love.
  Fool that I was! I fancied that the war
  Had kept me all too long away from here;
  Too late, as I had reckoned, I returned.
  But you inform me that I was in error, 790
  And with surprise I now perceive that I
  Have dropped inopportunely from the clear sky.
ALCMENA: I don't know . . .
AMPHITRYON: No, Alcmena,
  Forgive me. With those words you cast cold water
  Upon the flames of my impassioned love.
  Since I have been away, you have not cast
  A single fleeting glance upon the sundial.
  Here not a single throbbing of Time's wings
  Was heard, and in this palace five whole months
  Have all been whiled away in raucous pleasures 800
  As if they merely were as many minutes.
ALCMENA: I find it difficult, dear friend, to grasp
  What grounds you have for making this reproach.

If coldness on my part is your complaint,
Then you behold me at a loss to know
How I could satisfy you. Yesterday
When you appeared around the hour of twilight,
I did discharge the debt that you remind
Me of, and amply, from my ardent heart.
But if you want still more, expect still more,   810
I must confess my insufficiency,
Because I really gave you all I had.

AMPHITRYON: What's this?

ALCMENA: Can you still ask? Last evening, when
You pressed that stealthy kiss upon my neck—
You stole into the room, and I was spinning,
Lost to the world—did I not fly to you?
Can one rejoice more deeply in a lover?

AMPHITRYON: What are you saying to me?

ALCMENA: Oh, what questions!
You were yourself full of unbounded joy
To find yourself so loved; and as I laughed   820
And as my intermittent tears flowed down,
You swore an oddly solemn oath that Hera
Had never so delighted Jupiter.

AMPHITRYON: Eternal gods!

ALCMENA: And then, as day was dawning,
No plea of mine could hold you any longer.
You would not so much as wait for the sun.
You left; I threw myself down on the bed;
The morning was too warm, I could not sleep;
I got up to make offerings to the gods,
And here I come upon you in the forecourt!   830
I think you owe me, faith!, some explanation
If your return now takes me by surprise,
Or, if you will, throws me in consternation;
But reason there is none for your reproaches.

AMPHITRYON: Can it be that a dream foreshowed me to you,
Alcmena? Could you have received me in
Your sleep, so you imagine that you have
Already paid the debt that love demands?

ALCMENA: Can you have been robbed of your memory,

Amphitryon, by evil demons? Can   840
A god have made your cheerful mind confused
So you now mock the chaste love of your wife
And seek to strip it of morality?
AMPHITRYON: What? Do you dare to tell me that I stole
In here around the twilight hour last evening?
And kissed you on the neck in jest . . . Damnation!
ALCMENA: What? Do you dare deny that yesterday
You did steal in here round the hour of twilight?
Permitting yourself every liberty
That can be at a husband's disposition?   850
AMPHITRYON: You're jesting. Let's return to seriousness,
For jesting of this kind is out of place.
ALCMENA: You're jesting. Let's return to seriousness,
For jesting of this kind is coarse, unseemly.
AMPHITRYON: —Permitted myself every liberty
That can be at a husband's disposition?—
Were those your words?
ALCMENA: Leave me, ignoble creature!
AMPHITRYON: O heaven! What a blow has struck me! Sosia
My friend!
SOSIA: She needs five grains of hellebore;
She's not quite level in her upper story.   860
AMPHITRYON: Alcmena! By the gods, you do not weigh
The consequences that such talk can lead to.
Reflect a minute. Gather up your wits.
And then say what you will and I'll believe you.
ALCMENA: Come what come may, Amphitryon, I want
You to believe me; you must not consider
Me capable of such unseemly jesting.
You see how calm I am about the outcome.
If you can seriously deny the fact
That you were at the palace yesterday   870
Without the gods' most direly striking you,
All other baser motives do not matter.
My inner peace you cannot trouble, nor,
I trust, the world's opinion of me either;
My heart alone will feel the laceration
Of having my beloved seek to hurt me.

AMPHITRYON: Unhappy woman! What a thing to say!
   Have you already got your testimony?
ALCMENA: Who ever heard the like? The entire corps
   Of servants in this palace bears me witness.   880
   The very stones you trod upon, the trees,
   The dogs that wagged their tails about your knees
   Would testify about you if they could.
AMPHITRYON: The entire corps of servants? Impossible!
ALCMENA: Must I, incomprehensible man, present
   You now with finally decisive proof?
   From whom did I receive this belt I'm wearing?
AMPHITRYON: What's this? A belt? To you? From me? Already?
ALCMENA: The head-band, you told me, of Labdacus,
   Whom you had killed amid the final battle.   890
AMPHITRYON: You traitor there! Now what am I to think?
SOSIA: Let me step in here. These are sorry dodges.
   I hold that head-band right here in my hands.
AMPHITRYON: Where?
SOSIA: Here. *(He draws a casket from his pocket.)*
AMPHITRYON: The seal has not been broken yet.
      (He observes the girdle at Alcmena's bosom.)
   And yet—if all my senses don't deceive me . . .
                  (to Sosia)
   Quick, break the lock.
SOSIA: My goodness! Why, it's empty.
   The devil has made off with it; there is
   No head-band of King Labdacus inside it.
AMPHITRYON: O ye almighty gods who rule this earth!
   What destiny have you ordained for me?   900
SOSIA: What destiny's ordained for you? You're double,
   Amphitryon with the stick was here before you,
   And I would say you're lucky . . .
AMPHITRYON: Quiet, rascal!
ALCMENA *(to Charis):* What in the world can he find so upsetting?
   And why should shock and consternation grip him
   When he looks at this jewel that he knows?
AMPHITRYON: I have heard tell of marvels in my time,
   And of unnatural phenomena, of objects
   Which had strayed down here from another world;

But this cord from beyond has looped itself   910
  Around my honor and is strangling it.
ALCMENA *(to Amphitryon):* After this testimony, my odd friend,
  Will you go on denying that you came
  And that I paid my obligation to you?
AMPHITRYON: No. But you will recount how matters went.
ALCMENA: Amphitryon!
AMPHITRYON: You hear? I do not doubt you.
  The jeweled head-band can't be disallowed.
  But certain reasons merely make me want
  To have you tell the story in detail
  Of what went on while I was in the palace.   920
ALCMENA: My friend, you are not ill, then?
AMPHITRYON: No—not ill.
ALCMENA: Perhaps your head is heavy with some worry
  About the war that presses hard upon you
  And deadens your mind's cheerful competence . . . ?
AMPHITRYON: That much is true. My head does feel all numb.
ALCMENA: Come in and rest a little.
AMPHITRYON: Let it be.
  It isn't urgent. As I said, it is
  My wish, before I go inside the house,
  To hear the tale of yesterday's arrival.
ALCMENA: It is soon told. Twilight was coming on,   930
  I sat there spinning in my room and dreaming,
  Amid the spindle's hum, dreams of myself
  Out on the field among the warriors' weapons,
  When I heard the glad cries by the outer gate.
AMPHITRYON: Glad cries from whom?
ALCMENA: Our servants.
AMPHITRYON: Well?
ALCMENA: It
       [passed

  Out of my thoughts again. Not even in
  My dream did I consider what a joy
  The gods had destined for me, and I was
  Just taking up the thread again, when through
  My every limb there passed a sudden shock.   940
AMPHITRYON: I know.

ALCMENA: You know of that.
AMPHITRYON: And then?
ALCMENA: And then
There followed lots of talking, lots of jesting,
And questions overlapped in quick exchange.
Then we sat down—and then in warrior's language
You told me all about what happened at
Pharissa, and about King Labdacus,
And how he went down to eternal night,
—And all the gory episodes of battle.
And then you gave the splendid head-band to
Me as a gift, and that cost me a kiss.   950
We long examined it by candle-light
—And I arranged it like a sash around me,
Which your own hand then tied across my breast.
AMPHITRYON *(aside):* Can daggers be more keenly felt than this?
ALCMENA: Then supper was brought in, but neither you
Nor I paid very much attention to
The partridge pasty waiting there before us,
Nor to the bottle. You said playfully
That you lived on the nectar of my love,
You were a god, and other things besides,   960
As your gay sportiveness would prompt you to them.
AMPHITRYON:
—As my gay sportiveness would prompt me to them!
ALCMENA: Yes, as you thought of them. Then, after that . . .
But why so somber, friend?
AMPHITRYON: Then, after that . . . ?
ALCMENA: We got up from the table, and . . .
AMPHITRYON: And then?
ALCMENA: And after we had got up from the table . . .
AMPHITRYON: And after you had got up from the table . . . ?
ALCMENA: We went . . .
AMPHITRYON: You went . . . ?
ALCMENA: Why, then we went . . .
                                                  [of course!
Why do such blushes mount into your cheeks?
AMPHITRYON: This dagger cuts me to the very heart!   970
No, no, deceiving wife, it was not I.

Whoever stole in here last evening at
The twilight hour as Amphitryon
Was the most dastardly of vagabonds!

ALCMENA: Revolting husband!

AMPHITRYON: Faithless, thankless wife!—
Farewell now to restraint, and to love also,
Which up till now has paralyzed my honor,
Farewell to memory, hope, and happiness,
Henceforth I'll revel in revenge and fury.

ALCMENA: Farewell to you as well, ignoble spouse,   980
From you my bleeding heart I wrench away.
Your guile is loathsome, it outrages me.
If your affections have turned to another,
Compelled to do so by Love's dart, your wish,
Confided properly to me, would have
As soon succeeded as this coward's ruse.
You now see me determined to dissolve
The bond that galls your vacillating soul;
Before the present day has seen its evening
You shall be free of every tie that binds you.   990

AMPHITRYON: Considering the ignominy of this
Offense that has been done to me, that is
The least my wounded honor can demand.
That a deception has been perpetrated
Is clear, although my mind does not yet grasp
The whole nefarious web. But I shall now
Call witnesses who'll rip it all apart.
I shall call on your brother, the commander,
And on the entire army of the Thebans,
Out of whose midst I had not stirred until   1000
The first ray of this morning's dawning light.
Then I shall probe down to this riddle's root,
And woe! I say to him who has deceived me!

SOSIA: Sir, shall I . . . ?

AMPHITRYON: Silence! I don't want to listen
To anything. Stay here and wait for me.

                          (Exit.)

CHARIS: My lady . . . ?

ALCMENA: Silence! I don't want to listen

To anything. I want to be alone.

(Exit.)

CHARIS: Well, that was what I'd call a scene! But he
  Is crazy, thinking he can claim that he
  Had spent last night asleep down there in camp.—   1010
  But once her brother comes, we'll clear this up.

SOSIA: This is a nasty blow my master's had.
  —I wonder if I've had somewhat the same?
  I think I'll beat the bushes for a bit.

CHARIS *(aside):* What's this? He has the gall to stand right there
  And sulk away and turn his back on me.

SOSIA: I feel a cold chill running down my back
  Now that I'm coming to the ticklish point.
  I'm almost tempted to forgo the asking,
  But it won't make much difference, though,   1020
  As long as it's not scrutinized too closely.—
  So come, let's take a chance. I have to know!
  —Greetings to you, Charis!

CHARIS: What? You dare come near me,
  Deceiver? You still have the impudence
  To speak up boldly to me while I'm angry?

SOSIA: Ye righteous gods, what is the matter with you?
  When people meet again, they greet each other.
  The way you get so ruffled over nothing!

CHARIS: And what do you call "over nothing?" What
  Do you call "nothing?" Tell me that, you wretch!   1030

SOSIA: To speak the honest truth, what I call "nothing"
  Means simply "nothing," both in verse and prose,
  And "nothing," as you know, means just about
  Plain nothing, or, at least, not very much.

CHARIS: Oh, if I only knew what holds my hands
  As if tied down. They itch so I can hardly
  Restrain myself from scratching out your eyes
  To show you what a raging woman is.

SOSIA: Now heaven shield me! What a wild attack is here!

CHARIS: So I suppose you call it "nothing," then,   1040
  The shameless way that you behaved to me?

SOSIA: How was it I behaved to you? What happened?

CHARIS: What happened? Oh, just see the innocence!

The next thing, he'll be claiming, like his master,
That he did not come here to Thebes at all.
SOSIA: My goodness, as to that, I'll tell you now
That I'm not playing any mystery-man.
What happened was: we drank some devil's wine
That washed the thoughts clean out of our poor heads.
CHARIS: Do you think you'll escape me with that dodge?   1050
SOSIA: No, Charis. On my word. Call me a rascal
If I did not arrive here yesterday.
But I don't know a thing of what went on.
To me the world seemed nothing but a bagpipe.
CHARIS: Would you be claiming you don't know the way
You treated me when you arrived last evening?
SOSIA: The devil take it! Just as good as nothing.
So tell me. I'm a good sort, as you know,
And I'll condemn myself if I've done wrong.
CHARIS: You good-for-nothing! It was well past midnight,   1060
And the young couple had been long at rest,
And there you were up in Amphitryon's
Apartments still, without so much as showing
Your face in your own quarters. Finally
It was your wife that had to go and start
The hunt for you. What was it that I found?
Where did I find you then, you duty-shirker?
I found you all stretched out upon a cushion,
As if you were at home where you belonged.
And at my tenderly concerned complaint   1070
You said it was Amphitryon's command
Lest you should oversleep the hour of parting,
Because he wanted to leave Thebes quite early,
And more unlikely stories of the sort.
Not one kind word did I get out of you.
And then when I bent down in loving fashion
To kiss you, over to the wall you turned,
You lout, and said that I should let you sleep.
SOSIA: O good old Sosia, full of honor!
CHARIS: What!
I do believe you're glad about it. Are you?   1080
SOSIA: My goodness, you should thank your stars I did.

I had been eating some horseradish, Charis,
   And rightly turned my breath away from you.
CHARIS: Nonsense! I noticed nothing of the sort.
   At dinner time we had horseradish too.
SOSIA: I didn't know. But no one smells it then.
CHARIS: You won't worm your way out of it like this.
   Sooner or later the contempt with which
   You treated me last night will be avenged.
   I can't get over all those things that I   1090
   Was forced to listen to at dawn today;
   That liberty you gave me I will put
   To some use yet, as sure as I am honest.
SOSIA: What was the liberty that I gave you?
CHARIS: You said, and well you knew what you were saying,
   You wouldn't mind a pair of cuckold's horns,
   In fact, you'd even be quite satisfied
   If I took up with that young Theban who,
   As you well know, has lurked about my path.
   So, very well, my friend: your will be done.   1100
SOSIA: It was some donkey told you that; I didn't.
   Joking aside: I won't take blame for that.
   And on that score you will be reasonable.
CHARIS: But can I help myself, in any case?
SOSIA: Be quiet now! Here comes Alcmena.
              (Enter Alcmena.)
ALCMENA: Charis,
   What has befallen your unhappy mistress?
   O tell me what has happened! See this jewel.
CHARIS: What jewel is this, may I ask, my lady?
ALCMENA: It is King Labdacus's head-band jewel,
   The splendid present from Amphitryon,
   And has his monogram engraved upon it.   1110
CHARIS: This? This King Labdacus's head-band jewel?
   Why, this is not Amphitryon's monogram.
ALCMENA: Unhappy woman, have you lost your senses?
   It's not, so one can read it with one's finger,
   Engraved in gold, and clearly, capital A?
CHARIS: Indeed it's not, my lady. What odd fancy?
   Here is a different and quite strange initial.

This is a "J."
ALCMENA: A "J?"
CHARIS: A "J." There's no
  Mistaking it.
ALCMENA: Alas, then, I am lost.   1120
CHARIS: What is it, tell me, that upsets you so?
ALCMENA: How shall I find the words, dear Charis, to
  Explain to you the unexplainable?
  As I regained my room bewildered and
  Uncertain if I was awake or dreaming,
  Still baffled by the crazy notion that
  Some other man had spent the night with me,
  Yet thinking of Amphitryon's impassioned
  Grief and of his final words to me
  That he was going to summon my own brother—   1130
  Just think of it!—to testify against me;
  And as I asked myself: "Can I be wrong?"—
  For error must be mocking one of us,
  Since neither he nor I could be deceitful;
  And as that jest of double meaning darted
  Through my memory, when my beloved,
  Amphitryon—I don't know if you heard it—
  Was slandering Amphitryon, my husband;
  And as I shuddered and was gripped with horror
  And all my faithless senses fled from me—   1140
  Then, dearest Charis, I seized up this jewel,
  This dear, this priceless token which alone
  Can serve as evidence without deception.
  I clutched it and was just about to press
  Its precious monogram, my cherished liar's
  Own refuter, to my delighted lips,
  When I perceived a strange and different letter—
  And stood there as though thunderstruck—a "J!"
CHARIS: O horrible! Could you have been mistaken?
ALCMENA: Mistaken!
CHARIS: In the monogram, I mean.   1150
ALCMENA: As to the monogram . . . It almost seems so.
CHARIS: And therefore . . . ?
ALCMENA: What: "and therefore . . . ?"

CHARIS: Calm
                                                                      [yourself.
    Everything still will turn out for the best.
ALCMENA: O Charis!—I'd sooner be mistaken in
    Myself! I'd sooner take this firm conviction
    That I drank in while at my mother's breast
    And which assures me that I am Alcmena,
    And say I was a Parthian or Persian.
    Is this hand mine? And is this bosom mine?
    Is my reflection in the mirror mine?   1160
    Would he be stranger to me than myself?
    Remove my eyes and I will hear him still;
    My ears, I'll feel him still; my touch, I'll breathe him;
    Take eyes and ears and touch and sense of smell
    And all my senses, and but leave my heart,
    And you will leave me with the bell I need
    To find him anywhere in this wide world.*
CHARIS: Of course! Could I have doubted it, my lady?
    How could a woman err in such a case?
    Wrong clothes, wrong household items one might take,   1170
    But husbands are known in the dark.
    And didn't he appear before us all?
    And did the entire staff of grooms not greet
    Him at the gate with joy when he appeared?
    It still was daylight, and a thousand eyes
    Would have to have been cloaked in midnight here.
ALCMENA: But still there is this curious initial.
    Yet why did such an alien symbol, which
    No sense impaired could possibly mistake,
    Not catch my eye then from the very first?   1180
    If I could not distinguish, dearest Charis,
    Between two names like that, could they belong
    To two men—is that possible?—between
    Whom I could not distinguish any better?
CHARIS: But you are sure of this, I hope, my lady?
ALCMENA: As of my own pure soul and innocence!
    Else you would misconstrue my exaltation

* The heart emits a bell-tone, as also in line 1399.

In finding him more beautiful than ever
Last night. I could have thought him his own picture,
A painting of him by an artist's hand,   1190
Quite true to life, yet heightened to the godlike.
He stood before me as if in a dream,
And an ineffable awareness of
My happiness, such as I never knew,
Came over me, when in a shining glory
The victor of Pharissa came to me.
It was Amphitryon, the son of gods!
He seemed to be one of the glorified
Himself; I would have liked to ask him whether
He had descended to me from the stars.   1200
CHARIS: Imagination, Princess. Love's conception.
ALCMENA: Ah, Charis, that ambiguous jest of his
     That kept recurring, making a distinction
     Between him and Amphitryon. If it
     Was he to whom I gave myself, why did he
     Keep saying he was only the beloved,
     The thief, who merely stole a dainty morsel?
     To think I took the jest so smilingly
     If it did not come from my husband's lips!
CHARIS: Let no such over-hasty doubts torment you.   1210
     Did not Amphitryon acknowledge the initial
     When you showed him the head-band jewel today?
     There surely is some error here, my lady.
     If this strange letter did not puzzle him,
     It must be in the nature of the stone,
     And *yesterday* illusion blinded us,
     While all *today* is as it should be.
ALCMENA: What if he only hurriedly observed it,
     And now comes back with all the field commanders
     And frantically repeats his former claim   1220
     That he did not set foot across this house's threshold!
     Not only would *all* evidence be forfeit,
     This jewel would be evidence *against* me.
     Confounded then, what answer could I make?
     Where shall I flee from pain and from destruction
     Once those suspicious men examine it?

Must I not then confess that this initial
Simply does not start Amphitryon's name?
And further that a present with a different
Initial could not be a gift from him? 1230
And if I swear upon the altar that
He gave me this gem yesterday himself,
Can I be sure that yesterday I did
Receive from him *this* token now before us?
CHARIS: Be calm! He's coming. All will be resolved.
(Enter Jupiter.)
ALCMENA: My husband and my lord, permit me, on
My knees, to proffer you this jewel here.
My life I loyally lay at your feet;
If you gave me this stone, observe it well,
With the initial of a strange name on it, 1240
I'll kiss it for sheer joy and weep upon it;
If you did not, if you disclaim it to me
And disavow it, let death be my lot
And everlasting darkness hide my shame.
JUPITER: My lovely wife! Shall I take up this jewel
When such great worth lies in the dust before me?
Arise. What do you wish? Compose yourself.
ALCMENA: My over-confidence offended you,
I then felt sure of innocence and strength.
But since observing this strange monogram 1250
I mistrust my most intimate emotion.
I now think . . . someone else . . . appeared before me,
If your lips will assure me of that fact.
JUPITER: My noble wife! How you put me to shame.
What falsehood is this that has crossed your lips?
How could another have appeared before you?
Who can come near you, you, before whose soul
Are one and only one man's features ever?
You are, my saint, encinctured with a zone
Of diamond against all other comers. 1260
Even the lucky man whom you receive
Leaves you still pure and guiltless, for all who
Approach you turn into Amphitryon.
ALCMENA: But O my husband! Will you kindly tell

Me: was it you? Or not? O say it was!

JUPITER: It was. No matter who it was. Be calm.
All that you saw and touched and thought and felt
Was I. Who else, besides me, could there be,
Beloved? For, whoever crossed your threshold,
You still received, my dearest, none but me,   1270
And for whatever favors you bestowed
I am your debtor, and I thank you for them.

ALCMENA: No, no, Amphitryon, that is not right.
So now farewell forever, my beloved,
I was prepared for that event.

JUPITER: Alcmena!

ALCMENA: Farewell! Farewell!

JUPITER: How can you?

ALCMENA: Go, go, go . . .

JUPITER: Star of my eyes!

ALCMENA: Go, go, I say.

JUPITER: But hear me!

ALCMENA: I will not hear. I do not want to live
Unless my heart is irreproachable.

JUPITER: My wife whom I adore, what are you saying?   1280
What law, my holy one, could you transgress?
No matter if a devil came to you
And spat the slime of sin and slaver from
The depths of hell itself upon you, still
He would not spoil the splendor of my wife's
Breast with a single blemish! This is madness!

ALCMENA: Oh, I was shamefully deceived!

JUPITER: He was
The one who was deceived, my idol! *He*
Was cheated by his wicked craftiness,
Not you, not your unfailing sense! If he   1290
Imagined he had you in his embrace,
You lay upon Amphitryon's dear breast,
And if he dreamed of kisses, you were pressing
Your lips upon Amphitryon's dear mouth.
He has a sting in him, you may be sure,
Which all the skill of all the gods can not
Extract from his enflamed, love-smitten heart.

ALCMENA: If only Zeus would hurl him at my feet!
   O God! The two of us must part forever.
JUPITER: The kiss that you bestowed on him has linked   1300
   Me far more firmly to you now than all
   The love for me that ever fired your heart.
   And if out of the rushing dance of days
   I could, my dearest wife, shoot yesterday
   And drop it like a jackdaw from the air,
   Not for the bliss of all Olympus, not
   For Zeus' immortal life, would I do it.
ALCMENA: And I would deal my heart ten deaths. Now go!
   You'll never see me in your house again,
   Nor show me to a woman in all Hellas.   1310
JUPITER: To all the host of the Olympians,
   Alcmena!—I will introduce you into
   The radiance-darting host of all the gods.
   And were I Zeus, once you approached their ranks,
   Eternal Hera could not other than
   Rise up, and Artemis the strict, to greet you.
ALCMENA: Your favor crushes me. Go! Let me flee.
JUPITER: Alcmena!
ALCMENA: Let me flee!
JUPITER: Wife of my soul!
ALCMENA: Amphitryon, I want to leave at once.
JUPITER: You think you can escape out of these arms?   1320
ALCMENA: Amphitryon, I want to leave. Release me.
JUPITER: And if you fled across far lands among
   The hideous races of the wilderness,
   As far as to the ocean's strand, I would
   Pursue you, overtake you, kiss you, weep,
   And lift you in my arms, and carry you
   In triumph home again and to my bed.
ALCMENA: If you will have it so, I swear to you,
   And summon all the host of gods, the dread
   Avengers of false oaths, to be my witness: 1330
   While I have breath, I'll sooner take this heart
   Down to my grave than back into your bed.
JUPITER: By power innate in me I will shatter
   That oath and strew its fragments on the winds.

It was no mortal man that came to you
Last night, but Zeus himself, the god of thunder.
ALCMENA: Who?
JUPITER: Jupiter.
ALCMENA: Who, madman, did you say?
JUPITER: He, Jupiter, I said.
ALCMENA: He, Jupiter?
    Wretch, do you venture . . . ?
JUPITER: Jupiter, I said,
    And I repeat it. No one less than he   1340
    Appeared before you in the night just past.
ALCMENA: You dare blame the Olympians, you godless
    Man, for the sacrilege that was committed?
JUPITER: Blame the Olympians for sacrilege?
    Rash woman, never let me hear your lips
    Pronounce a thing like that again.
ALCMENA: Not let my lips . . . ? Is it not sacrilege . . . ?
JUPITER: Silence, I say! I so command.
ALCMENA: Doomed man!
JUPITER: If you care nothing for the honor of
    Ascending up the ladder-rungs to the immortals,   1350
    I do! And you'll permit me to be so.
    If you do not feel envy for Callisto
    The glorious, nor for Leda and Europa,
    So be it; but I envy Tyndarus
    And long for sons like the Tyndarides.*
ALCMENA: Feel envy for Callisto? For Europa?
    Those women venerated throughout Hellas?
    The high elect of Jupiter himself?
    Who dwell in the eternal realms of aether?
JUPITER: Most certainly! Why should you envy them?   1360
    Contented as you are completely with
    The fame of seeing one lone mortal at your feet.
ALCMENA: O, the unheard-of things that you suggest!
    Dare I so much as think of such a thing?
    Would I not perish in such radiance?

* The sons of Tyndarus—the "Tyndarides"—were the heroic brothers
Castor and Pollux.

If he had been the one, would I still feel
Life coursing joyously through this warm heart?
I, all unworthy of such grace! A sinner!
JUPITER: Whether you are worthy of such grace
   Or not, is not for you to judge. As he   1370
   Deems you to be, you will submit in patience.
   Would you presume, short-sighted woman, to
   Judge him who knows the human heart?
ALCMENA: Good, good, Amphitryon. I understand you,
   Your magnanimity moves me to tears.
   You threw out that remark, I realize,
   In order to distract me . . . But my soul
   Returns to take up once again its painful thought.
   Go, my own darling, you who are my all,
   Go find yourself another wife, be happy,   1380
   And let me weep out all my days to think
   Of how I cannot make you happy.
JUPITER: My dear wife, how you touch my heart!
   Look at the jewel now that you are holding.
ALCMENA: Celestials, save me from illusion!
JUPITER: It *is* his name? Where *mine* was yesterday?
   Are all these things that happen here not marvels?
   Did I not hold this head-band gem today
   Inside its casket under lock and key?
   And opening it to give the gem to you,   1390
   Did I not find a mere dent in the cotton?
   And see it glittering at your breast already?
ALCMENA: Is that how I should see it? Jupiter?
   The sire of men and of eternal gods?
JUPITER: Who else could ever have deceived you in
   The instantaneous gold-scales of your feelings?
   Who else could so elude your woman's soul
   That so acutely senses all around it
   On those fine chimes of bells within your heart
   That quiver into sound at a whispered breath?   1400
ALCMENA: His very self!
JUPITER: Almighty ones alone
   Dare come to you as boldly as that stranger,
   And over such a rival I prevail!

I willingly see those omniscient ones
Seek out and find the way into your heart
And watch those omnipresent ones approach you,
For are they not themselves obliged, beloved,
To be Amphitryon, and steal his features,
If your soul is to grant them access to you?

ALCMENA: That's true. *(She kisses him.)*

JUPITER: My goddess!

ALCMENA: Oh, I am so happy! 1410
And oh! how glad I am to be so happy!
How glad I will be to have borne the pain
That Jupiter has given me
If only all is well, as once it was.

JUPITER: So, shall I tell you what I'm thinking?

ALCMENA: Well?

JUPITER: And what, short of a revelation to us,
I even feel inclined now to believe?

ALCMENA: Well? Well? You frighten me . . .

JUPITER: . . . What if you have
Provoked—Do not be frightened—his displeasure?

ALCMENA: I? His displeasure?

JUPITER: Do you believe in him? 1420
Do you perceive the world, his handiwork?
Do you behold him in the sunset's glow
As it slants through the silent greenery?
And hear him in the rippling of the waters,
In the song of the sumptuous nightingale?
Does not the mountain towering to the sky
In vain proclaim him to you, not in vain
The cataracts that cliffs dash into spray?
And when the sun aloft lights up his temple
And, rung in on the throbbing pulse of joy, 1430
All races of created things sing praise
To him, do you not go down in your heart's
Abyss and there adore your idol?

ALCMENA: What are you saying? Can he be adored
In any way more reverent or more childlike?
Has any day burned out to darkness but
That I knelt at his altar giving thanks

For life, for this heart, and for you, beloved?
And did I not just now, by starry night,
Bow down before him, fervently adoring,   1440
And send my ardent prayer like incense up
To heaven from the seething depths of feeling?
JUPITER: Why did you bow before him?—Was it not
Because amid the lightning's jagged script
You recognized a certain well-known letter?
ALCMENA: O dreadful! But how do you know of that?
JUPITER: Who is it that you pray to at his altar?
Is it to him up there above the clouds?
Can your engrossed mind ever comprehend him?
Or can your feelings, in their wonted nest   1450
Dare spread their pinions in such flight? And is
It not Amphitryon, your beloved, always,
Before whom you bow to the dust?
ALCMENA: Unhappy woman! How confused you make me.
Can even our involuntary actions
Be blamed? Must I pray to white marble walls?
To think of him, I need some form and features.
JUPITER:
You see? That's what I said. And don't you think that such
Idolatry offends him? Does he enjoy
Not having your fair heart? Does he not also   1460
Yearn to feel your fervent adoration?
ALCMENA: Ah yes, of course he does. Where is the sinner
Whose homage is not pleasing to the gods?
JUPITER: Of course! So, *if* he came to you, he came
Down only to *compel* your thoughts toward him,
To take revenge on you for your neglect.
ALCMENA: O horror!
JUPITER: Have no fear. He will not punish
You more than you deserve. But in the future
When at his altar, you must think of none
But him who came to you by night, not me.   1470
ALCMENA: That I swear holily to do. I know,
Down to the last detail, just how he looked,
And I will not confuse him with you.
JUPITER: Do that. Else you will risk his coming back.

As often as you see his monogram
Engraved upon that head-band gem, you are
To think most fervently of his appearance,
Recalling each detail of that occurrence,
Recalling how, in that immortal presence,
The shock went through you at your distaff, how   1480
You then received the jewel from him, and who
Helped you adjust the sash, and what took place
Around the partridge pasty. If your husband
Should intervene as a distraction, ask him
To leave you for an hour to yourself.
ALCMENA: Good, good, you will be satisfied with me.
  For the first hour every morning I
  Shall not so much as think one thought of you,
  And then no longer think of Jupiter.
JUPITER: But if the everlasting Thunderer of   1490
  The clouds, touched by such great improvement,
  Were now to come to you in all his glory,
  Beloved, how would you comport yourself?
ALCMENA: How dread a moment that would be! If only,
  When at his altar, I had thought of him,
  As long as he so slightly differs from you.
JUPITER: You have not yet seen his immortal face,
  Alcmena. Ah, beholding it, your heart
  Will leap up in delight a thousandfold.
  What you will feel for him will seem like fire,   1500
  And ice what you feel for Amphitryon.
  Yes, if he were to touch your soul this moment
  And then depart and go back to Olympus,
  You would experience the incredible
  And weep that you could never follow him.
ALCMENA: No, no, Amphitryon, do not believe that.
  If I could just live backwards one day's time,
  And shut myself away inside my room
  From gods and heroes, under lock and key,
  I would be willing . . .
JUPITER: Really? Would you do that?   1510
ALCMENA: With all my heart I would be willing to.
JUPITER (aside): Curse the illusion that enticed me here!

ALCMENA: What is it? Are you angry? Have I hurt you?
JUPITER: Ah, would you then, my worthy child,
Not sweeten his atrocious life for him?
Would you deny your breast when his head seeks it,
His head that orders all the worlds,
To rest upon its downy softness? Oh, Alcmena,
Olympus too is empty without love.
What good are nations prostrate in the dust   1520
With adoration, to a heart athirst?
He wants their love, not their illusion of him.
Enshrouded in eternal veils,
He craves to mirror himself in a soul
And be reflected in a tear of rapture.
Beloved, see! Twixt earth and heaven he
Pours forth such vast infinities of joys,
If you were chosen now by fate
To pay the gratitude of many millions
Of creatures and to pay back all his claims   1530
Upon creation with a single smile,
Would you, perhaps . . . Oh! I can not believe that . . .
Oh, do not let me think . . .
ALCMENA: From me far be it
To oppose the high decree of gods.
If I was chosen for such sacred duty,
May my creator rule and govern me!
And yet . . .
JUPITER: Well?
ALCMENA: If the choice were mine . . .
JUPITER: The choice . . .
ALCMENA: . . . were mine, my reverence would go to him,
And all my love to you, Amphitryon.
JUPITER: But if to you I were this god . . . ?
ALCMENA: If you . . .   1540
—What strange sensation . . . If you were this god
To me . . . I don't know whether to fall on
My knees, or not, before you . . . Are you? Are you?
JUPITER: Yours the decision. I am Amphitryon.
ALCMENA: Amphitryon . . .
JUPITER: Amphitryon—to you.

But still I ask you: if I were this god
To you, in love descending to you from
Olympus, how would you comport yourself?
ALCMENA: If you, beloved, were this god to me—
    I would not know where my Amphitryon was,   1550
    And I would follow you no matter where,
    Yes, even like Eurydice, to Orcus.
JUPITER: If you did not know where Amphitryon was,
    Yes. But what if Amphitryon appeared?
ALCMENA: If he appeared?—Oh, you are torturing me.
    How can Amphitryon appear to me
    When I now hold Amphitryon in my arms?
JUPITER: And yet you might well have the god in your embrace
    Because you thought he was Amphitryon.
    Why should your feelings then cause you surprise?   1560
    If I, the god, held you in my embrace
    And your Amphitryon were to appear,
    How would your heart declare itself?
ALCMENA: If you, the god, held me in your embrace
    And now Amphitryon were to appear,
    Yes—I would then be sad, and I would wish
    That he were then the god, and that you would
    Remain Amphitryon, as you surely are.
JUPITER: O my sweet creature whom I so adore,
    In whom I call myself so blessèd, blessèd!   1570
    One truer to the ultimate divine
    Conception, both in form and mould,
    Has not in eons gone forth from my hands!
ALCMENA: Amphitryon!
JUPITER: Be calm, be calm, be calm!
    All will yet be resolved for your sheer triumph.
    The god longs to reveal himself to you,
    And yet, before the starry hosts have danced
    Their way across the silent fields of night,
    Your heart shall know for whom it burned in ardor.
    Sosia!
SOSIA: Sir!
JUPITER: Up now, my faithful servant,   1580
    In order that this day may be made glorious!

Alcmena has, in love, made peace with me,
And you shall go and summon to a feast
All guests that you find anywhere in camp.
              (Exeunt Jupiter and Alcmena.)
CHARIS *(aside):* What have you overheard, unhappy woman!
    There may have been gods from Olympus here?
    And that the one who passes here for Sosia
    May also be one of the deathless ones—
    Apollo, Hermes, maybe Ganymede?
SOSIA *(aside):* It may have been great Zeus, the god of lightning!
CHARIS *(aside):* O shame upon me for the way I acted.   [1590
SOSIA *(aside):* My goodness, he was not served badly.
    The fellow stood up stoutly to his man
    And like a panther battled for his lord.
CHARIS *(aside):*
    Who knows but what I'm wrong? I'm going to test him.
                    (aloud)
    Come, Sosia, let us also make our peace.
SOSIA: Another time. Right now I'm much too busy.
CHARIS: Where are you going?
SOSIA: I must invite the captains.
CHARIS: Grant me a word before you go, my husband.
SOSIA: Your husband . . . ? Oh, with pleasure.
CHARIS: Did you hear   1600
    How to my lady in the twilight yesterday,
    And to her faithful servant too,
    Two mighty gods descended from Olympus,
    How Zeus, the god that rules the clouds, was here,
    And Phoebus the magnificent was with him?
SOSIA: Yes, if it's true. I'm sorry to have heard it.
    I always did dislike that sort of union.
CHARIS: Dislike? Why so? I can't imagine why . . .
SOSIA: Well, if you want to know the honest truth,
    It's much like horse and donkey.
CHARIS: Horse and donkey!   1610
    A princess and a god! *(aside)* Then he must not
    Come from Olympus . . . *(aloud)* You are pleased
    To make a jest with your unworthy servant.
    A triumph such as has befallen us

Was never known in Thebes before.
SOSIA: As far as I'm concerned, it costs me dear.
A proper measure of disgrace would be
As welcome to me as these devilish trophies
That gleam on both my shoulders now.
But I must hurry.
CHARIS: Yes, but I was saying—   1620
Who ever dreamed of having guests like that?
Who thought that in those wretched human bodies
Two of the high immortals would be hidden?
There certainly was many a good trait
Left deep inside from carelessness, that could
Have been turned outside much more than was done in this case.
SOSIA: My goodness, how I could have used it, Charis!
For you were just about as tender with me
As wildcats might have been. Do mend your ways.
CHARIS: I don't recall offending you exactly,   1630
Or doing more than . . .
SOSIA: Not offending me!
Call me a scoundrel if this morning you
Did not deserve as sound a thrashing as
Has ever rained down on a woman's back.
CHARIS: What ever did I do?
SOSIA: What did you do,
You silly creature! Didn't you say you
Were going after that oaf of a Theban
That I threw recently out of the house?
You didn't promise me a pair of horns?
You didn't call me cuckold to my face?   1640
CHARIS: Oh, I was joking! Really!
SOSIA: Joking! Try
That joke on me again, and I will smack you,
The devil take me . . . !
CHARIS: Heavens! What's coming over me?
SOSIA: The dirty dog!
CHARIS: Don't look at me so fiercely!
I feel my heart is shattering within me!
SOSIA: You ought to be ashamed, blasphemous woman,
For making mock of sacred marriage duty!

    Go and be party to this sin no more,
    That's my advice.—And when I get back, I'll
    Be wanting cabbage with fried sausages.   1650
CHARIS: Just as you say. But why do I postpone
    And keep delaying? Is he? Isn't he?
SOSIA: Well, am I what?
CHARIS: Behold me in the dust.
SOSIA: What's wrong?
CHARIS: Behold me in the dust before you.
SOSIA: Are you out of your mind?
CHARIS: You are! You are!
SOSIA: What am I?
CHARIS: Why do you deny yourself?
SOSIA: Has everyone gone mad today?
CHARIS: Did I
    Not see the flaming anger of your eyes,
    Far-darting and betokening Apollo?
SOSIA: Apollo? Is the devil in you?—One   1660
    Calls me a dog and one calls me a god?—
    I'm no one but the old familiar donkey
    Sosia!
                  (Exit.)
CHARIS: Sosia! What? The old
    Familiar donkey Sosia, nothing more?
    Clown, it's a good thing that I know;
    There'll be no sausage fried for you today.   (1666)
                  (Exit.)

Act III

[*Amphitryon alone before his house.*]

AMPHITRYON: Oh, how repugnant are the faces of
These captains. Each one wants to offer me
Congratulations on the victory won,
And I must clasp each one in my embrace   1670
Right when I'm cursing all of them to hell.
Not one of them would have the sort of heart
That I could pour out my full heart to him.
    That jewels can be stolen from a sealed
Receptacle and not disturb the seal:
Agreed; a mountebank some distance off
Can trick us out of things held in our hands.
But taking over some man's shape and manner
And making payment to his wife in full besides,
That is a nasty trick of Satan's doing.   1680
In rooms where candlelight was shining fair
No one who had five healthy senses has
Mistaken friends until today. Mere eyes
Wrenched from their sockets and laid on the table,
Mere limbs, ears, fingers, severed from the body
And packed in boxes, would have been enough
To recognize a husband by. But now they will
Be branding husbands of necessity
And hanging bells around their necks like rams.
    She is as capable of such deception   1690
As her turtle-dove, and I will sooner
Believe in honesty of thieves escaped
From nooses than this woman's trickery.
—She is insane, and when dawn comes tomorrow
I'll surely have to send out for physicians.
—If only I could find a way to start.
                (Enter Mercury on the balcony.)
MERCURY *(aside)*: This following you, old father Jupiter,
Upon this earthly love-adventure is
True friendship on the part of Mercury.

For, by the Styx, it bores me thoroughly!   1700
And playing husband, more deceptively
Than need be, to that lady's maid, that Charis,
Is something I can't say I'm eager for.
—I'll pick out an adventure of my own
And drive that jealous lout down there to madness.

AMPHITRYON:
Why should this house be all locked up this way in daytime?

MERCURY: Hey! Easy there! Who's knocking?

AMPHITRYON: Me.

MERCURY: Who's me?

AMPHITRYON: Ah! Open up!

MERCURY: Why should I? Who are you
To raise this racket and to talk that way?

AMPHITRYON: I guess you don't know me?

MERCURY: Oh, yes.   1710
Yes, I know everyone that pulls that latch.
—Do I know him!

AMPHITRYON: Has all Thebes eaten mad-wort
Today and gone out of their senses too?—
Hey, Sosia! Sosia!

MERCURY: Yes, my name is Sosia.
The rascal shouts my name into my ears
As if he were afraid I might forget it.

AMPHITRYON: Just gods, man, don't you see me?

MERCURY: Perfectly.
What's up?

AMPHITRYON: You clown! "What's up," he says.

MERCURY: What isn't up?
Well, speak, if I'm supposed to talk with you.

AMPHITRYON: You rascal, just you wait! I'll bring a stick   1720
Up there and teach you how to speak with me.

MERCURY: Ho, ho! Down there's a rough and ready customer.*
Don't be offended.

AMPHITRYON: Devil!

MERCURY: Calm yourself.

AMPHITRYON: Hey! Isn't anybody home?

* Reading *Rüpel,* not *Riegel,* in this uncertain line.

MERCURY: Hey! Philip! Charmion! Where are you all?

AMPHITRYON: You low-born rascal!

MERCURY: But you must be tended to.
　But if you don't wait patiently until
　They come, and if you lay hand on that knocker
　So much as one more time, I'll send you down
　A whizzing embassy from up above here.   1730

AMPHITRYON: The shameless impudence of him! A fellow
　I've often kicked, whom, if I felt like it,
　I could send off and have him crucified.

MERCURY:
　Well? Are you through now? Have you looked me over?
　Have you surveyed me with those staring eyes
　Of yours? How wide, wide open he does stretch them!
　If looks could bite, he would have gotten to me
　By now and torn me limb apart from limb.

AMPHITRYON: I tremble, Sosia, myself to think
　Of what you're getting into by such talk.   1740
　What monstrous blows you are accumlating!
　—Come down and open up this door.

MERCURY: At last!

AMPHITRYON: Don't keep me waiting any longer, this
　Is urgent.

MERCURY: You'll declare your errand then.
　You say you want that door there opened?

AMPHITRYON: Yes.

MERCURY: All right. You could have said as much politely.
　Who is it that you're after? . . .

AMPHITRYON: that I'm after . . . ?

MERCURY: Yes. Are you deaf? Whom do you wish to see?

AMPHITRYON:
　. . . I wish to see? You cur, I'll kick your every bone in
　Once I get inside of that house.   1750

MERCURY: Do you know something, friend? Take my advice
　And go along. You gall me. Go along.

AMPHITRYON: You low-born scoundrel, you will soon find out
　What kind of treatment comes to servants
　Who make fun of their masters.

MERCURY: Of their masters?

I make fun of my master? You're my master?
AMPHITRYON: Now I hear him deny it yet!
MERCURY: I know
  Of only one, and that's Amphitryon.
AMPHITRYON: Who else but me, then, is Amphitryon?
  You blear-eyed rascal taking day for night?   1760
MERCURY: Amphitryon?
AMPHITRYON: Amphitryon, I tell you.
MERCURY: Ha, ha! You Thebans, come on over here.
AMPHITRYON:
  Oh, that the earth would swallow me! What shame!
MERCURY: Good friend, do tell me which the tavern was
  Where you got such a jolly jag on.
AMPHITRYON: Heaven!
MERCURY: And was the wine new wine or old?
AMPHITRYON: Ye gods!
MERCURY: And why not just one snifter more? You could
  Have drunk yourself to be the king of Egypt.
AMPHITRYON: Now it's all up with me.
MERCURY: Just go along,
  Dear lad. I'm sorry for you. Go sleep it off.   1770
  Here dwells Amphitryon, the Theban captain.
  Just go, and don't disturb his rest.
AMPHITRYON: What's that? Amphitryon's inside this house?
MERCURY: Yes, he's inside this house, he and Alcmena.
  But once more: go along, and don't disturb
  The happiness of that enamored pair,
  Unless you want him to come out here now
  And punish you himself for your offense.
                    (Exit.)
AMPHITRYON *(alone):*
  Oh, what a blow has struck you, luckless man!
  A crushing one, and all is up with me.   1780
  I am already buried, and my widow
  Already wedded to another husband.
  What decision ought I now to make?
  Should I reveal the shame that has befallen
  My house to all the world, or should I hide it?
  Here's nothing that needs sparing! Nothing's heard

Amid this meeting of the council but
The fiery hot consensus of revenge;
Be it my one and only care now that
The traitor does not get away alive.   1790
    (Enter Sosia with Commanders of the Army.)
SOSIA: Sir, these were all that I was able to
  Round up and bring you here to be your guests.
  My goodness, even if I don't dine at
  Your table, I deserve the meal.
AMPHITRYON: Ah! There you are.
SOSIA: Eh?
AMPHITRYON: Dog! How you shall die!
SOSIA: Me? Die?
AMPHITRYON: Now you'll find out just who I am.
SOSIA: The Devil! Don't I know?
AMPHITRYON: You did know, then, you traitor?
    (He puts his hand on his sword.)
SOSIA: O gentlemen, protect me now, I beg you.
FIRST COMMANDER: Forgive me! *(He grabs his arm.)*
AMPHITRYON: Let me go.
SOSIA: What have I done?
AMPHITRYON: You still ask that?—Away, I tell you. Let   1800
  My righteous vengeance find its satisfaction.
SOSIA: When someone's hanged, at least they tell him why.
FIRST COMMANDER: Do be so kind.
SECOND COMMANDER: And say what wrong he did.
SOSIA: Sirs, stand your ground, if you will be so good.
AMPHITRYON: What! Just a little while ago this scurvy
  Knave here shut that door right in my face
  And hurled down such abusive streams of insults,
  Each one enough to get him crucified . . .
  Die, cur!
SOSIA: I'm dead already. *(He falls to his knees.)*
FIRST COMMANDER: Calm yourself.
SOSIA: Commanders! Ah!
SECOND COMMANDER: What?
SOSIA: Is he stabbing at me?   1810
AMPHITRYON: Hands off, I tell you once again! He must
  Have payment, to the full, there for the shame

That he has heaped on me within this hour.
SOSIA: But when can I have possibly done wrong
    When for the last nine hours, by the clock,
    I've been down there in camp and at your orders?
FIRST COMMANDER: That's true. He asked us to your dinner table.
    It's two hours now that he has been in camp
    And never once out of our sight.
AMPHITRYON: Who gave that order?
SOSIA: Who? Why, you yourself!
AMPHITRYON: When? I?
                                              [1820
SOSIA: Right after you had made up with
                                [Alcmena.
    You were so happy and at once gave orders
    For festival throughout the palace.
AMPHITRYON: O heavens! Every hour, every step
    Just gets me deeper in the labyrinth.
    What am I now to make of this, my friends?
    Did you hear what he said has happened here?
FIRST COMMANDER: What this man here has told us is so poorly
    Designed for comprehension that right now
    Your prime concern must be to rip apart   1830
    The riddle of this whole deceitful web.
AMPHITRYON: All right, so be it! I shall need your help.
    My lucky star has brought you here to me.
    I shall assay the fortune of my life.
    Oh, my heart is afire for clarification,
    And yet I dread it worse than death.
                    (He knocks.)
                  [Enter Jupiter.]
JUPITER: What noise obliges me to come down here?
    Who's knocking at the door? What! You, Commanders?
AMPHITRYON: Who are you? Ye almighty gods!
SECOND COMMANDER: What do I see? Gods! Two Amphitryons!
AMPHITRYON: My very soul is frozen numb with horror!   [1840
    Alas for me! The riddle has been solved.
FIRST COMMANDER: Which of you two then is Amphitryon?
SECOND COMMANDER:
    Indeed! Two creatures so exactly like each other,
    No human eye can make distinction of them.

SOSIA: Sirs, this one is Amphitryon. The other
  Is a wretch deserving punishment.
                (He goes and stands at Jupiter's side.)
THIRD COMMANDER *(pointing to Amphitryon)*:
  Incredible! Is this one an impostor?
AMPHITRYON: Enough of this disgraceful witchery!
  I'm going to break this mystery open.   1850
                (He puts his hand on his sword.)
FIRST COMMANDER: Stop!
AMPHITRYON: Let me be!
SECOND COMMANDER: What now?
AMPHITRYON: I'm going to
                                                    [punish

  This vilest of deceits. Hands off, I say.
JUPITER: Composure there! No zeal is needed here.
  A man so much concerned about his name
  Must have but shaky grounds for bearing it.
SOSIA: That's just what I say. He has padded
  His belly out, and painted up his face,
  The cheat, to make himself look like the master.
AMPHITRYON: You traitor, your revolting babble will
  Be punished with three hundred blows of whips   1860
  Administered by three arms alternating.
SOSIA: Ho, ho! My master is a man of spirit,
  And he'll teach you to beat his servants up.
AMPHITRYON: Don't keep me any longer now, I say,
  From washing out my shame in scoundrel's blood.
FIRST COMMANDER: Excuse us, Sir. We can't allow this fight:
  Amphitryon against Amphitryon.
AMPHITRYON: What? Can't allow . . . ?
FIRST COMMANDER: You must compose
                                              [yourself.
AMPHITRYON: Is this your friendship for me too, Commanders?
  This the support that you had vowed to lend me?   1870
  Instead of taking vengeance for my honor,
  You back the vile deceiver's cause and block
  The righteous fall of the avenging sword?
FIRST COMMANDER: If you judged fairly, as you are not doing,
  You would give your approval to our steps.

Which one of you two is Amphitryon?
Why, you are. Very well—but so is he.
Where is God's finger that could point out for us
Inside which bosom, one just like the other,
The traitor heart is lurking in concealment?   1880
Once it has been identified, doubt not
But we'll have found the object of our vengeance.
But since the sword-blade could do no more here
Than rage with futile indiscrimination,
It surely would be better in its scabbard.
Let us investigate the matter calmly,
And if you feel you are Amphitryon,
As we in this odd situation truly
Hope that you are, but yet must feel some doubt,
It will be no more difficult for you,   1890
Than it will be for him, to prove the point.
AMPHITRYON: To prove the point . . . ?
FIRST COMMANDER: With cogent evidence.
And till then, nothing will be done about this.
JUPITER: You're quite right, Photidas. And this resemblance
Prevailing here between the two of us
·Excuses your suspended judgment for me.
Nor shall I feel resentment if between me
And him comparison is to be made.
Only, no coward's settlement by swords!
I mean to summon all of Thebes myself   1900
And in the thronged assembly of the people
Establish of what blood I am descended.
My nobleness of line he shall himself
Acknowledge, and that I am lord in Thebes.
Before me, to the dust, he shall bow down.
All fertile fields of Thebes he shall call mine,
Mine all the herds that feed among the pastures,
Mine too this house, and mine its lady mistress
That quietly commands throughout its rooms.
The entire realm of earth shall be informed   1910
That no shame has befallen Amphitryon.
As for suspicions that the fool has roused,
Here stands one who can set them all at naught.

Thebes presently will be assembled here.
Meanwhile come in and kindly grace the table
To which Sosia has invited you.
SOSIA: My goodness, this is just what I had thought.
Sirs, this announcement casts all further doubts
To the four winds. The real Amphitryon
's the one at whose house dinner is now served.   1920
AMPHITRYON: Ye everlasting and ye righteous gods!
Can any man be so humiliated?
To be robbed of my wife, dominion, name,
And honor by so infamous a trickster!
And friends of mine should tie my hands?
FIRST COMMANDER: No matter who you are, you must be patient.
A few hours yet, and we will know. And then
Without delay revenge will be exacted.
And woe, I say, on whom it falls.
AMPHITRYON: Faint-hearted lot! Go, honor the impostor!   1930
I still have other friends besides you two.
There still are men in Thebes here who will come to me
And share the suffering in my heart and not
Refuse their arms to be avenged for it.
JUPITER: All right! You call them. I shall wait for them.
AMPHITRYON: You rascal mountebank! You in the meantime
Will sneak out by the back way and be off.
But you will not elude my vengeance!
JUPITER: You go and call and bring your friends to me,
Then I shall say a word or two; not now.   1940
AMPHITRYON: By Zeus, there you are right, the god of clouds!
For if it is my lot to find you then,
You won't say more than two words, filthy cur,
Before my sword is hilt-deep down your throat.
JUPITER: Go call your friends. I won't say anything,
I'll speak in glances only, if you wish.
AMPHITRYON: Come on, then, fast, before he slips away.
You must, ye gods, grant me the joy of sending
Him down this very day into your Orcus!
Soon with a band of friends I shall return,   1950
Armed friends, who'll cast a net around this house,
And like a wasp I'll jab my stinger through

His breast and pluck it, sucking, out again
So winds will whistle through his withered bones.
(Exit.)
JUPITER: Come, Sirs, then, if you please, and by your entrance
Do honor to this house.
FIRST COMMANDER: Now, by my oath,
My wits are all awry from this adventure.
SOSIA: Now call a truce to your astonishment.
Go in to table and carouse till morning.
(Exeunt Jupiter and the Commanders.)
And how I'm going to pull my chair up too!   1960
What tales I'll tell
When they all get to talking of the war.
I'm dying to report on how they cut
Their way into Pharissa. And in all
My life I've never been so wolfish-hungry.
(Enter Mercury.)
MERCURY:
Where to? I'll bet you're sticking your nose in here too,
You shameless sniffer-out of kitchens, you.
SOSIA: No!—By your leave.
MERCURY: Away there! Off, I say!
Or do I need to fix your wagon for you?
SOSIA: What's this? Magnanimous and noble me,   1970
Restrain yourself. Go just a wee bit easy
On Sosia, Sosia. Who would always want
To be dead set on beating up himself?
MERCURY: So you're back up to your old tricks again?
You take my name away, you good-for-nothing?
You rob me of the name of Sosia?
SOSIA: Oh, nonsense! God forbid, my doughty self,
Now would I ever be that stingy with you?
So jealous of you? Take half of this name,
It's trash. Or if you like, take all of it.   1980
If Castor were the name, or Pollux, what
Would I not gladly share with you, my brother?
I tolerate you in my master's house,
So tolerate fraternal love in me,
And while those two Amphitryons go breaking

Each other's necks in jealous rivalry,
Why should the Sosias not sit down together
In mutual understanding and clink glasses
And drink to wish each other good long lives?
MERCURY: No, none of that!—Now, what a silly notion.   1990
    Should I sit meanwhile gnawing Hunger's paw?
    The table's only set for one.
SOSIA: What difference does that make? One mother's womb
    Gave birth to us, one cottage gave us shelter,
    We both have slept together in one bed,
    We've shared one set of clothes fraternally,
    One fate, so why not eat out of one dish?
MERCURY: I know of no such life in common. From
    My childhood I have been all on my own,
    And never have I shared a bed, a set   2000
    Of clothes, or any bite of food.
SOSIA: Reflect a minute. We are two twin brothers.
    You are the elder; I'll take second place,
    You'll take precedence over me completely.
    You'll take the first and all odd-numbered spoonfuls,
    I'll take the second and all even-numbered.
MERCURY: No, none of that. I want my own full serving,
    And anything that's left, I'll save for later.
    And anyone that reaches toward my plate
    I'll show a thing or two, by the high gods.   2010
SOSIA: Well, then at least let me become your shadow
    That falls behind your chair while you are eating.
MERCURY: Not so much as my footprint in the sand!
SOSIA: O you barbaric heart! You man of iron,
    Forged like a thunderbolt upon an anvil!
MERCURY: Do you think I should sleep outside the gates
    On grass, as if I were a journeyman,
    And live by breathing the blue air of heaven?
    No horse has earned a good square meal today,
    By God, as thoroughly as I have earned one.   2020
    Did I not come up here by night from camp?
    And didn't I walk back down there this morning
    To round up guests to come up for this dinner?
    And on those devilish trips have I not just

About run these old busy legs of mine
Right off and worn them out up to the thighs?
We're having sausages and warmed-up cabbage,
Just what I need to get my spirits back.

SOSIA: You're right there. Going over all those damned
Pine-root gnarls all that way is just about   2030
Enough to break your legs—and break your neck.

MERCURY: Well, then!

SOSIA: Poor me, deserted by the gods.
So Charis has fixed sausages . . . ?

MERCURY: Yes, fresh ones.
But not for you. There was a pig to slaughter.
And I have patched my quarrel up with Charis.

SOSIA: Ah, good. I'll just lie down and die. And cabbage?

MERCURY: Yes, cabbage. Warmed-up, yes. And anyone
That might find his mouth watering at the thought
Should not start anything with me and Charis.

SOSIA: For all I care, eat cabbage till you choke.   2040
What need do I have of your sausages?
The god that feeds the birds of heaven won't,
I think, neglect to feed old honest Sosia.

MERCURY: You still dare call yourself by that name, traitor?
You dare, you scurvy cur . . . ?

SOSIA: Go on! I didn't mean myself.
I meant a former relative of mine
Named Sosia. Long ago he used to work here—
And used to beat the other servants up—
Till someone dropped out of the sky one day
And turned him out of doors at dinner time.   2050

MERCURY: Watch out, I say, and no more now about it.
Just watch your step, I'm telling you, if you
Still want to count yourself among the living.

SOSIA (to himself):
How I would like to knock you, if I had the courage,
You whoreson, bastard rascal that you are,
Puffed up with arrogance.

MERCURY: What's that you're saying?

SOSIA: What?

MERCURY: You said some words . . . ?

SOSIA: Me?
MERCURY: You.
SOSIA: I never made a
                                                          [sound.
MERCURY: I heard you mention "knocking," if I'm not
    Mistaken; also "whoreson bastard rascal."
SOSIA: There must have been a parrot talking somewhere.   2060
    They chatter when the weather's nice.
MERCURY: So be it.
    For now, farewell. But if your back gets itchy,
    I'm always to be found here at this house.
                        (Exit.)
SOSIA: You overbearing devil! I just hope
    That slaughtered pig will be the death of you!
    "He'd show the man that reached out toward his plate!"
    I'd sooner have a shepherd's dog to share
    A dinner-dish with, than I would with him.
    He'd let his father starve before his eyes
    Before he'd let him have as much as he   2070
    Has sticking in between his middle teeth.
    —Go on! You have been rightly served, deserter.
    If I now held a sausage in each hand
    I wouldn't take a bite of either one.
    Leaving my poor good master in the lurch
    When greater force turned him out of his house!
    —There he approaches with his sturdy friends.
    —Here crowds are coming this way too! What is this?
            *(Enter Amphitryon with Colonels from one
               side and citizenry from the other.)*
AMPHITRYON: Welcome, my friends! But who has summoned you?
ONE OF THE CITIZENS: All through the city heralds are proclaiming
    That we're to gather here before your palace.   [2080
AMPHITRYON: Heralds! But to what purpose? Why?
THE CITIZEN: They told us that we would be witnesses
    To a decisive statement from your lips
    That would clear up the riddle that has thrown
    The whole town in dismay.
AMPHITRYON *(to the Colonels):* The gall of him!
    Can impudence be carried any further?

SECOND COLONEL: Then he'll appear at last.
AMPHITRYON: What if he does?
FIRST COLONEL: Don't worry. Here's Argatiphontidas.
  Just let me get to look him in the eye   2090
  And his life will be dancing here upon this sword-point.
AMPHITRYON (to the citizenry):
  You citizens of Thebes, listen to me!
  I was not the one who summoned you,
  Although the surging tide of your assemblage
  Is very welcome to me. It was he,
  That lying spirit up from hell, who wants
  Me out of Thebes, and out of my wife's heart,
  Out of the world's remembrance, if he could,
  Out of the fortress of my consciousness.
  So muster all your senses now, and even   2100
  If every man of you, like Argus, had
  A thousand eyes and could at midnight's hour
  Tell crickets from their footprints in the sand,
  Do not spare any effort now, but open
  Your eyes up wide the way that moles will do
  When they are looking for the sun at noon;
  Direct your glances in a single mirror,
  Then turn that full and total ray on me,
  Survey me head to foot and up and down,
  And then pronounce and speak and answer me: 2110
  Who am I?
THE CITIZENRY:
            Who are you? Amphitryon!
AMPHITRYON: All right. Amphitryon. So much for that.
  Now when that son of Darkness comes in sight,
  That monster of a man upon whose head
  Each individual hair curls just like mine,
  And when your dazzled senses presently
  Discover no more marks than mothers need
  When they identify their youngest babes,
  And when you are obliged to choose between us
  As though between two drops of water, one   2120
  All sweet, pure, genuine, and silvery,
  The other poison, guile, deceit, and death—

Be sure then to remember *I*'m Amphitryon,
You citizens of Thebes,
The one that bent his helmet crest like this.
THE CITIZENRY: What are you doing? Don't break off the crest
    As long as you stand in your prime before us.
SECOND COLONEL: Do you think we would . . . ?
AMPHITRYON: Friends, don't
                                                [interfere.

My wits are clear and I know what I'm doing.
FIRST COLONEL: Do as you like. Meanwhile I trust that you   2130
    Have not done such a silly thing for my sake.
    If your Commanders hesitated when
    That ape appeared, it does not follow that
    Argatiphontidas would do the same.
    If some friend needs us in a matter of
    His honor, down we pull our helmets over
    Our eyes and close in on the adversary.
    To stand and listen to opponents' bragging
    Is something for old women. As for me,
    I'm always for the shortest course of action;   2140
    In cases of this sort the only way
    To start is: run the adversary through
    Straight off—not stand on any ceremonies.
    So, short and sweet, Argatiphontidas
    Will show you all a thing or two today,
    And not at any other's hand than mine,
    By Ares, shall this rascal bite the dust.
AMPHITRYON: Come on, then!
SOSIA: Here I kneel before your feet,
    My true, my noble, persecuted master.
    I now am in a state of full repentance   2150
    To take the wages of my impudence.
    So hit me, box my ears, beat, push, and kick me,
    Yes, kill me, and I won't so much as whimper.
AMPHITRYON: Get up. What's happened now?
SOSIA: Not so much as a
                                                [smell

Of dinner would they let me have in there.
The other me, that serves the other you,

The very devil was in him again,
And in a word, I've been de-Sosia-ized
The way that you are dis-Amphitryon-ated.
AMPHITRYON: Hear, citizens!
SOSIA: Yes, citizens of Thebes!   2160
Here stands the actual Amphitryon.
The one inside at table there
Deserves to have the ravens eat him up.
Go storm the house, if you will be so kind,
The cabbage may just still be warm.
AMPHITRYON: So follow me.
SOSIA: Look! There he comes now. He and
                                                    [she.

(Enter Jupiter, Alcmena, Mercury, Charis,
and the Commanders.)

ALCMENA: Appalling! A mortal man, you say, and you
Would shamefully expose me to his sight?
THE CITIZENRY: Ye everlasting gods! What's this we see?
JUPITER: The entire world, Beloved, must be shown   2170
That *no one* else came near your soul
Save your own husband, save Amphitryon.
AMPHITRYON: Lord of my life! The poor unlucky woman!
ALCMENA: What? No one! Can you alter lots once cast?
THE COLONELS: All ye Olympians! Amphitryon there.
JUPITER: You owe it, Dearest, to yourself and me,
You *must,* you will, my life, bring yourself to it.
Come, pluck your courage up; a triumph waits you.
AMPHITRYON: Lightning, hell, and devils! This to me?
JUPITER: I bid you welcome, citizens of Thebes.   2180
AMPHITRYON: You dirty dog, they're here to bring you death.
Come on! *(He draws his sword.)*
SECOND COMMANDER *(blocking his way):*
                Stop there!
AMPHITRYON: Come on, I say, you Thebans!
FIRST COMMANDER *(pointing to Amphitryon):*
Thebans, seize him, I cry. There's the impostor!
AMPHITRYON: Argatiphontidas!
FIRST COLONEL: Am I bewitched?
THE CITIZENRY: Can any human eye here tell the difference?

AMPHITRYON: Death! Devil! Rage and no revenge!
Annihilation!
(He collapses in Sosia's arms.)
JUPITER: Fool, listen to a word or two from me.
SOSIA: My goodness! He can't hear you. He is dead.
FIRST COLONEL: What good now is the bent-down helmet crest?
"Open your eyes up wide the way that moles do . . ." [2190
The one his wife accepts must be the real one.
FIRST COMMANDER: Commanders, here's the real Amphitryon.
AMPHITRYON *(reviving):*
Which one does his own wife accept?
FIRST COLONEL: The other,
The one with whom she issued from the house.
Around whom would she, vine-like, wreathe her tendrils
If it is not her tree, Amphitryon?
AMPHITRYON: To think I do not have enough strength left
To crush in dust the tongue that said that!
Accept him she does not.
(He gets to his feet again.)
FIRST COMMANDER: Ah, that's a lie! 2200
Do you think you'll becloud the people's judgment
When they can see with their own eyes?
AMPHITRYON: I say again that she does not accept him!
—If she can recognize her husband in him,
I will inquire no further who I *am*,
But I will hail him as Amphitryon.
FIRST COMMANDER: Agreed. Pronounce.
SECOND COMMANDER: Declare yourself now,
[Princess.
AMPHITRYON: Alcmena! My young wife! Declare yourself,
Grant me once more the light of your dear eyes!
Say you accept that man there as your husband, 2210
And faster than that lightning-thought can flash
This sword will rid you of the sight of me.
FIRST COMMANDER: That sentence will be carried out at once.
SECOND COMMANDER: You know that man?
FIRST COMMANDER: You know that
[stranger there?
AMPHITRYON: Can it be that you should not know this heart,

Of which your listening ear so often told you
How many loving beats it throbbed for you?
Or could you fail to recognize my voice
Which you so often stole with glances from
My lips before it could attain to sound?   2220
ALCMENA: Could I but sink into eternal darkness!
AMPHITRYON: I knew it. Citizens of Thebes, you see
    The swift Peneus will reverse its streams,
    The Bosporus will make its bed on Ida,
    The dromedary will traverse the ocean,
    Before she will accept that stranger there.
THE CITIZENRY: What? He, Amphitryon? She hesitates.
FIRST COMMANDER: Pronounce!
SECOND COMMANDER: Speak!
THIRD COMMANDER: Tell us!
SECOND COMMANDER: Princess, speak
                                                    [one word!
FIRST COMMANDER: We're lost if she is silent any longer.
JUPITER: Lend, lend your voice unto the truth, my child.   2230
ALCMENA: Amphitryon, my friends, is here beside me.
AMPHITRYON: That is Amphitryon! Almighty gods!
FIRST COMMANDER: So be it, then. Your lot is cast. Withdraw.
AMPHITRYON: Alcmena!
SECOND COMMANDER: Go, impostor, go, unless
    You'd have us carry out that sentence for you.
AMPHITRYON: Beloved!
ALCMENA: Worthless, shameless wretch!
    Do you still dare address me by that term?
    Before my husband's awe-inspiring face
    Can I not be secure from your affront?
    You monster! More abhorrent to me   2240
    Than any bloated things that nest in swamps!
    What did I do, that you should come to me
    Beneath the hellish cloak of darkness
    And spew your venom out upon my pinions?
    What more, O evil man, than having gleamed
    In silence like a glowworm in your sight?
    I now see what delusion blinded me.
    I needed the bright splendor of the sunlight

To tell the venal body of a lout
From the high glory of these regal limbs,   2250
To tell the bullock from the royal stag!
A curse upon the senses that fall prey
To such a gross deception, and upon
The heart that uttered such false sounds !
A curse upon the soul that could not even
Remember and identify her own beloved!
Oh, let me flee up to the mountain tops,
To dead waste regions where not even owls
Will visit me unless some guardian
Attends me and preserves my heart in blamelessness!—   2260
Go! You succeeded in your vile deceit,
And all my peace of soul is broken down.
AMPHITRYON: Unhappy woman that you are! Was I
   The one that came to you in this past night?
ALCMENA: Enough of this! Release me now, my husband.
   You will now kindly charm away somewhat
   This bitterest hour of my life.
   Let me escape these thousand stares that beat me,
   Like cudgels intercrossing, to the ground.
JUPITER: Divine one! Yet more radiant than the sun!   2270
   For you a triumph waits, the like of which
   Befell no princess ever yet in Thebes.
   And you must tarry for a moment yet.
                  (to Amphitryon)
   Do you believe now *I*'m Amphitryon?
AMPHITRYON: Do I believe now *you*'re Amphitryon?
   You creature . . . . horrible
   Beyond what breath has power to convey!
FIRST COMMANDER: Impostor! You refuse?
SECOND COMMANDER: You still deny it?
FIRST COMMANDER: You would not be about to try to prove
   The Princess has played false with us?   2280
AMPHITRYON: Oh, every single word of hers is true—
   And gold ten times refined is not more true.
   Not if I read what lightnings write upon
   The night, not if I summoned up the voice
   Of thunder, would I trust those oracles
   As I trust what her faithful lips have said.

I now take oath upon the very altar
And straightway go to die death sevenfold
In the unshakeable conviction that
He is Amphitryon to her. 2290
JUPITER: Good, then.—You are Amphitryon.
AMPHITRYON: I am!
—And who are you, dread spirit, then?
JUPITER: Amphitryon. I would have thought you knew that.
AMPHITRYON: Amphitryon! No mortal man can grasp this.
Speak so we understand.
ALCMENA: What talk is this?
JUPITER: Amphitryon! You fool! And still you doubt?
Argatiphontidas and Photidas,
The citadel of Cadmus, Greece itself,
Light, aether, and the element of water,
All things that were, and are, and ever shall be. 2300
AMPHITRYON: Come gather, friends, around me now, and let us
See how this riddle is to be resolved.
ALCMENA: Oh, monstrous!
THE COMMANDERS: What are we to make of this?
JUPITER (to Alcmena): You think Amphitryon appeared to you?
ALCMENA: Leave me forever in my error, if
Your light is not to shade my soul forever.
JUPITER: A curse upon this bliss you gave me, if
I must not be forevermore beside you!
AMPHITRYON:
Then out with your pronouncement now: Who are you?
(A flash of lightning and a peal of thunder.
The stage is enveloped in clouds. An eagle with
the thunderbolt swoops down out of the clouds.)
JUPITER: You seek to know?
(He seizes hold of the thunderbolt.
The eagle flies off.)
THE CITIZENRY: Ye gods above!
JUPITER: Who am I? 2310
THE COMMANDERS AND THE COLONELS:
It is the dread god Jupiter himself!
ALCMENA: Protect me, ye celestials!
(She falls into Amphitryon's arms.)
AMPHITRYON: Worship to you

From here in dust. You are the mighty thunderer!
And yours is all that I possess.
THE CITIZENRY: The god! To dust, to dust bow down your faces!
　　(*All prostrate themselves, except Amphitryon.*)
JUPITER: Amid your household Zeus has been well pleased,
　　Amphitryon, and of his divine favor
　　A sign shall be made manifest to you.
　　Let your black woe and care be now dispelled,
　　And open up your heart to triumph.　　　　　　　2320
　　What you, in me, did to yourself, will not
　　Harm you before my everlasting nature.
　　If you find your reward amid my fault,
　　Then I hail you in friendly words, and leave you.
　　Your fame shall henceforth find, as my world finds,
　　Its boundaries and limits in the stars.
　　But if you are not satisfied with thanks,
　　Then you shall have your fondest wish fulfilled,
　　And I permit it voice before me now.
AMPHITRYON: No, father Zeus, I am not satisfied!　　　2330
　　And now my tongue grows unto my heart's wish.
　　What you once did for Tyndarus, do likewise
　　Now for Amphitryon: grant him a son,
　　Great like the sons of Tyndarus.
JUPITER: So be it. To you will be born a son
　　And "Hercules" shall be his name; no hero
　　Of former ages shall match his renown,
　　Not even my eternal Dioscuri.
　　Twelve mighty labors shall he raise aloft,
　　A monument beyond comparison.　　　　　　　2340
　　And when that pyramid has been completed
　　And lifts its brow up to the hems of clouds,
　　He shall ascend its steps as far as heaven
　　And I shall greet his godhead in Olympus.
AMPHITRYON:
　　My thanks—You will not take this woman from me?
　　She is not breathing.
JUPITER:　　　　　　She shall be left with you.
　　But let her rest, if she is to remain.—
　　Hermes!

*(He disappears amid the clouds which
in the meantime have opened at their top
to reveal the summit of Olympus where
the Olympians are assembled.)*

ALCMENA: Amphitryon!

MERCURY: I follow you at once, divine one!—   2350
As soon as I have told that oaf down there
About how sick and tired I am of wearing
His ugly face, and how I'll take ambrosia now
And wash it off of my Olympian cheeks,
And how his beatings may make lofty poems,
And how I am no more nor less than Hermes,
The wing-foot messenger of the high gods.

(Exit.)

SOSIA: If only you had left me unfit for
Those lofty poems! Never in my life
Did I see such a devil in his thrashings!   2360

FIRST COMMANDER:
Well! Here is such a triumph . . .

SECOND COMMANDER: Such high fame . . .

FIRST COLONEL: You see, we're overwhelmed . . .

AMPHITRYON: Alcmena!

ALCMENA: Ah!   (2362)

IV. AMPHITRYON SINCE KLEIST

Continental Romanticisms tended on the whole to force themes from classical antiquity into retirement. Nor did the succeeding movements of Realism, Naturalism, and the various neo-Romanticisms at the end of the century foster much of a resurgence of interest in those themes. Thus nineteenth century *Amphitryons* are rare and obscure. Professor Shero lists only one item, an unsuccessful opera of *Amphitryon,* libretto by Beaumont and Nuitter, music by Paul-Jean-Jacques Lacome d'Estaleux, which was produced in Paris on April 5, 1875. Professor Lindberger, after mentioning this item, was able to add only two instances of an Amphitryon influence, the first a case of partial influence on Karl Gutzkow's comedy of 1844 entitled *Das Urbild des Tartüffe* (The Prototype of Tartuffe), which had for its hero Molière himself, the second a case of partial influence on a forgotten comedy of 1901 called *Die Zwillingsschwester* (The Twin Sisters) by Ludwig Fulda. In the early twentieth century classical themes began to emerge once again after their prolonged retirement. We notice, for instance, such operas of Richard Strauss as *Ariadne auf Naxos, Elektra,* and *Daphne*—and the plays of Jean Giraudoux.

1. GIRAUDOUX' *Amphitryon 38*

At mid-twentieth century, theater-goers were most likely to recall the age-old story in the form given it by Jean Giraudoux in his second work for the stage, the three-Act prose comedy entitled *Amphitryon 38,* which had its première at the Comédie des Champs-Elysées on November 8, 1929 with the celebrated Louis Jouvet in the role of Mercure. The "38" of the title presumably implies thirty-seven previous versions, and by that conspicuous advertisement the author asserted the prerogative of writers to rework old themes rather than to be constrained to invent "fables" anew at every turn. Precisely how the scholarly Girau-

doux arrived at the total of 37-plus-1 is not known; the figure
may have been based on some calculation or it may have been
merely whimsical. We have mentioned about sixty predecessors
in these pages, including the mythographers.

Even if the "38" was merely fanciful, however, Giraudoux
must have had first-hand acquaintance with a fair number of
these predecessors. His opening scene suggests possible use, as a
point of departure, of that south-Italian vase painting which,
since Winckelmann's time two centuries ago, has been accepted
at representing Jupiter and Mercury outside Alcmena's window.
As the two gods stand talking, Mercury's reminder to Jupiter
about trans-mural eyesight seems to echo Dryden's Mercury
seeing through Phaedra's clothes to inventory her pockets. The
divine brilliance upon Jupiter's face recalls a passage in Rotrou
about the god's strange youthfulness as opposed to the real Amphitryon's features. Jupiter's and Alcmena's oath-swearing near
the end of Act I surely echoes Plautus. More striking still is the
recurrence of the Kleistian idea of the god humanized by love
of a mortal woman, to say nothing of the conversion of Kleist's
pantheistic *tirades* into a creation myth in terms of modern
science. Here it is noteworthy that Alcmena disconcerts the god,
not the other way around.

But more important than the influences are the "non-influ-
ences," for it is evident that Giraudoux was at pains to avoid
competition, or even comparison, with Molière. The grateful
role of Sosia, for example, which Molière created for himself, has
been reduced almost to supernumerary status. Much of the best
comic matter is now assigned to Mercury, no doubt with the
finesse of actor Louis Jouvet in mind from the outset. The role
of Alcmena has been expanded far beyond the modest part she
had in Molière, so that she now dominates the total work. In
compensation, the titular hero is reduced to second magnitude,
not without the substitution of a somewhat passive, pathetic,
manipulated husband for an angry, active, and challenging one.
Gone are the identification tokens, for there is here neither King
Pterelas' golden goblet nor his diamond-cluster nor his Grecian
headband with the single monogrammed jewel. Even the Taph-
ians/Teleboans have disappeared. The war is now a fanciful
contrivance of Mercury's magic and the author's will for a few

hours' time. Wholly new roles have been introduced: the Trumpeter; the Warrior, who is like a figure in an allegory; Ecclissé, who resembles a Racinian nurse-confidente, like Phèdre's Oenone, turned comic, but whose name seems to have been coined from the Greek word *ekklesia*—"community," to denote her function as speaker for the people at large; and above all, Leda, the *grande dame* bemused by her former experience with Jupiter and not averse to having a second try at amatory submission to a god. New characters mean new scenes, so that the Warrior episode in Act I and the Leda scene in Act II are wholly new inventions without precedent in the "thirty-seven" foregoing *Amphitryons*.

Even the time analysis has been ingeniously altered. Temporally, Act I would come before the action of Molière's Act I, indeed before Molière's very prologue. Act II would correspond to undisclosed off-stage action before Jupiter's morning farewell near the end of Molière's Act I. And if the final Acts of both plays deal with the conclusion of the fable, Giraudoux makes that conclusion consist primarily of a long dialogue between Alcmena and Jupiter. The voice out of heaven is now an impersonal one and it speaks at the beginning of Act III rather than at the end, and Jupiter now closes the play with the words of a comic, if cosmic, puppeteer.

Amphitryon 38, in spite of its title, is Alcmena's play throughout. Miscast an actress in that role and the whole play will collapse, let the supporting cast be ever so fine. This fundamental reallocation of dramatic weight within the plot is in contrast to all foregoing versions and necessarily alters the character of the total work. Yet in this Alcmena lies also the problematic quality of Giraudoux' product, for this heroine, who can subtly control the "kosmokrator" himself, to say nothing of bending Leda to her will with a few words, must also dominate Amphitryon's soul and self. Benign and lovely as she is, able as she is to stand firm against great odds, sincere as she is in her devotion to her husband, she is basically of the type known as "deadlier than the male."

Still, not even she is allowed to win every move in this complex chess game. Belatedly she realizes that she sent her husband, not the impostor, to Leda. She suspects that Jupiter is lying when he denies having impersonated Amphitryon and in the end she accepts the gift of oblivion which alone will allow her to bear Jupiter's child in good conscience as Amphitryon's child. But if she is deceived, so is everybody else in the cast. Amphitryon possesses Leda under the impression he is possessing his wife and Amphitryon accepts at face value Jupiter's reassurance that the child Hercules will be his, Amphitryon's, child. Leda honestly fancies she has had her second encounter with the king of the gods. As for Jupiter, he has been evaded, discomfited, and put out of countenance throughout the entire adventure; Alcmena does not want him or any advantage he can bestow, not even immortality, not even the kind of son he means to have by her. The Theban people themselves are deceived into congregating for a divine visit when, actually, the occasion is a divine farewell. Ecclissé is thwarted in her ambitions for her mistress and even the Warrior gets only a paltry little war. Mercury alone is unaffected, having been coolly detached all along. The irony-ridden work ends with a pact of friendship—which may mean something just a little different to each of the individuals involved.

The Giraudoux whose higher schooling was devoted to German language and literature cannot have failed to acquire from that source certain notions of "Romantic irony" that are reflected in *Amphitryon 38* both on the larger plane and in smaller details. Jupiter greets Alcmena's house with the aria-title from Gounod's *Faust:* "Salut, demeure chaste et pure," and when he inquires why Mercury should smile at the words, the latter replies that he has heard them in advance: "The future centuries call them out to me." That sort of comic fillip Giroudoux could have found in the practice of Ludwig Tieck and Clemens Brentano. The specifically theatrical irony of I, 5, on the other hand, where the human actor plays a god who is about to transform himself into a human, smacks rather of Neo-Romantic subtlety; a parallel would be *Der Rosenkavalier* of Hugo von Hofmannsthal and Richard Strauss, where a female singer must impersonate a young man who presently disguises himself as a chambermaid.

Alien to Molière's almost exclusively verbal art is Giraudoux' twentieth-century exploitation of electrical stage lighting possibilities, not for extra show but as intrinsic to the play. Mercury not only tells the audience about the protracted night he has produced, he also demonstrates some of his cosmic magic before their eyes. At the beginning of Act II he is seen, his reclining body mysteriously aglow, in stage blackout. Then he summons rays from the sun, first a green one, then a sickly bluish-purple one, and finally a saffron-yellow one, which he approves; whereupon the obliging sun floods Alcmena's chamber with a glory of morning light. This is technology subordinated to poetic use. There is about it also something of that nineteenth century German notion of the theater as a magic box that produced the most wondrous illusions within the darkness to which spectators came. One thinks of Grillparzer's *The Dream is a Life,* and still more of Wagner's *Ring* operas, especially in their Bayreuth house. What is significant here is the qualitative difference from any paltry "machines" that might have been available for Molière's production of 1668.

The use of prose in a twentieth century play was all but inevitable, yet Giraudoux must have been happy not to be obliged to vie with Molière even on this score. In this case the prose is normal educated speech judiciously combined with poetic turns. Classical antiquarianism is deftly introduced on occasion, as when Amphitryon gives the names of his horses as Elaphocéphale and Hypsipila (Elephant Head and High Gate), although there is an almost studied avoidance of "Grecian local color," either Homeric or Classical. These gods and mortals are thoroughly French and of 1929, so much so that we need to look twice to catch the verbal irony of Mercury's saying that Jupiter's eyes show "not a sign of lachrymal glands." One notes also a fin-de-siècle preference for things unusual—unusual animals like the ocelot and "young wild boar" (marcassin), unusual flowers like verbena and zinnia, and Alcmena professes a post-Huysmans preference for unusual colors: "du mordoré, du pourpre, du vert lézard"—bronze-gold, magenta, lizard-green. Jupiter-Amphitryon's reply to this remark of hers is a passage that would have astonished Kleist and made Molière or Plautus stare. Such hues, says the would-be husband, creating Jupiter left to the dyers;

"But, to come back to the different vibrations of the ether, he arranged, by means of the impact of molecular double impact, as well as by means of the counter-refractions of the original refractions, that there should be stretched across the universe a thousand different networks of sound and color, perceptible or not—after all, it's nothing to him!—to human organs."

Witty, skillful play that it is, modern readers and theater-goers are mistaken if they fancy that *Amphitryon 38* is simply an old work brought up to date. *That* description may apply to Molière, to Rotrou, to Dryden even. Those writers sought conscientiously to bring Plautus up to date, but they all remained as faithful as possible to the ancient scenario as they cut and trimmed in conformance with prevailing fashions. Giraudoux, on the other hand, extracted certain elements of the old fable and reorganized them into a wholly new pattern. What with Kleist had been a partial, hesitant dislocation of the fable, almost as an afterthought, is here a systematic and thorough dislocation. Only a little distance more and this would not be an Amphitryon play at all.

2. *Amphitryon 38* IN ENGLISH

In 1937 an English-language version of *Amphitryon 38,* adapted by S. N. Behrman, enjoyed success with the famous husband-wife team of Alfred Lunt and Lynn Fontanne in the roles of Jupiter and Alcmena respectively. It should be made clear that this well-known version is a very free adaptation of Giraudoux' work, faithful to the general intentions of the original, unfaithful in a sufficient number of ways to make it about one-third a new play.

Giraudoux's opening scene, which we have mentioned as being possibly connected with that ancient vase-painting that showed Jupiter and Mercury below Alcmena's window, had about it the quality of a prologue in so far as it broached the entire adventure casually in conversation between the two gods. Behrman made it frankly a Prologue, converting the neutral earthbound scene to a cloud on which the naked divinities are outstretched as they gaze down toward Alcmena's window below them. Their dialogue proceeds much as before, with some speeches translated and others paraphrased, but more rapidly paced and more realistic in tone than the somewhat deliberately stylized original. By and large, this is the formula of adaptation throughout. Long speeches characteristic of French drama are regularly broken up or condensed, sometimes transposed elsewhere in a scene, and sometimes omitted altogether. Only Alcmena is allowed continuous discourse to the extent of what might be called a paragraph, though Mercury is given his full scene to himself at the beginning of Act II. There, for some reason, he conjures only the green ray from the sun, omitting the bluish-purple one, before approving the saffron-yellow light of morning to suffuse the chamber. The role of Ecclissé is omitted completely. In her place stand two serving girls, Kleantha with three lines to speak, and Nenetza with two. Necessarily, Leda has been retained, and with the same bemused character as before, but her dialogue with Alcmena has been much reduced in length. In place of the aria title from Gounod's *Faust* now stands Hamlet's line to Ophelia, "Nymph, in thy orisons be all my sins remembered," with the "my" wickedly altered to "thy"—unless this is a misprint like the "thousands of leaves" in Mercury's soliloquy where the French should yield "thousands of leagues." With the beginning of Act III the adaptation becomes ever more free. The Voice out of Heaven is eliminated completely, and the two dialogues of chief importance, between Alcmena and Amphitryon and between Alcmena and Jupiter, are to all intents and purposes new invention.

All these changes were apparently made in the interests of getting on with the story. All imply audiences who detest a "talky play." All seem to have been made in accordance with the concept of dramatic writing which claims that the best part of any script is the blank spaces between the lines that leave good actors free to act. The text suggests a skillfully designed vehicle for the Lunts—and for the stage manager.

3. GEORG KAISER: *Zweimal Amphitryon*

Georg Kaiser was the successful author of forty-one plays when, in 1933, he fled his native Germany to seek political asylum in Switzerland. In exile he wrote eighteen further plays, of which the final three, *Pygmalion, Zweimal Amphitryon* (Amphitryon Doubled), and *Bellerophon*, were posthumously published in Zürich in 1948 under the collective title of *Griechische Dramen*. The Amphitryon play was given its première in Zürich in the spring of 1944, a year before the close of the war that dictated much of its spirit and a year before the author's death.

The scenario of this five-Act drama in blank verse may be summarized as follows: A messenger from Alkmene to Amphitryon in his battle tent returns to say that it has been impossible to carry out his commission; Amphitryon refused to receive any message except the word of capitulation from the besieged city of Pharsala; not even Alkmene's brother Alexandros could gain access to him. Dialogue between Alkmene and her old nurse reveals that Amphitryon's attention was exclusively claimed at his wedding festivities by a suit of armor, a gift from his Captains, and that, once having donned the armor, he departed immediately, with his marriage unconsummated, to "consecrate" the armor in battle. Her message to him was an abject plea to be allowed to come to him and serve at menial tasks in his tent so long as the siege continued. The neglected bride now kindles a fire at the house-altar, commits her letter to its flames, and earnestly begs Zeus to send Amphitryon to her in the status of the lowliest goatherd so that she will not be too base to love him. The fire-smoke parts to disclose Zeus in Amphitryon's form and clad in a shaggy goatskin. As he lifts her lovingly into his arms, the altar divides before a flight of gleaming steps, and while he is carrying her up those steps, the altar closes again and the curtain descends on Act I.

The scene of Act II is the interior of Amphitryon's tent. The starving defenders of Pharsala had opened their gates to drive in a herd of unmilked goats, the besiegers had outraced the goats and entered the city, and now Amphitryon stands gloating over the burning town and the smell of roasting human flesh. At the conference of Captains everyone is startled to hear that a report of the victory is to be sent to Thebes. Why, it is asked, are they not all going home, now that victory has been achieved? Amphitryon mocks them and outlines his plans to reconnoiter beyond the mountains for some other town to capture. When no one else will go, he announces that he will go himself, disguised as an innocent goatherd. Miraculously there are found right there in the General's tent a shaggy goatskin, a staff, a girdle, and a scrip. Amphitryon sets out for the mountains.

Act III presents a banquet given by Zeus-Amphitryon for the Elders and ladies of Thebes. A singer rehearses the "goat song" of the fall of Pharsala. The astonished guests ask how Amphitryon can be home when none of his men have returned. To which Zeus-Amphitryon replies that the greedy Captains insisted on pushing up into the mountains to reconnoiter further towns to pillage, mocking at the love of their wives and at the authority of the Elders, while he himself has slipped away in the disguise of a goatherd to be with Alkmene. In outrage the Elders send a deputation of three of their number to remonstrate with the refractory Captains.

In the fourth Act the deputation hears with amazement that the case was precisely the reverse of what they had been told. As all agree to return to Thebes at once to confront the lying Amphitryon, the tentflaps are opened and there stands the real Amphitryon in his goatherd disguise. He has reconnoitered the mountain region, made a map of paths and fords, and calls for immediate advance against a wealthy and unsuspecting population—whose very name he does not know. To his bewilderment they arrest him.

His trial is in progress in the marketplace of Thebes as the fifth Act begins. Accused and accusers repeat exactly what each has experienced. Amphitryon is offering his map of reconnoitered territory to be put to the test when Alkmene enters to declare that Amphitryon's story would be true, were it not for the fact that she is pregnant by him. The Elders bid him consult the god by sacrifice and if the god denies him, he will be killed. In the fire-smoke appears Zeus, clad in a goatskin and in the shape of Amphitryon. Solemnly he announces that he had been on the point of destroying the entire human race from sheer loathing of their senseless blood-lust when Alkmene's prayer moved him to descend to her from Olympus. From her he learned human love. Her unborn child will be Herakles, of his own seed, and the labors of the future hero shall be for the betterment of mankind. Until the child is born Amphitryon must serve as a real goatherd. The crowd parts to let Amphitryon pass toward his penance, the god vanishes, and Alkmene faints into the arms of her old nurse as the final curtain falls.

This impressive play may be marred by bluntness of message and by undistinguished verse, but it is dramatically powerful and conceived with brilliant originality. Kaiser's compositional process resembles that of Giraudoux in that he extracted elements of the old legend from their traditional settings and assigned them new values in an entirely new pattern. Zeus still impersonates Amphitryon while the latter is away at the wars, Alkmene is still deceived by the god in her husband's shape, Herakles is still begotten by the god upon the mortal woman, but all these points have a completely new meaning. If there is neither Mercury nor Sosia, we remind ourselves that these personages were not in the earliest myth. Of husband-wife jealousy there is almost none. Comedy has vanished, but the author has not attempted a reconstitution of pre-Plautine Amphitryon tragedy either. As with Giraudoux, there has been once again a redistribution of dramatic weight among the characters, but this time it is Alkmene whose role is subordinated. Amphitryon and Zeus now carry almost the entire story. The heroine's brother, Alexandros, has little to say or to do, and all other persons are unnamed, chorus-like figures—Elders, Captains, the nurse, the messenger, the mute populace—reminiscent of Kaiser's earlier Expressionist practice.

As an anti-war play, *Amphitryon Doubled* has the authentic ring of heartsickness on the part of an author who wrote while a monstrous and inhuman war was still raging only a few miles from his none-too-secure refuge. There is no mistaking his fury in having Zeus declare his intention of destroying the human race. There Zeus speaks like the Jehovah of the Deluge or of the extinction of the Cities of the Plain. Like the Christian God, Zeus imposes penitential service upon the sinning hero until the birth of Herakles, not unsimilar to Zachary's being struck dumb until the birth of John. And the son of this god shall be a savior, for Herakles will set mankind a model of energies properly directed. In the myth Kaiser saw Biblical parallels other than the Annunciation. Yet this Zeus, who is a god of righteousness, is deflected from his destructive purposes, not by finding one upright man, but by experiencing the love of a mortal woman. If, however, through Alkmene he learns the hidden worth of mortals and is himself somewhat humanized thereby, that is left as a minor motif. This is a play of men and of ideas, not of romantic love. All the rest is "goat song"—*trag-oedeia*, and Greek. Alkmene is the relatively slight bar from which depend the heavy scales of Hellenic and Judaeo-Christian traditions. A post-chivalric attitude toward women is also seen in her portrayal.

This rare blend of Greek and Christian elements was realized in the high heat of the author's anger. For this anger and for his thundering message Kaiser makes no apology, for he sees literature's duty as lying in the guidance of mankind. In Act III Zeus recalls not only the potters and the cabinet-makers and all the other tradesmen who are forced away from their useful work by soldiering, but also the *Schreiber*—here the author plays on the double meaning of "scribes" and "literary authors"—

> . . . .
> Auch von den Schreibern, die die Hüter sind
> aus eingebor'nem Recht und gleicher Pflicht
> des über alle Grenzen ausgespannten Reichs
> des Geists, der in Vollendung führt die Schöpfung.
>
> And of the writers too, who are the guardians,
> by innate right and no less innate duty,
> of the frontier-transcending kingdom of
> the mind, that toward fulfillment leads Creation.

Kaiser's sermon-message is of such urgency that it seems improper to interpose objections to his lack of esthetic objectivity. Yet it may be mentioned that Euripides composed *The Trojan Women* in the midst of a war no less dismal to *him,* composed it with righteous anger,—and contented himself with objective portrayal of human miseries afflicting victor and vanquished alike, while over all the actors streamed the flame and smoke of burning Troy.

4. AMPHITRYON PLAYS IN RUSSIA

Apart from minor Scandinavian items, all the Amphitryon dramas so far mentioned were created in areas once located within the Roman Empire; we see the German works as repre-

senting eastward extensions of the old Rhine and Danube zones
of that Empire. Of Slavic items west of Russia we have found
no trace, but we note a Russian *Race of Hercules, with Jupiter
as primary personage* (Poroda Gerkulesova, v nei zhe pervaya
persona Iupiter) as being performed in Red Square in 1702.
That this was a Molière derivative is indicated by two further
titles from the six-title repertory, *Doktor prinuzhdennyi* and
Dragya smeyaniya, which are surely *Le Médecin malgré lui* and
Les Précieuses Ridicules. These texts seem to have been lost and
no further Amphitryons are known to us in Russia before the
twentieth century.

Dated from the summer of 1912, however, there is a fine verse
translation of Molière's play by the symbolist poet Valeri
Bryusov, published in Volume XV of his *Collected Works,* St.
Petersburg, 1914. The Russian line count is identical with the
French, but Bryusov felt free to adjust line lengths and rhyme
patterns to suit his needs so long as he maintained the general
effect of what the seventeenth century termed "free verse."
Speeches vary from quite literal renditions to looser paraphrase,
but always within the spirit of the French text.

Bryusov either chanced on a very early edition of Molière or,
more likely, sought out a text as near as possible to the 1668
printing, because his translation lacks several stage directions
as well as the lines which appear in our version as 453a–d, both
things having first appeared in the 1682 edition. Tiny departures
from the original are too trifling to mention, but we observe that
King Pterelas' cluster of five diamonds (*le noeud de diamants*)
is understood as a diamond crown (*venets almaznyi*), so that we
wonder how Alcmena can wear it as a girdle. Kleist's bit of
antiquarian lore was unknown to Bryusov.

The scholarly poet furnished an eight-page Introduction (pp.
282–9) in which he briefly reviews several of the lost Greek plays,
Plautus, Rotrou's two versions, and alludes to the various Amphitryon plays from Italy, Spain, and Portugal. Since his Introduction regards only Molière's comedy, he says nothing of versions since 1668. Rotrou's *Les Sosies* was, he remarks, "if not on
Molière's table, (it was) in his memory," but he justly cites
Molière's fresh inventions in the Prologue, in the new character
of Cléanthis, and in many a poetic turn. Sosia he sees as a

raisonneur and traces his down-to-earth sense to the author's bourgeois youth amid poverty. He dismisses any notion of parallels with Louis XIV and Mme de Maintenon. He comments on the elusive verse patterns, he notes the anachronism of Sosia's "devil" in line 1889, and he sees the remarks about doctors (lines 1160 ff.) as relevant to the author's impending death. In speaking of costumes he erroneously claims that Molière played the title role, whereas Molière played Sosia and the costume partially described by Bryusov derives from the post-mortem inventory of Molière's wardrobe:

"... un tonnelet de taffetas vert, avec une petite dentelle d'argent fin, une chemisette de même taffetas, deux cuissards de satin rouge, une paire de souliers avec laçures garnies d'un galon d'argent, avec un bas de soie céladon vert pâle, les festons, la ceinture et un jupon, brodé or et argent fin."

All in all, the very fussy livery of a *valet* to a very lofty *seigneur* of the seventeenth century.

We puzzle at the lack of Amphitryon translations and Amphitryon derivatives in Russia between the lost version of 1702 and Bryusov's excellent rendition of 1912. The theme in any form, we suppose, jested too close to Imperial severity and too close to churchly solemnity to warrant its use in the theater.

5. OTHER TWENTIETH CENTURY *Amphitryons*

Considering the resources which motion pictures could bring to an *Amphitryon* scenario, it suddenly occurs to us to wonder why no movie version has ever been made. The answer to our question is the startling one that such a film *was* made, albeit an ill-starred one. Entitled *Amphitryon,* it was Nazi-financed and made in Berlin, but in the French language and with French actors in the leading roles. It was written and directed by Reinhold Schunzel and Albert Valentin, with dialogue and songs by Serge Veber and a musical score by François Doelle. Professor Shero reports that it was shown in various American cities in 1936–7, reviewed in *The New York Times* of March 24, 1937, but closed in New York after only a week's showings because of anti-Nazi boycotting and picketing. Its most unusual feature was a part for a frumpish virago of a Juno who frustrated Jupiter's desires to the point where even Alcmena felt sorry for him.

Further reported by Professor Shero is the 1950 musical entitled *Out of This World*, with book by Dwight Taylor and Reginald Lawrence and with music by Cole Porter, though in this case the characters bore quite different names and the plot freely shifted from *Amphitryon* outlines.

Still nearer the present moment and again from New York, he reports a play which *The New York Times* of February 21, 1957 termed "an often uproariously funny burlesque." Its title was *A God Slept Here* and represented an English adaptation by Lloyd George and John Fostini of a Brazilian original work by Guilherme Figueiredo. Here Alcmena was seduced by her own husband who was pretending to be Jupiter in disguise.

All three of these items, it will be noted, prolong the familiar comic tradition stemming from Plautus. Meanwhile, the Swiss composer Robert Oboussier has attempted an operatic treatment which seeks to combine comic elements with more serious ones, looking to Molière for the former and to Kleist for the latter. For this opera of *Amphitryon* the composer wrote his own libretto. The work bears the date of 1950 and had its première in Berlin in March of 1951.

Most recent of all versions, to our knowledge, is the *Amphitryon* of Peter Hacks (1928–   ), the German writer who has also adapted Halévy-Meilhac's libretto for Offenbach's *La Belle Hélène* and Aristophanes's *Peace* for the Berlin stage. According to the *New York Times* of May 29, 1970, this *Amphitryon,* in English translation by Ralph Manheim, "winked—minus a leer, into the Forum Theater last night." Wink-swift it was gone again before the present writers had a chance to see it. The *Times* praised it as "a snug, briskly cheerful 'Amphitryon' with a tart, take it or leave it tone . . ." and spoke of its "simple costumes, untricky lighting, exotic half-masks, uncluttered sets."

As we write, the Amphitryon tradition is still alive, its comic aspect predominant but not without representation of its serious aspect also.

V. A WORD ON THE DESTINIES
OF AMPHITRYON

In discussing the Amphitryon theme in classical antiquity through Part I of the present volume, a triple distinction was made relative to the myth, the tragic dramas, and the comic dramas.

Some story of Alcmena, we said, was known to Homer and located by him in the heroic age of Greece a generation before the Trojan War. Significant surely, though we do not know precisely in what way, is the fact that the heroine figures in a "catalogue of women" in the *Iliad,* in the *Odyssey,* and in the "Hesiodic" poem of the "Or-Like's" and its continuation, *The Shield of Herakles.* Allegedly the heroine lived before 1200 B.C., we place the *Iliad* between 850 and 800 B.C., and we were probably over-bold in suggesting that *The Shield of Herakles* could be dated as late as somewhat after 699 B.C. Except for a fragment of Pherecydes between 500 and 450 B.C., no further mythographic evidence is available until the period just before and just after the opening of the Christian era, though allusions in Pindar, Theocritus, and others confirm the continuity of the myth. The fullest account is provided by "Apollodorus," who wrote probably in the first or second century A.D. Two salient features of the myth were mentioned: the fact that Amphitryon and Alcmena were figures in an exceedingly complex tangle of political legend about the dynasties of Mycenae, and the fact that their Theban adventure with Zeus served primarily as a prelude to the career of Hercules—which was in turn entangled in that web of Mycenean dynastic legend. Nothing in the late mythographers contradicts the brief statements in the *Iliad,* the *Odyssey,* or *The Shield of Herakles,* but it is unsafe to assume that all elements of the story had been conjoined as early as Homer. Rather, there is some slight evidence for important modifications around 500 B.C. The myth treated the Theban episode only briefly, attaching more importance to the dynastic legends of Mycenae on one side of it and to the career of Herakles on the other side. Thus we observed that the myth provided a framework for drama and the raw material for drama without giving any dramatic focus. Most curiously, the later mythographers, who wrote after the entire four-hundred-year evolution of the dramatic *Amphitryons* had closed, seem to ignore the dramas and to write in an independent mythographic tradition, which no doubt went back to origins and sources well before 500 B.C.

Dramas on the Amphitryon theme began, it would seem, with Aeschylus, who died in 456 B.C., and until late in the fifth century those dramas were tragic or at least of high seriousness. Of the tragedies by Aeschylus, Sophocles, and Ion of Chios, we know next to nothing; about the tragic version by Euripides we have only informed guesses. The loss of these works is doubtless a most regrettable loss, but it is also a fact of capital importance that dramatists from the Renaissance forward were not embarrassed by their serious treatments of pagan religion which might well have deterred them from handling the Amphitryon theme at all.

Comic treatments of the Amphitryon theme began late in the fifth century "Old Comedy" phase of Greek literature and included a comic *Amphitryon* by Archippus and a comic *Long Night* by Plato "Comicus," both lost. If Greek "Middle Comedy" from 404 B.C. to the 330's B.C. or so, produced no known Amphitryon plays—some belated tragedies from that period are attested—still, "Middle Comedy" practices, particularly the practice of burlesquing stories about the gods, was to influence the later work of Plautus. The urbane "New Comedy" that developed after the 330's was to remain the established form of literary comedy throughout the remainder of classical antiquity and its very extensive repertory—almost totally lost—was what Roman poets sought to translate and adapt into the Latin language for Roman audiences from 240 B.C. forward. Philemon's "New Comedy" of *The Long Night,* however, was not the model for Plautus' *Amphitruo* in the 190's, nor was Rhinthon's south-Italian, Greek-language travesty of *Amphitryon* from, say, the 290's. What Greek comedy Plautus translated is unidentifiable, and his "carelessness"—or carefulness—in adapting it is a matter of puzzled dispute. The fact of supreme importance for later centuries is that of all the fourteen (or more) Amphitryon plays

of classical antiquity, tragic and comic alike, only this one trans-
lation-adaptation in comic vein survived. Its sole presence provided the very idea of an Amphitryon play for those later centuries. Its being in Latin rather than in Greek made it accessible
to readers, indeed made it accessible to copyists. As a comedy
it predisposed all Amphitryon plays of later eras to be comedies
and its seeming irreverence toward the pagan gods made it
acceptable in Christian times.

The mythographers apparently thought of Alcmena as a Mycenean princess suitably royal to become the mother of Herakles
by the seed of Zeus. What Aeschylus, Sophocles, and Ion of
Chios thought of her we do not know. We suspect that Euripides
portrayed her as a woman deeply wronged by her husband, who
sought to kill her, and quite possibly wronged by Zeus as well.
How the Greek comic poets conceived of her we, again, do not
know. Social conditions in Rome around 200 B.C., we believe,
obliged Plautus to represent her as a young (Roman) matron of
total uprightness; her lack of sentimentality is likely to have
reflected Plautus' own preferences and those of his audiences as
well.

Amphitryon's role must all along have been to misunderstand,
to protest, and ultimately to accede to a higher will. In the myth
he was considered privileged to do so. In fact, Euripides' tragedy
of *The Raging Herakles* showed him and Herakles united in
the deepest ties of affection. Yet we suspect that in Euripides'
Alkmene he may have raged cruelly, even inhumanly. We do
not know how the comic poets treated him, except for Plautus,
who allows him a princely anger and a nobleman's dignity amid
his plight. Moreover, in the tragicomedy of *Amphitruo* domestic
cuckoldry is overshadowed by the awesomely proclaimed commission of foster-parenthood. His situation is absurd, *he* is not.
Nowhere does Plautus make a monkey out of him.

What is perennially problematical in the story is the god's
motivation. The myth begged that question. In the far-off heroic
age a god might act as he pleased and a child by him honored
both mortal mother and mortal foster-father. What the tragic
poets did about this question is unknown. What the Greek comic
poets did about it is unknown. Plautus' Jupiter acts somewhat
as a high nobleman might act toward lesser persons, but he is

not malicious, he is moved by the most understandable of passions, and he does not depart without bestowing a certain glory on Amphitryon's house. (Mercury's gratuitous mischief is a separate concern.) As a dramatized myth, *Amphitruo* was not obligated to motivate the god's conduct; or the siring of Herakles might afford all the explanation an audience might need. Some degree of religious mystery still invests Plautus' Jupiter, comic though he may be. He comes and goes and acts according to laws above human laws. He is a very great personage whose presence was troublesome at the time, yet wonderful to look back on—like many men's war experiences.

For Plautus and his audience the play as a whole still had some religious significance. The Romans of 200 B.C. were not disbelievers. The play was not a mockery of a discarded belief. We are in no position to evaluate that religious component but we must suspend Judaeo-Christian notions long enough not to confuse comedy with blasphemy. As for what moderns would call the psychological implications of the story, those were not yet dreamed of in Plautus' day. The play deals with "a certain situation" and is not a "study" of anybody or anything. Alcmena is the hinge on which the plot turns but she is not the chief personage. She appears in only three scenes, is on stage during 369 lines out of 1,146, and actually speaks only about 100 lines. Amphitryon, Jupiter, Mercury, and Sosia all have longer roles than hers, yet though the play is named *Amphitruo,* the husband is not the chief personage either. Like a Mozart opera, this play is a team affair and "everybody sings."

After the long leap down through time, to the court performances at Ferrara in 1487 and 1491, we witness successive changes in all the factors we have mentioned.

In Christian times, both before and after the Reformation, the heathen god-stories were dubious matters for literary treatment. Comic god-stories might appear relatively harmless, but the difficulty with *Amphitruo* was that it got serious toward the end. Moreover, drama itself encountered opposition from the church. Three points may be made relative to the Ferrara performances: they were private court entertainments not open to the public at large, lavish spectacle obscured the dramatic import, and the text was altered to glorify a reigning family. As Professor Lindberger remarked, that proclamation of Hercules' birth, once it was expanded to express hope for an infant Ercole d'Este to come, tended to set the Dukes of Ferrara equal to gods. The pagan religious element had been duly exorcised—and replaced by an idolatry of princes. Therein lay a fateful prognostic.

That was in 1487 and 1491, at the beginning of the story's new lease on life. In 1787 Swedish King Gustavus III added (or caused to be added) four "Intermèdes" to a performance of Molière's *Amphitryon* given before his court in the Drottning-holm Palace, in the last of which "Intermèdes" he himself appeared in apotheosis as victor in war and lover of peace. Through that three-hundred-year span, 1487–1787, most Amphitryon plays, operas, vaudevilles, etc. either subtly glorified monarchs or oligarchs or else served as expensive courtly toys. One does not have to be a Marxist to see that the greatest proliferation of *Amphitryons* occurred in the period from 1680 to 1787 when European aristocracies were most self-assertive, most oppressive, and most useless. The striking interruption in modern Amphitryon history comes not with Romanticism but with the French Revolution. Rotrou's Mercury seems rather to mean what he says when he declares that social rank will oblige the chaste Moon to abet what, in lesser persons, would be vice. Dryden's Jupiter more cynically voices the same notion in the lines we quoted in our discussion of that work, and Dryden's arrogant courtiers offend our bourgeois-democratic sensitivities by their aristocratic insolence. One need not be an uncritical libertarian rebel in the sense of Schiller's *Kabale und Liebe* to be irritated *politically* by Dryden's play.

Renaissance enthusiasm for classical antiquity will, of course, account for some *Amphitryons* of the three-century period in question, and for their particular qualities. Thomas Heywood seems not to have perceived any qualitative difference between the Amphitryon story and all the other god-stories he put pell-mell together in his 20-Act *Four Ages,* and that "classical revue" was intended for the public theaters as well as for court performances. Heywood boggled only at minor details of religion, carried away as he was with his Grecian enthusiasms. Johannes Burmeister went to the opposite extreme of creating a bogus antiquity that obliterated pagan elements altogether. But the typical *Amphitryons* made the gods courtiers and courtiers gods.

How comes it then, it will be asked, that Molière's *Amphi-*

tryon of 1668, squarely in the middle of the aristocratic era and composed in the heyday of Louis XIV, should have escaped being aristocratically tendentious? Primarily, we answer, by virtue of the author's transcendent genius. We hasten to add that Molière's *Amphitryon* is not anti-aristocratic! But the down-to-earth dialogue of Sosia and Cleanthis does much to widen the range of human feelings in the play, and, more important, there is no positive claim for high-born persons' being above the laws of the rest of humanity. In the Prologue Mercury makes the same request of the Lady Night that Rotrou's Mercury made of the Moon, but when he alleges Rotrou's reason, he does so with profound irony (lines 126–131):

> Un tel emploi n'est bassesse
> Que chez les petites gens.
> Lorsque dans un haut rang on a l'heur de paroître,
> Tout ce qu'on fait est toujours bel et bon;
> Et suivant ce qu'on peut être,
> Les choses changent de nom.

Molière was a monarchist and a patriot and, with good reason, he relied heavily on the king's personal support; he was also a bourgeois by birth, a man who had known hardship and debtor's prison, a member of a socially despised profession, and a follower of the free-thinking religious opposition, along with Cyrano de Bergerac and the "dangerous" philosopher Gassendi. Opposites conjoined in him to broaden his humanity.

In designating the 1668 *Amphitryon* as the sane norm of Amphitryon comedy, we may give some reasons for the choice and some explanation of how it was achieved. In the flawless perfection of the Prologue we are confronted with a brand new invention. If its source was a dialogue of Lucian, then that choice was a stroke of genius, as is evident from comparison with the pedantic borrowing that Rotrou made from Seneca, to say nothing of the irrelevancy of Rotrou's Juno. Otherwise Molière followed Plautus as long as Plautus was humanly sound. He sensed the eerie mystery inherent in Plautus' opening scene, where a lone man coming home in the dark of night is driven from his own door by—himself, and made the most of it without being deflected from his comic purpose. The melodramatic close of the old Latin tragicomedy has, on the other hand, been almost completely converted to high comedy "with just a little thunder," and the gods are made to withdraw almost as lightly as the *Midsummer Night's Dream* fairies. His three-Act structure is based on the ever effective principle of triple gradation in jest: Act I, the servant meets his double; Act II, the lady claims to have met her husband's double; Act III, the master meets *his* double —and the double is a god. It is all as simple as common sense. The five-Act structure is too big to fit the material, and intrusive ballets slacken the dramatic tension just as intrusive songs spoil wit with sentiment. These wrong choices have been avoided. The plot builds from level to level just as the time builds from pre-dawn into full light, from enigma into clarification. Other dramatists often undermined this simple logic (which was there in Plautus) by staging showy first scenes where Jupiter's arrival was enacted, as if audiences would not get the situation straight if they did not see it with their own eyes. No sub-plot distorts this clear line of development, as with Dryden's tasteless complications with Phaedra and Judge Gripus. Amphitryon is angry enough but he has no exaggeratedly Iberian *point d'honneur*. The mythological strings that hampered Plautus in the last Act have been neatly clipped. Piquantly sexy wit is managed without a bedroom scene. Alcmena is exquisitely feminine without being either weak or sentimental, but, as in Plautus, she is kept discreetly on the second plane of the action. The story depends on her but she does not dominate the story. The play does not wallow in fantasies about the unfathomable mystery of the female. If the language is marked with some degree of courtly mannerisms, it is eminently clear. The first lines spoken by Jupiter amount to a transfiguration of *préciosité*. Banal realism was not allowed to reduce the dialogue to commonplace chatter; the verse is worthy to be put into the mouths of gods and in speaking it all the characters become poetically like gods. It is as though Molière, like a character in *The Arabian Nights*, had passed by every door of false choice and gone instinctively to the one that opened into the treasure chamber.

Up until the French Revolution, we have said, Amphitryon plays, operas, etc. tended to be court toys. Since 1800 they have more often than not been problematic works, "des *Amphitryons* à thèse." Falk's play of 1804 was one such, though its "ideas"

were second-hand and a quarter of a century old at least. Its
ideal of *humanitas* or *Menschheit,* while admirable in itself, had
received definitive poetic statement in Goethe's *Iphigenie auf
Tauris* in 1787, so that Falk's *Amphitryon* was redundant. Its
pantheism echoed earlier works of Goethe's Sturm-und-Drang
of the 1770's. In so far as it sought to create a gallery of types
"from the world of Philemon and Menander," it ventured beyond its depth, "the world of Philemon and Menander" being
known only in scholarly generalities; and in so far as it sought
to Hellenize directly from Hellas and not via Versailles, it attempted what had been often preached in Germany since the
1760's and what Goethe had already discovered was next to impossible. *Iphigenie auf Tauris* is no doubt a finer work than,
say, Voltaire's *Mérope,* but it is doubtful if it is any closer to
ancient Greece. Perhaps, however, these second-hand ideas of
Falk's could have been brought together in a great work if his
poetic talent had matched his ambition. Still, that *Amphitryon*
of 1804, with its planned dislocation of the legend for the sake
of expressing timely ideas, was symptomatic of what was to
follow.

Kleist's play we regard as a magnificent failure and, as such,
vastly more interesting than many a slick success. It is particularly significant that its newness in 1807 was the result of a
psychological approach. The drama "dealing with a certain
situation" here yields place to a process of searching the soul
of Alcmena. The yearning god, lonely in his omnipotence and
immortality, seeks and cannot win this one beloved. His desperate, even cruel, testing of her soul only reveals her ever more
distant retreats from him. What happens on stage is less important than the evocation of Alcmena's inner thoughts and
feelings. By no coincidence, the Jupiter-Alcmena scene is a poetic
idealization of a hypnotist's eliciting of self-revelations from a
subject. Mesmer was himself alive in 1807 and his theories were
the topic of endless speculation in German literary circles. By no
coincidence either, that hypnotist-and-subject parallel anticipates
the twentieth century parallel of psychoanalyst and patient.

For almost a century and a quarter after 1807 the Amphitryon
theme suffered neglect. Kleist, who was most certainly a Romanticist by European standards, could not be labeled a *Romantiker*

precisely because of such a work as his *Amphitryon,* which was
both classical and neo-classical in subject and based directly on
a famous product of "Versailles culture." But if all the varieties
of European Romanticism did not avoid classical and neo-
classical subjects quite with the determination of the German
Romantik, there was nevertheless a general tendency to do so.
Yet it is strange that the Amphitryon theme should not have
attracted that belated classicist Grillparzer, particularly in tragi-
comic, rather than comic, form. One would think the subject
readier to the purposes of Friedrich Hebbel than the thin parable of Gyges and his ring. It is astonishing, if true, that there
were no Russian *Amphitryons.* The imagination runs riot with
the thought of what an operatic *Amphitryon* by Verdi or Puc-
cini might have been, or a comedy of *Amphitryon* by Bernard
Shaw. For these omissions there were reasons in the changing
climates of literary opinion between 1807 and 1929, and in the
climates of political and sociological opinion no doubt as well.
The old favorite of courts was very likely suspect in a democ-
ratizing century.

At any rate, the long spell of neglect was not broken until
Giraudoux' play of 1929. Neither high wit nor the charm of its
multiple ironies can obscure the fact that *Amphitryon 38* is
basically a sophisticated comedy about the battle of the sexes.
Nor the fact that it is a "vehicle play" for Alcmena. Nor the
fact that it concerns a woman's strategy and tactics in the battle
to save a marriage. So learned a man as Giraudoux, and so
respectful of the heritage of the French classics, would, we have
said, go to great lengths not to challenge Molière, and this fact,
we feel, explains more than any other the deliberate dismemberment of the legend and its reorganization into a wholly new
pattern, though Giraudoux' procedure is not without analogy in
painting and sculpture since 1913. The durability of this French
play remains yet to be tested. The present writer has doubts
about that durability, though he feels the non-realistic approach
of Giraudoux was the right approach and though he finds the
French dialogue marked with distinction.

With Kaiser's *Amphitryon Doubled* we encounter another
deliberate dismemberment of the legend and reorganization of
selected portions of it into a wholly new pattern, but for pur-

poses very different from those of Giraudoux. The supplementary
matter is fresh invention, independent of the ancient myth and
yet strikingly consonant with the tone of Greek myth in general.
Kaiser seems to have worked out his suspenseful alternation of
scenes in terms of the principle of duality which lies at the very
heart of the story. The cast of characters lists both Zeus and
Amphitryon, but the two appear in exclusively separate scenes
until the final confrontation. At that point Amphitryon is kneel-
ing amid a crowd with his hands over his face and Zeus is seen
in the dense fire-smoke of the altar above him. With appropriate
stage equipment and a little ingenuity on the part of the stage
manager, a single actor could play both parts even there. Such
a dual role would make a dazzling tour de force to challenge
the ability of the most gifted actor. Not the least surprising thing
about this scenario compounded of elements old and new is the
conventional coherence of its story, as opposed, for instance, to
Giraudoux's situational play with its assortment of dispensable,
peripheral characters. Moreover, Kaiser, the one-time Expressionist, here returned to the main channel of German-language
dramaturgical tradition, so that this work could have been
acceptable to Lessing, to Goethe, to Schiller, to Grillparzer, perhaps even to Hebbel. If we have some reservations about the
forthrightness of Kaiser's moral parable, it is nevertheless our
opinion that this strong play deserves wider appreciation. It is
surely meaningful in the troubled era of the second half of the
twentieth century.

The years since 1944 have already yielded an *Amphitryon*-
derived musical and an *Amphitryon*-derived burlesque, testify-
ing to the story's persistent tendencies toward opera, toward
farce, and toward that combination of the two which we may
term vaudeville. The perennially fascinating tale is easily drawn
in those directions, and no doubt there will be more musicals
and more farces in the future, but the history of *Amphitryons*
suggests that durable works are not likely to be realized in those
genres. Noteworthy achievements in the past have been on the
level of high comedy. On that plane it would seem impossible
to improve on Molière, hence the significant reorganization of
the legend by Giraudoux. With the relaxation of religious objections, the logical step would be toward non-comic treatments of

the theme. Kaiser's play of 1944 took that step but still reorganized the scenario. The future alone holds the answers to questions of whether scenario-reorganization is unavoidable, whether *Amphitryons* of high seriousness will be realized, and whether the standard comic tradition or the latent tragic tradition will prevail. It will be interesting to see what the next great author will do with the theme.